Arkansas Legal Research

CAROLINA ACADEMIC PRESS
LEGAL RESEARCH SERIES

Suzanne E. Rowe, Series Editor

❧

Arizona, Second Edition — Tamara S. Herrera

Arkansas, Second Edition — Coleen M. Barger, Cheryl L. Reinhart &
Cathy L. Underwood

California, Third Edition — Aimee Dudovitz, Hether C. Macfarlane,
& Suzanne E. Rowe

Colorado — Robert Michael Linz

Connecticut — Jessica G. Hynes

Federal, Second Edition— Mary Garvey Algero, Spencer L. Simons,
Suzanne E. Rowe, Scott Childs & Sarah E. Ricks

Florida, Fourth Edition — Barbara J. Busharis, Jennifer LaVia & Suzanne E. Rowe

Georgia — Nancy P. Johnson, Elizabeth G. Adelman & Nancy J. Adams

Idaho, Second Edition — Tenielle Fordyce-Ruff & Kristina J. Running

Illinois, Second Edition — Mark E. Wojcik

Iowa, Second Edition — John D. Edwards, M. Sara Lowe, Karen L. Wallace &
Melissa H. Weresh

Kansas — Joseph A. Custer & Christopher L. Steadham

Kentucky — William A. Hilyerd, Kurt X. Metzmeier & David J. Ensign

Louisiana, Second Edition — Mary Garvey Algero

Massachusetts, Second Edition — E. Joan Blum & Shaun B. Spencer

Michigan, Third Edition — Pamela Lysaght & Cristina D. Lockwood

Minnesota — Suzanne Thorpe

Mississippi — Kristy L. Gilliland

Missouri, Third Edition — Wanda M. Temm & Julie M. Cheslik

New York, Third Edition — Elizabeth G. Adelman, Theodora Belniak
Courtney L. Selby & Brian Detweiler

North Carolina, Second Edition — Scott Childs & Sara Sampson

North Dakota — Anne Mullins & Tammy Pettinato

Ohio, Second Edition — Sara Sampson, Katherine L. Hall
& Carolyn Broering-Jacobs

Oklahoma — Darin K. Fox, Darla W. Jackson & Courtney L. Selby

Oregon, Third Edition Revised Printing — Suzanne E. Rowe

Pennsylvania — Barbara J. Busharis & Bonny L. Tavares

Tennessee, Second Edition — Scott Childs, Sibyl Marshall & Carol McCrehan Parker

Texas, Second Edition — Spencer L. Simons

Washington, Second Edition — Julie Heintz-Cho, Tom Cobb
& Mary A. Hotchkiss

West Virginia — Hollee Schwartz Temple

Wisconsin — Patricia Cervenka & Leslie Behroozi

Wyoming, Second Edition — Debora A. Person & Tawnya K. Plumb

❧

Arkansas Legal Research

SECOND EDITION

Coleen M. Barger
Cheryl L. Reinhart
Cathy L. Underwood

Series Editor
Suzanne E. Rowe

CAROLINA ACADEMIC PRESS
Durham, North Carolina

Library of Congress Cataloging-in-Publication Data

Names: Barger, Coleen M., 1951- author. | Reinhart, Cheryl L. | Underwood, Cathy L.

Title: Arkansas legal research / Coleen M. Barger, Cheryl L. Reinhart, and Cathy L. Underwood.

Description: 2nd edition | Durham, North Carolina : Carolina Academic Press,
[2016] | Series: Legal research series | Includes bibliographical references and index.

Identifiers: LCCN 2016027517 | ISBN 9781531000141 (alk. paper)

Subjects: LCSH: Legal research--Arkansas.

Classification: LCC KFA3675 .B37 2016 | DDC 340.072/0767--dc23

LC record available at https://lccn.loc.gov/2016027517

Carolina Academic Press, LLC
700 Kent Street
Durham, North Carolina 27701
Telephone (919) 489-7486
Fax (919) 493-5668
www.cap-press.com

Printed in the United States of America
2018 Printing

Contents

List of Tables and Figures

Series Note

The Legal Research Series published by Carolina Academic Press includes titles from states around the country as well as a separate text on federal legal research. The goal of each book is to provide law students, practitioners, paralegals, college students, laypeople, and librarians with the essential elements of legal research in each jurisdiction. Unlike more bibliographic texts, the Legal Research Series books seek to explain concisely both the sources of state law research and the process for conducting legal research effectively.

Preface and Acknowledgments

Access to the law has never been easier. Ask a question, get an answer—okay, get hundreds or thousands of answers. How will you know which is the right answer? Does it represent the law in your own state? Does it represent federal law? Are there things governed solely by state law? Solely by federal law? Is it from an official or even trustworthy source? Does the quick answer give you everything you need to know? Does the quick answer help you find even more (or better) authority on the point of law you're researching? Access isn't everything.

Even as it has become easier for today's legal researchers to access sources of the law online, that abundance can be overwhelming, whether the researcher is a first-year law student or an attorney with several years' experience. Therefore, deciding how and where to start, refine, and filter results for any legal research project is more important than ever.

In preparing this second edition of *Arkansas Legal Research*, we discovered how quickly the tools of legal research are evolving. This edition has undergone significant updating to cover current sources of and methods for finding and evaluating Arkansas law. It is intended to be useful for legal researchers of various levels of experience and training, whether they use materials in print, online, or in combination.

The opening chapter walks users through the legal research process. The second chapter introduces readers to the eclectic mix of secondary materials that provide users with the concepts, vocabulary, and overview needed when researching unfamiliar areas of the law. Each of the remaining chapters focuses on particular sources of law, beginning with the ultimate source of state law, the Arkansas Constitution, and continuing through cases, statutes, legislation, administrative rules, and rules of court. This edition includes a new chapter on updating sources and using online citators, plus two new appendices. Appendix A briefly explains and illustrates citations to the most common sources of law, both in practitioner format (including those used in local practice) and academic format. Appendix B contains a wealth of references to current online and print resources of particular interest to Arkansas legal researchers.

It has been rewarding to work together on this new edition and to draw upon each other's experiences, skills, and wisdom, but we could not have written it without a lot of help. We would like to thank in particular Suzanne Rowe, director of the legal writing program at the University of Oregon School of Law, Series Editor for the state legal research series at Carolina Academic Press, and the authors of those other states' texts for new ideas, inspiration, and encouragement. Specifically, our thanks go to Barbara Busharis, *Florida Legal Research*; Mark Wojcik, *Illinois Legal Research*; Wanda Temm, *Missouri Legal Research*; Beth Adelman, *New York Legal Research*; and Sibyl Marshall, *Tennessee Legal Research*, for allowing use of their materials in Chapter 4, and to Suzanne Rowe, *Oregon Legal Research*, for allowing use of her materials in Chapters 2 and 4.

We owe many thanks to the law librarians of the University of Arkansas at Little Rock, William H. Bowen School of Law, including Director Jessie Burchfield, and Professors Kathryn Fitzhugh, Melissa Serfass, and Jeff Woodmansee. We would also like to thank Susan P. Williams, Reporter of Decisions for the Arkansas Supreme Court, for patiently answering questions for us.

Christina Jack from Fastcase, Hannah Barnhart from Lexis, and Peter Lippmann from Westlaw graciously verified the accuracy of information about their products. Thanks go to John Wesley Hall for his practical advice, and to Pulaski Technical college paralegal students Sally Porter and Sarah Keech for reviewing the chapter on case law.

Coleen M. Barger
Cheryl L. Reinhart
Cathy L. Underwood
March 2016

Arkansas Legal Research

Chapter 1

The Research Process and Legal Analysis

I. Introduction to Arkansas Legal Research

The fundamentals of legal research are the same in every American jurisdiction, though the details vary. While some variations are minor, others require specialized knowledge of the resources available and the analytical framework in which those resources are used. That knowledge and analytical framework are the heart of legal representation; they form the basis of a lawyer's ethical obligation to "provide competent representation to a client."[1] Such competence "requires the legal knowledge, skill, thoroughness and preparation reasonably necessary for the representation."[2] Legal research provides the foundation for those requirements, even when the representation involves matters unfamiliar to the lawyer. "Perhaps the most fundamental legal skill consists of determining what kind of legal problems a situation may involve, a skill that necessarily transcends any particular specialized knowledge. A lawyer can provide adequate representation in a wholly novel field through necessary study."[3]

As advocates, lawyers have another important ethical obligation, to "disclose to the tribunal legal authority in the controlling jurisdiction known to the lawyer to be directly adverse to the position of the client . . . ."[4] This obligation, known as the *duty of candor*, directs researchers to search for *unfavorable* mandatory law as well as law that is helpful to their clients' cases.[5]

---

1. Ark. R. Prof. Conduct 1.1.
2. *Id.*
3. *Id.* cmt. 2.
4. Ark. R. Prof. Conduct 3.3(a)(2).
5. An even more practical reason to search for both favorable and unfavorable law is to make an objective assessment of the strengths and weaknesses of opposing positions on a question of law.

This text provides instruction in how to conduct competent, ethical, effective, and efficient research into Arkansas law. It focuses on the resources and analysis required to be thorough and effective in researching Arkansas law. It supplements this focus with brief explanations of more general resources, although it does not detail materials for researching federal law or address the laws of other states.

Because legal materials are available in both electronic and print media, this text discusses the use of both kinds of sources. While electronic media deliver the materials to your computer, you have to balance the convenience of those media against not only their cost, but also their currency, completeness, and coverage. In choosing whether to use online or print media as research sources, therefore, you must keep these differences in mind. Some sources are more reliable than others. Some are more complete. Some are less expensive. To the extent that it is practical and reliable, lawyers choose — or wisely combine — research media according to their effectiveness and efficiency, considering that research costs are ultimately borne by the lawyer's clients.

II. Types of Legal Authority

American law — federal and state — has its source in one or more of the three branches of government, as defined in the United States Constitution or the constitutions of the individual states.

The *judicial branch*, represented by trial and appellate courts, has perhaps the most complex set of responsibilities in determining law. Rather than develop law in an abstract or general sense, courts employ law to decide existing controversies between litigants. A court may decide a case by applying a statute to particular conduct, by interpreting a constitutional provision, or by using *common law*, i.e., finding similarities and differences in the way similar controversies have been treated by courts in the past and extending those principles to decide the current controversy.

The *legislative branch*, whether Congress or a state legislature such as the Arkansas General Assembly, enacts laws that reflect the public policies of the jurisdiction. These laws have general application to citizens of that jurisdiction, both current and future.

The *executive branch*, headed by the president or the state's governor, is charged with carrying out the jurisdiction's enacted laws, and to do so, issues rules and regulations through the government's administrative agencies.

Table 1-1. Arkansas Legal Authority at a Glance

Governmental Branch	Type of Authority	Promulgator(s) of Authority
Judicial	Judicial opinions (cases)	Arkansas Supreme Court
	Court rules	Arkansas Court of Appeals
		Arkansas circuit courts
Legislative	Statutes, session laws, and slip laws	Arkansas General Assembly
Executive	Administrative rules and regulations; agency decisions	Arkansas administrative agencies
	Executive orders	Arkansas governor

In every research situation, the goal is to find the constitutional provisions, statutes, administrative rules, or judicial opinions (or at times, some combination of these) that control the client's situation. In other words, you are searching for primary, mandatory authority.

Law is often divided along two lines. The first line distinguishes primary authority from secondary authority. *Primary authority* is law created by one of the branches of government authorized by the constitution: the judicial, legislative, or administrative branch. The primary authority created by the judicial branch is *case law*. *Statutes* are the form of primary authority created by the legislative branch. The executive branch of government promulgates primary authority in the form of *agency regulations* and *executive orders*. Table 1-1 identifies the most important forms and sources of Arkansas legal authority.

Another division is made between mandatory and persuasive authority. *Mandatory authority* is binding on the court that would decide a conflict if it were being litigated. For example, in conflicts involving Arkansas law, mandatory authority includes Arkansas's constitution, legislation enacted by the Arkansas General Assembly (and later codified as statutes), Arkansas administrative rules, and opinions of the Arkansas Supreme Court and the Arkansas Court of Appeals. Because Arkansas is also a state within the federal system of government, opinions of the Supreme Court of the United States are mandatory on issues involving the federal constitution or federal statutes. If a case is pending before either the United States District Court for the Eastern District of Arkansas or the Western District of Arkansas (federal trial courts), decisions of the United States Court of Appeals for the Eighth Circuit are mandatory authority.[6]

Unlike mandatory authority, *persuasive authority* is not binding, although a court may elect to follow the guidance of relevant and well reasoned persuasive authority. For example, in a conflict involving Arkansas law, an Arkansas court might consider the Tennessee Supreme Court's holding on a similar issue (a primary authority, but not mandatory because it is the law of another state) or a relevant law review article (a secondary authority). The Arkansas court is not bound by either of these persuasive authorities, however. Only mandatory authority is binding.

In each jurisdiction, the primary authorities bear a hierarchical relationship to one another. In other words, where a legal issue is governed by more than one kind of primary authority, some primary authorities are superior to others. The constitution of each state is the supreme law of that state. If a statute from that state is on point, then it comes next in the hierarchy, followed by administrative rules. Judicial opinions may interpret or apply the statute or rule but cannot disregard either. A judicial opinion may, however, determine that a statute violates the constitution or that a rule oversteps the authority of the agency issuing it. If there is no constitutional provision, statute, or administrative rule on point, common law controls the issue.

In contrast to primary authorities, *secondary authorities* are written by scholars, practitioners, and other commentators who explain, evaluate, criticize, or suggest changes to the law. Examples of secondary authority include treatises, law review articles, practice manuals, law dictionaries, and legal encyclopedias. While secondary authority may exert some persuasive influence in legal analysis, secondary authority is *not* the law itself. Table 1-2 outlines the distinctions among primary, secondary, mandatory, and persuasive authorities in Arkansas and gives examples of each.

III. The Research Process

Clients expect their lawyers to be effective and efficient researchers. Legal researchers are effective when they find the best authority that applies to the facts. They are efficient if they can do so without wasting time and energy (and money) by looking in the wrong sources or following unproductive leads.

---

6. Specialized courts such as federal bankruptcy courts are similarly bound by higher courts.

Table 1-2. Hierarchy of Authority in Arkansas Legal Research

	Mandatory Authority	Persuasive Authority
Primary Authority	U.S. Constitution and U.S. Supreme Court cases (for federal constitutional issues) Arkansas Constitution Arkansas statutes Arkansas administrative rules Opinions of Arkansas Supreme Court and Arkansas Court of Appeals Arkansas rules of practice, procedure, and professional conduct	Opinions of Arkansas Attorney General Opinions of other state or federal courts interpreting or applying similar constitutional or statutory provisions Opinions of courts in other jurisdictions involving similar common-law issues Non-majority parts of opinions of Arkansas courts (dicta, concurring, and dissenting opinions) Similar constitutional provisions, statutes, rules, or common law in other jurisdictions
Secondary Authority		Treatises Restatements Law review articles Practice aids Dictionaries Legal encyclopedias

Effective and efficient legal researchers plan their research, following a regular and thorough process that leads them to the authority that controls the legal issue. Table 1-3 outlines the steps of this fundamental research process.

The process of research does not necessarily follow the later steps in order — sometimes you can skip ahead; other times you will circle back or repeat a step. For example, you've found a secondary source's reference to a case that you need to read immediately, not later in the process. If you are unfamiliar with an area of law, however, it's wiser to follow each step of the process in the order indicated.

As you gain experience in researching legal questions, however, you'll customize this basic process for each new research project. To customize, consider

Table 1-3. Overview of the Research Process

1. Make a research plan.
2. Identify the issues and the scope of your assignment.
3. Determine the relevant jurisdiction and type of law.
4. For each issue, generate a list of research terms, from broad to narrow.
5. Consult secondary sources, finding tools, or practice aids for additional research terms and citations to primary authority.
6. Retrieve, read, and evaluate relevant primary authority in print or online sources.
7. Update and validate relevant materials.
8. Decide when to stop.
9. If necessary, return to earlier steps for follow-up research.

whether you need to follow all of these steps, and if so, in what order. For example, if you know that a situation is controlled by a statute, begin your research with an annotated version of the statute, rather than a secondary source.

A. Make a Research Plan

A research plan is your own plan, so it need not follow any particular format or order. By creating a general template for planning research, you can not only keep track of your research but you can also report more efficiently your research to others (such as your supervising attorney, or a judge, to name a few).

At a minimum, your research plan template should identify or consider the following:

- a preliminary description of the issue you are researching (and if multiple issues, make a separate research plan for each);
- the governmental units or sources that supply *mandatory* authority for the issue (and if there is more than one such unit or source, their hierarchical order, unless you have a reason to order them differently);
- the places where you plan to look for that authority (and if you have a choice of places to obtain the same information, giving some thought to which is the "best");
- whether it would be helpful or instructive or time-saving to find a source that has already researched (fully or partially) the same issue, and if so, what source(s) that might be;
- the methods you'll use to update or validate relevant authority and a way to record *when* you do so;

- a way to keep track of the sources you have *finished* searching, so that you don't unnecessarily repeat unproductive steps or follow unproductive leads; and
- a self-reminder to get all the data needed for full *ALWD* or *Bluebook* citations[7] for each source you actually consulted and that you are likely to use (if done while you still have the source in front of you, you won't need to revisit the source for that information).

Develop a systematic and thorough note-taking system, including the date(s) of research, what you found (or didn't find) in each specific source you consulted, and the steps you have taken to ensure the currency and validity of the sources you ultimately chose. It's critical to record your steps at each stage of the research process. You could be interrupted. You might forget where you left off or where you've already looked. You might have to turn the project over to someone else. You might need to justify why you spent the amount of time you did on the project. You might not find anything and have to explain to a supervisor what you did and where you looked.

Legal research is complex and time-consuming. You will consult many different sources, and you will not likely do it all at one sitting. Having a complete set of research notes — essentially a journal of your research — not only helps keep track of your work but keeps you out of trouble.

B. Identify the Issues and Scope of the Project

The beginning steps are to identify — at least preliminarily — the issues that are present and to determine the scope of the research project. Even when a supervising attorney gives you the issues to research, be alert to additional issues and sub-issues that are necessary to address the research project. Often the key to identifying these issues is to look at the outcome sought by the client. Does she seek to enforce a legal right? Has she been charged with some sort of crime? Is she negotiating a business relationship with another party?

Determining the project's scope is particularly important for those performing the research under the supervision or direction of another lawyer.

---

7. See Appendix A for an overview of the basic components required for citations to legal sources. Appendix A identifies relevant citation rules for both the *ALWD Guide to Legal Citation* (5th ed. 2014) and the *Bluebook* (20th ed. 2015). Although parallel citations to official and unofficial reporters are not *required* unless used in briefs to an Arkansas appellate court, this book uses parallel citations to all Arkansas cases. *See* Ark. R. Sup. Ct. & Ct. App. 4-2(a)(7).

The answers to the following questions help to establish the parameters of your research:

- What does the research project entail?
- How will this project be used? If written, who will read it?
- How much depth is expected or required?
- How much time should I spend (or not exceed)?
- When are the research and analysis needed?
- If I need additional facts, where should I go?

Once you have a sense of the kind of problem you're tasked with researching and the scope of your expected research, it's time to examine the facts present in the client's situation. Identifying key facts in the client's problem helps researchers refine their sense of the issues and begin to shape their research strategy.

Assume that Rachel Goshen comes to your law firm with two documents: a written employment contract she signed three years ago when she started working for Blackacre Realty Company in Morrilton, Arkansas, and a letter she just received from Blackacre's law firm, advising her that she has violated her employment contract's non-compete provision and threatening her with a lawsuit. The contract provided that Ms. Goshen would not work for a competitor for two years after terminating her employment with Blackacre.

Ms. Goshen tells you that she resigned her position as a real estate agent for Blackacre four months ago and has started her own company. Her new company does business in Hot Springs, Arkansas, which is in a different county, and her listings are primarily residential and urban, whereas Blackacre specializes in commercial and rural agricultural properties. She wants to know whether Blackacre can prevent her from operating her own company.

The biggest issue is, of course, whether Blackacre has a viable cause of action against Ms. Goshen for breach of the employment contract; within this big issue, however, there are several smaller issues, all of which may affect the research and the course of action the lawyer chooses to pursue on Ms. Goshen's behalf.

Whatever you identify as preliminary issues, be prepared to amend them as your research progresses. As you locate relevant authorities, you may discover new sub-issues you hadn't previously recognized or realize that something you thought was an issue is unimportant.

C. Determine the Relevant Jurisdiction and Type of Law

In researching any legal task, lawyers must determine the *jurisdiction* to which the task is tied. Jurisdiction refers to the governmental entity whose laws apply. A state's laws apply within its boundaries; federal law applies across the nation, regardless which state one is in. For example, when your task involves finding solely the law of a particular state, such as Arkansas, your research plan will direct you to state law materials (e.g., the *Arkansas Code of 1987*, Arkansas administrative rules, and cases from Arkansas courts). However, a matter may implicate the laws of another state, whose state law materials you will similarly need to examine. Further, matters involving United States law invoke federal jurisdiction, and research into such matters involves the use of federal materials (e.g., the *United States Code*, federal regulations, federal court rules, and cases from federal courts).

Pay attention to the *type of law* the task involves. The type of law gives you important cues to the type of research materials to consult. Does the task concern itself with the application of statutory law to the client's problem? Do administrative rules and regulations apply? Is the issue one of common law? As a beginning step, identify and prioritize the research materials you plan to use.

Early in a research project, avoid making assumptions that limit your search. If you don't know whether the research problem involves federal or state law, determining the jurisdiction is the first research step. If you don't know whether the problem involves statutory or common law, find out whether a statute governs the situation before jumping into case law.

D. Generate a List of Research Terms

Many legal resources in print use lengthy indexes as the starting point for finding legal authority. Electronic sources often require the researcher to enter words that are likely to appear in a synopsis or in the full text of relevant documents. To ensure your research is thorough, prepare a comprehensive list of words, terms, and phrases — whether legal terms or common words — to locate relevant law. Whether you use online or print resources, or a combination of the two, the terms on this list are your *research terms*.

Organized brainstorming is a great way to compile a comprehensive list of research terms. Some research experts recommend asking the journalistic questions: *Who? What? Where? When? Why?*[8] Others suggest a comprehensive analysis of facts suggesting likely issues for research.[9] Whether you follow

---

8. *See, e.g.,* Christina L. Kunz et al., *The Process of Legal Research* 25–26 (8th ed. 2012).

9. *See, e.g.,* Amy E. Sloan, *Basic Legal Research* 27–30 (6th ed. 2015) (using factual categories for parties and their relationships, places and things involved, potential claims and defenses, and the relief sought); Steven M. Barkan et al., *Fundamentals of*

one of these suggestions or develop your own method, generate a broad list of research terms regarding the facts, issues, and desired solutions to the client's legal problem. Include in the list both specific and general words for the concepts present in the client's situation. Think of synonyms and antonyms when you are uncertain which terms an index includes. A legal dictionary or thesaurus is a good resource for finding additional terms.

Order your research terms from the most general to the most specific. In constructing searches for online sources, consider the breadth or narrowness of the research terms being developed. Construct too broad a search, and you'll retrieve thousands of documents, the vast majority of which have no application to the issue. Construct too narrow a search, and you'll miss relevant and important documents that use slightly different language to address the issue. If you are researching in print sources, look at their indexes. Indexes are organized by general topics, with the more specific topics listed underneath. While the most narrow of your research terms may not appear in an index, you may encounter them in statutory language or case law once you begin to locate applicable primary authority. And if you don't find any of your narrow terms, this is a signal to broaden the research to include analogous concepts.

Update the list of terms as you go along. Once you begin work, you are likely to find new terms for the list and to conclude that you can delete others. This sort of insight is particularly likely as you read secondary sources and cases repeating the key words judges use in discussing particular topics. Or you may learn a *term of art*, a word or phrase that has special meaning in a particular area of the law. For example, the word "consideration" has particular legal significance in the law of contracts. Add terms of art to the list of research terms.

Using the employment contract example set out above, Table 1-4 provides examples of research terms related to this project. Compare the terms generated by each method: Which concepts are similar? How do they differ? Similar terms will likely make up the key research terms; different terms may be important for more subtle issues.

E. Consult Secondary Sources, Finding Tools, and Practice Aids

Secondary sources offer you the broadest possible array of information, from the most basic to the most esoteric. When new projects force you to work

---

Legal Research 15–16 (9th ed. 2009) (using the acronym "TARP" for organizing facts as "Thing," "Action," "Relief," and "Persons or parties").

Table 1-4. Generating Research Terms

Journalistic Approach

Who: employee, employer, competitor, real estate agent

What: contract, employment, employment contract, competition, non-competition, covenant not to compete, commercial and agricultural properties, residential real estate

Where: Arkansas, cities in different counties

When: two-year contractual restriction, four months since resignation

Why: lawsuit, demand letter, action for breach of contract's non-competition clause

---

TARP Approach

Thing: contract, employment, employment contract, real estate, restraint on trade, non-competition clause, covenant not to compete, two-year restraint

Action: promise, breach, hiring, resignation, sale of real estate, creation of new company

Relief: lawsuit, injunction, damages, defenses

Persons or parties: employee, employer, competitor, real estate agent

---

in unfamiliar areas of the law, starting the research in a basic secondary authority, such as a legal encyclopedia, provides context and helpful background. In addition, you may discover additional or more focused research terms that assist in quickly locating the best materials. Secondary sources treating the issues within a given jurisdiction, such as law review articles or state law treatises, can provide citations to primary, mandatory authority.

Depending on the type of law that is involved in a research project, the materials may be organized chronologically or by subject. Unless you have precise clues to find a chronologically organized source, such as the exact date a judicial opinion was released, you will probably have better success locating materials according to subject. *Finding tools* are research aids that help you quickly gather citations to potentially relevant primary materials; these tools include digests, key numbers, indexes, annotations, directories, and search engines.

In other situations, a *practice aid* may be the best source to start with. Practice aids include handbooks and continuing legal education materials, form books, and jury instructions, to name a few. Usually written by local experts in particular topics, practice aids tend to be jurisdiction-specific.

Let's return to the employment contract example. If you had never re-searched employment contracts before, you might choose to begin your research by looking for the research terms in some secondary sources. You might start with a general overview of the topic, consulting a legal encyclopedia. The encyclopedia entry would not only help you to generally understand this area of law, but it might also give you additional ideas for research terms and even citations to primary authorities in the relevant jurisdiction.

F. Retrieve, Read, and Evaluate Relevant Primary Authority Online or in Print

The next step is finding and assessing primary authority. If the secondary sources or finding tools utilized in the previous step yielded citations to rele-vant primary authority in the jurisdiction, obtain those documents and be-gin reviewing them.

Use the research terms to search for secondary materials or primary sources on the Internet or in online databases such as Bloomberg Law, Fastcase, Lexis, and Westlaw, narrowing and filtering their extensive collections of materials organized by jurisdiction and type.[10] Carefully choose and arrange the words to use in the search engine mechanisms used by these databases. Computer-assisted legal research, while convenient, requires thoughtful planning in or-der to be both effective and thorough.

The most effective online searches target databases that are known to con-tain current, complete, and accurate authorities from the jurisdiction whose laws apply. Useful portals to reliable electronic resources and databases are maintained by the Arkansas Supreme Court Library,[11] the Federal Digital Sys-tem ("FDsys"), and the Law Library of Congress,[12] emphasizing sites that of-fer the full text of legal authorities.

Alternatively, go to print resources of the kinds of legal materials the issues have implicated. In print sources, review indexes for research terms, then read the relevant sections. Find (or rule out) controlling *constitutional provisions*, *statutes*, or *rules*. Use *annotated codes* (especially when researching constitu-tions and statutes) to find cases interpreting and applying the relevant sections.

---

10. For guidance on using these kinds of online resources, consult the remain-ing chapters of this book, which go into greater detail.

11. *Library Electronic Resources*, https://courts.arkansas.gov/courts/supreme -court/library (last visited Feb. 28, 2016).

12. *Guide to Law Online*, http://www.loc.gov/law/help/guide.php (June 22, 2015).

Find additional citations to cases using *digests*, especially if there is no controlling statutory authority.[13]

No matter how promising a source looks, you won't know exactly how it applies until you have carefully read it and determined its applicability. Effective researchers realize that skimming the headnotes of a case doesn't provide enough information to know the reasoning process used by a court. Just because a case contains some facts similar to the client's problem doesn't mean that the case addresses the same legal issues. To be effective, you must read the actual text to determine whether this source in fact addresses your issue.

At times, you will find several potentially applicable authorities, and part of your job is to evaluate and choose among those authorities. In general, the best authorities to rely upon are those which are the most recent, the most factually similar, and for cases, from the highest court in the relevant jurisdiction. This holds true even when the most pertinent authorities are *adverse*, meaning they do not favor the client's position.

G. Confirm the Currency and Validity of Relevant Materials

In one sense, research is like panning for gold. To find nuggets worth keeping, you must sift through a lot of material, examining it to determine what to discard and what merits a closer look. The next step in the process tests your nuggets to determine exactly how valuable they are.

Once you have selected appropriate authorities to apply to the facts of the client's situation, you must confirm their currency and continued validity, in a process commonly referred to as *updating*.[14] Online sources are typically edited to incorporate changes, whether additions or deletions. Because this editing means it's not easy to tell whether an online source has been modified from an earlier version, it is equally important to look for a date indicating the currency of the online version.

In contrast, the first step in updating a print source is to check for printed *supplements* to the original text. Supplements not only contain new information, but also indicate the deletion or amendment of materials in the original. Supplements are inserted into a pocket in a book's back cover (giving rise to the name *pocket part)* or available as separate documents. Pocket part supplements

---

13. For guidance on using resources in print, consult the remaining chapters of this book, which go into greater detail.

14. Chapter 9, Updating Your Research, details the processes used for updating online and print sources.

are frequently used to update statutory codes and secondary sources. With any supplement, look for a date indicating its currency.

Whether the authority being updated is in an online or a print source, the next step in updating that source is to use a *citator*. Citators retrieve subsequent sources that affect or refer to the authority you have found, and they help you to determine what effect, if any, they have on that authority.[15]

H. Decide When to Stop

Deciding when to stop is an important step in the research process. Some researchers stop too soon; more researchers find it difficult to quit researching, perhaps because they aren't ready to begin writing. We tend to ask ourselves, "When is it time to stop?" A better question is: "Why *isn't* it yet time to stop?"

It *isn't* time to stop just because research efforts have located some relevant materials. Experienced researchers know that even relevant materials may be superseded or rendered obsolete by newer or different authorities — a fact that careful updating reveals. You can feel comfortable about ending your research, however, when the various sources you're checking lead to the same ultimate authorities, and no matter which new path you try, you don't find anything new.

On the other hand, if you aren't finding anything relevant, while it's still not time to stop, *it is time* to re-evaluate your methods and the project. If your research has been fundamentally electronic, try using print sources, or vice versa. Expand the list of research terms, or add or substitute synonymous terms. Try other secondary sources or try another jurisdiction. If you find relevant materials in another state, for example, note any different research terms, key numbers, or citing references in that jurisdiction, and follow those leads. You may in fact have an *issue of first impression* in the jurisdiction, one that has never before been presented to courts in that state, in which case the persuasive primary authorities from other jurisdictions guide your analysis.

If you're having trouble finding relevant authority and you're doing this project for a supervising attorney, contact that person within a reasonable amount of time to discuss the status of the research. Research notes help demonstrate the following:

- What you were looking for (i.e., showing whether you understood the issue);
- The research terms you used;
- The jurisdiction and type of law you identified;

---

15. Citators are covered in detail in Chapter 9.

- The specific sources you reviewed; and
- The manner in which you updated that research.

With this information, you can show a supervising attorney that you in fact followed a careful and thorough research process. By memorializing the methods and leads that were not productive, you may save another person (or yourself, if you've forgotten where you looked and what you did) from unnecessarily duplicating those research dead-ends.

I. If Necessary, Return to Earlier Steps

Legal research rarely proceeds in a linear fashion. At times it's necessary to return to earlier steps in the research process. Sometimes that's because the researcher hasn't found enough useful materials in the sources he selected. Sometimes it's because his research illuminates additional issues he hadn't considered in the beginning. Sometimes it's because the sources he's finding reveal that facts he didn't consider being legally relevant are important to the resolution of the problem. Whatever the reason, this circling back is not a bad thing. Table 1-5 demonstrates graphically the non-linear process of research.

Table 1-5. The Recursive Process of Research

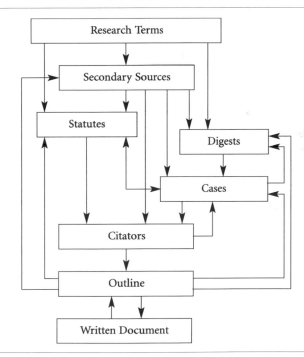

IV. Researching the Law — Organization of This Text

While Chapter 1 has introduced you to the general process of legal research, the remaining chapters in this book explain in detail how to conduct Arkansas legal research in a variety of sources.

Because the research process often begins with secondary sources, especially when the issue involves an unfamiliar area of the law, Chapter 2 addresses secondary authority and practice materials. Secondary authority includes not only Arkansas-based materials like handbooks and treatises, but also a rich variety of more general sources for helpful background information, additional ideas for research terms, and citations to primary authority. Practice materials include such things as form books and jury instructions, which address the law to apply in deciding the outcome of a trial.

Chapter 3 addresses the highest of all primary authorities in Arkansas, the state constitution. It provides some historical context for the creation and evolution of the current constitution — the Arkansas Constitution of 1874 — and its amendments.

Chapter 4 treats the judicial form of primary authority, i.e., case law. Although lawyers rarely *begin* their research with case law, it makes up a large portion of most research projects. The chapter begins with a description of the Arkansas court system and the anatomy of a judicial opinion, and it then discusses how to use online and print resources to find applicable cases.

Chapter 5 deals with enacted law at the state and local levels, i.e., statutes and ordinances. Current Arkansas statutes are collected in the *Arkansas Code of 1987 Annotated* and arranged by subject matter. The chapter also discusses earlier statutory compilations, as you may encounter references to them in your research.

Chapter 6 covers legislation and legislative history, including a close look at the Arkansas General Assembly and the lawmaking process, tracking legislation from bill to act to slip law to session law.

Chapter 7 discusses Arkansas administrative law, the product of the executive branch of government and its administrative agencies. Administrative materials include primarily the rules and regulations promulgated by agencies. They also include the opinions of the administrative law courts who adjudicate disputes between litigants and these agencies.

Chapter 8 deals with Arkansas court rules and rules of professional conduct, which regulate the way attorneys practice law and the manner in which courts handle cases. Court rules include the rules of civil and criminal procedure, appellate procedure, and evidence, among others.

Chapter 9 discusses the processes and tools available for updating your research to ensure that the mandatory sources upon which the research relies are current, valid, and accurate. It also includes how to find treatment of the case by later authorities, whether mandatory or persuasive.

Appendix A provides quick references to rules governing the citation of common forms of authorities. Appendix B contains bibliographic entries for miscellaneous resources that are valuable to Arkansas legal researchers, arranged by topic. These entries include references to practice aids, treatises, and other secondary sources on Arkansas-specific topics and to URLs for useful websites, e.g., the Arkansas Bar Association, the Arkansas Judiciary, and the Arkansas General Assembly.

Chapter 2

Secondary Sources and Practice Materials

I. Introduction to Secondary Sources

A. Overview

Despite their label, secondary materials are often the first sources that effective and efficient legal researchers consult. Secondary sources provide commentary on primary forms of law, taking the forms of explanation, summary, criticism, suggestions for change, suggestions for limitation, or evaluation.

For researchers unfamiliar with the issues and materials generated by their clients' problems, secondary sources can provide a basic understanding of the governing law, its context, and its vocabulary. Secondary sources can lead you to relevant material that helps to focus the research. Secondary sources also function as finding tools, providing shortcuts to primary authority by offering numerous references to existing cases, statutes, and rules on point. They may inspire you to pursue a creative and useful new theory, which — if successful — will add to the development of law. You may also use them as a tool for keeping current in a changing area of the law.

Never treat a secondary source as the definitive authority on a subject. Unlike primary authorities, created by governmental branches and binding within their jurisdictions, secondary sources are — at most — merely persuasive. They are written by lawyers, law professors, law students, or even judges (but not while they are acting in an adjudicative capacity). Depending on a secondary source's comprehensiveness and its authors' expertise, its degree of persuasiveness varies.[1] Therefore, direct your use of secondary materials in

---

1. The diminishing persuasive impact of secondary materials in opinions by the Arkansas courts is well documented and analyzed by A. Michael Beaird, *Citations to Authority by the Arkansas Appellate Courts, 1950–2000*, 25 U. Ark. Little Rock L. Rev. 301, 320–28 (2003).

general to two goals: first, learning more about the issues and law at stake; and second, discovering leads to primary controlling authority.

This chapter introduces a variety of secondary sources commonly used by legal researchers: legal encyclopedias; treatises and other books; annotations in *American Law Reports*; restatements, uniform laws, and model codes; legal periodicals (including law reviews, specialty journals, and bar journals); practice aids (such as jury instructions, practice handbooks, and form books); and continuing legal education ("CLE") publications.[2]

B. Using Secondary Sources and Practice Materials[3]

Depending on the project, some secondary sources are better than others. For a broad overview of an area of law, consult a legal encyclopedia or an annotation. For in-depth analysis on a narrow topic, a law review article is more likely to be helpful. On cutting-edge issues, CLE material, articles in the Social Science Research Network ("SSRN"), Bloomberg BNA Law Reports, and blogs will cover new areas of law quickly. In litigation, court-approved forms and uniform jury instructions are indispensable.

Consider your own background in the subject matter and the goals of your research, and select from these sources accordingly. A source that was not helpful in your last research project may be perfect for the current project. How many secondary sources you use depends on the success of your early searches and the time available to you.

Despite the value of secondary sources, rarely will you cite a secondary source in writing a memorandum or brief. Some sources, such as indexes for finding periodicals, are not "authority" at all. Rather, they are authority-finding tools; don't cite them. Cite legal encyclopedias, A.L.R. annotations, and CLE material only as a last resort, when no mandatory primary authority or persuasive primary authority addresses the point. Even sources that carry some authority, including law review articles and treatises, should be cited in-

---

2. Appendix B refers to many Arkansas practice materials. To locate more such materials, see library guides, articles, and bibliographies prepared by professional law librarians, including the following: Glen-Peter Ahlers, *Selected List of Legal Materials of Interest to the Practicing Bar of Arkansas*, 1994 Ark. L. Notes 83; A. Michael Beaird, *Citations to Authority by the Arkansas Appellate Courts: 1950–2000*, 25 U. Ark. Little Rock L. Rev. 301 (2003); Kathryn A. Fitzhugh, *Arkansas Practice Materials II: A Selective Annotated Bibliography*, 21 U. Ark. Little Rock L. Rev. 363 (1999).

3. The material in Section I.B. of this chapter is reproduced from *Oregon Legal Research*, Third Edition, by Suzanne E. Rowe, and is used with permission of the author.

frequently. By citing secondary sources, you are admitting to your reader that you could not find any primary authority supporting your arguments, thereby weakening those arguments substantially.

Three exceptions exist. First, when you need to summarize the development of the law and no case has provided such a summary, citing a treatise or law review article that traces that development could be helpful. Citation to secondary authority is also appropriate when there is no law on point for an argument you are making. This is likely to occur with new issues. It may also occur when you are arguing to expand or change the law. In these situations, your only support might come from a law review article. Finally, secondary authority may provide additional support for a point already cited to primary authority. For example, you can bolster an argument supported by a case, especially if it is from another jurisdiction, by also citing an article or treatise by a respected expert on the topic.

Whether or not you cite a secondary source in a document, you must decide the weight to give secondary authority in developing your own analysis. Consider the following criteria:

- *Who is the author?* The views of a respected scholar, an acknowledged expert, or a judge carry more weight than a student author or an anonymous editor.
- *When was the material published?* Especially for cutting-edge issues, a more recent article is more helpful. Even with more traditional issues, be sure that the material analyzes the current state of the law.
- *Where was the material published?* Treatises from leading publishers are considered more authoritative than opinions expressed on a blog. Law review articles published in established law journals are generally granted greater respect. A school's prestige and the length of the journal's existence can influence how well established a journal is. Thus, a journal that has been published for a century at a top law school may carry more respect than a new journal at an unaccredited school. A publication specific to your jurisdiction or dedicated to a particular topic, however, could be more helpful than a publication from another state or one with a general focus.
- *What depth is provided?* The more focused and thorough the analysis, the more useful the material will be.
- *How relevant is it to your argument?* If the author argues your exact point, the material is more persuasive than if the author's arguments are only tangential to yours.

- *Has this secondary source been cited previously by courts?* If a court has found a source persuasive in the past, it is likely to find it persuasive again. Remember that the text of a secondary source may become primary authority if it is adopted by a court or legislature.

II. Finding Secondary Sources and Practice Materials

Although secondary sources are increasingly available in electronic and online formats, the primary focus of this chapter is on print sources. Print sources are recommended for researchers who have no prior experience with a particular topic, as computer-assisted research may return results that are too narrow to give the researchers an appropriate overview of the topic or so broad as to be unmanageable. The process for researching secondary sources varies depending on the source. Table 2-1 provides a general outline for researching print sources.

Table 2-1. Outline for Researching Secondary Sources in Print

1. Generate a list of research terms.
2. Search library catalog for the location of relevant secondary sources in the topic area of the problem you're researching.
3. Consult the index of the secondary source to find references to the topics and terms of interest.
4. Find and read those references in the source's bound volumes (and pocket parts or supplements to those volumes, if any).
5. Skim the text and its footnotes for citations to primary authority in the jurisdiction that interests you.

A. Legal Encyclopedias and Dictionaries

1. Legal Encyclopedias

Legal encyclopedias provide general information on a wide variety of subjects. They are organized by subject matter under *topics*, which — in their print format — are presented alphabetically in bound volumes. The two national legal encyclopedias are *Corpus Juris Secundum* ("C.J.S.") and *American Jurisprudence, Second Series* ("Am. Jur. 2d"). Some encyclopedias treat topics in a single state, e.g., *California Jurisprudence, Third Edition* and *Pennsylvania Law Encyclopedia*. As of this writing, there is no encyclopedia treating solely Arkansas law.

To use a legal encyclopedia in print, review its soft-bound index volumes for the research terms generated so far (remembering that you may find additional research terms at this early stage).[4] The index provides references to the encyclopedia's topics (usually in the form of an abbreviated word or phrase) and their section numbers. Tables in the front of the index volumes explain the topic abbreviations, and the encyclopedia's bound volumes organize the topics alphabetically. When you find a promising topic, check the spines of the bound volumes to find the volume containing that topic.

When researching an unfamiliar area of the law, resist the temptation to rush straight to any specific section. Instead, skim text at the beginning of the topic for an overview and general information. This step helps you place the specific information you're seeking in context; it may also help you discover other relevant areas of inquiry.

Turn to the particular section number within that topic and read its text. Because the writer's goal is to summarize the law, the text of most encyclopedia entries is brief. Encyclopedia entries will identify jurisdictional variations in the law, but they will not resolve or explain those differences. Always check the pocket part (the additional pages inserted in the back cover) of the encyclopedia volume, where you may find updated commentary on the topic and section.[5]

One of the encyclopedia's most helpful features is the footnote. The footnotes in each section refer to primary authority from miscellaneous jurisdictions. If a footnote cites an authority for the jurisdiction whose law you are researching, even if it's dated, it provides a lead for discovering other, more recent authority on point; even if the case is from another jurisdiction, you can still use it to find relevant cases from the relevant jurisdiction.

An encyclopedia may also provide cross-references to other topics or sources. For example, C.J.S. includes cross-references to relevant topics and key numbers in the West digest system, discussed in Chapter 4. Similarly, Am. Jur. 2d cross-references *American Law Reports*, discussed later in this chapter.

Legal encyclopedias are available online in both Lexis and Westlaw.[6] You can restrict the search to encyclopedias before running it by choosing content type or a specific source, or you can filter the results after running the search.

---

4. Review Chapter 1 for information on generating search terms.

5. For more information about finding updated content in a source, see Chapter 9.

6. Both C.J.S. and Am. Jur. 2d are available on Westlaw (choose "Secondary Sources," then "Texts & Treatises"). Lexis has an online version of Am. Jur. 2d (in "Secondary Materials").

You may search using terms and connectors or natural language searches or by browsing the encyclopedia's table of contents.

Some free online services offer legal encyclopedias, but they typically do not have sophisticated searching options. They can, however, provide useful information at the early stages of research. One example is Wex, provided by the Legal Information Institute hosted by Cornell University.[7] Wex is a wiki website, which means that the content is provided by volunteer contributors.[8] Its list of terms is extensive and quite detailed, and it also provides a search box for keyword searching.

Because of their broad but shallow coverage of legal issues, legal encyclopedias are typically disfavored as authoritative sources, and attorneys are generally discouraged from citing them as authority in legal memos and briefs.[9]

2. Legal Dictionaries

Legal dictionaries define words and phrases used in legal contexts and indicate their correct pronunciation. Because some words mean something different in their legal sense as opposed to their ordinary sense, a good legal dictionary will help you understand those differences. The development of the law in Anglo-American jurisprudence also means that many Latin words and phrases remain in usage, and the legal dictionary translates and explains them.

The best known of all legal dictionaries is *Black's Law Dictionary.*[10] Not only is *Black's* available in its familiar hard-bound format, it is also available on Westlaw. Another venerable dictionary is *Ballentine's Law Dictionary* (3d ed. 1969), available in print and on Lexis. Online dictionaries have proliferated in recent years; one popular resource is *Findlaw Legal Dictionary.*[11] Another is *The People's Law Dictionary.*[12]

---

7. https://www.law.cornell.edu/wex.

8. Wex does, however, qualify its author contributors before allowing submissions, unlike Wikipedia.

9. One study found that Arkansas appellate courts occasionally cite legal encyclopedias for general propositions. In the year 2000, for example, a legal encyclopedia was cited 27 times by the Arkansas Supreme Court and 21 times by the Arkansas Court of Appeals. *See* Beaird, *supra* note 1, at 326.

10. *See Black's Law Dictionary* (Bryan Garner ed., Thomson Reuters 10th ed. 2014).

11. http://dictionary.lp.findlaw.com.

12. http://dictionary.law.com.

B. Books and Treatises

A book on a legal topic can provide a deeper discussion and more relevant references than what's in an encyclopedia entry. Legal texts include treatises, hornbooks, and *Nutshells*. All of these books share the purpose of covering a particular legal subject, such as contracts or civil procedure. They are distinguished mainly by their level of coverage. Treatises are generally more comprehensive statements on a subject than hornbooks, which offer more summarized views. *Nutshells* are a series of soft-cover books published by West offering an even more condensed explanation of the law on a particular subject. Accordingly, an attorney may use a treatise to become familiar with a new area of legal practice, while a law student may turn to a hornbook or a *Nutshell* to prepare for class or review for exams.

Locate a treatise or book by conducting a search in the library's catalog for the general subject matter of your research project. To use the treatise or book, begin with the table of contents or the index to find specific sections on point. In multi-volume treatises, the index is often found in the last volume of the series. Depending on the arrangement of material in the treatise or book, indexes may refer to page numbers, section numbers, or paragraph numbers.

Some treatises are so well known and widely respected that a colleague or supervisor may suggest that you begin research with a particular title. Examples include *Prosser & Keeton on the Law of Torts*; Wright & Miller's *Federal Practice and Procedure*; and *Corbin on Contracts*. The authoritative value of a book or treatise depends largely on the reputation of the author. For example, the late Dr. Robert A. Leflar of the University of Arkansas (Fayetteville) School of Law was a nationally-recognized expert on the conflict of laws, and early editions of his treatise, *American Conflicts Law*, have been cited hundreds of times by American courts.[13] Although the trend has been for courts to rely less on treatises (or any secondary sources) than they did in years past,[14] these materials are still useful for practitioners who need to learn more about a subject. Several well-known treatises and books on Arkansas law are included in Appendix B.

---

13. *See, e.g.*, Robert A. Leflar, *American Conflicts Law* (2d ed., Bobbs-Merrill 1968); Robert A. Leflar, Luther L. McDougal III & Robert L. Felix, *American Conflicts Law* (4th ed., Michie 1986). As of this writing, the most recent edition is Robert L. Felix & Ralph U. Whitten, *American Conflicts Law* (6th ed., Carolina Academic Press 2011).

14. *See* Beaird, *supra* note 1, at 320–22.

Many books and treatises are available online through Lexis or Westlaw.[15] Treatises and books published by Bloomberg BNA, the Practising Law Institute, and a few other publishers are available on Bloomberg Law.

Treatises are regularly updated.[16] Bound treatises are updated through the use of pocket parts, supplements, and new editions. Looseleaf treatises are produced in binders that are updated by replacing outdated pages throughout the binder with current material. Each page is dated to show when it was last updated. Also, new pages at the beginning of some looseleaf binders are highlighted by being printed on different color paper.

C. *American Law Reports*

American Law Reports ("A.L.R.") contains commentary articles called *annotations*. Annotations tend to focus on very narrow topics from a practitioner's perspective, and they provide a survey of the law on those topics in the federal system and the 50 states. Thus, locating an annotation on the exact topic of your research is extremely helpful.

The first volume of A.L.R. was published in 1919. Early volumes in the series contained both state and federal subjects. In 1969, A.L.R. began a new publication for federal topics, *ALR Federal*, now in its third series. Today, state subjects are discussed in the third through seventh numbered series of A.L.R.[17]

Annotations are written by lawyers who are knowledgeable about their topics but who are not necessarily recognized experts in those areas. Each annotation in the first through the sixth series and the first two federal series was accompanied by one full-length case. For example, A.L.R. features an annotation for a leading case, *Thornton v. Southwest Detroit Hospital*, dealing with the Emergency Medical Treatment and Active Labor Act, 42 U.S.C. § 1395dd (EMTALA). Although the *Thornton* case is reported at 895 F.2d 1131, the full text of the case is also reproduced in A.L.R. Following the case is an annotation, *Construction and Application of Emergency Medical Treatment and Active Labor Act (42 U.S.C.A. § 1395dd)*, written by attorney Me-

---

15. Texts and treatises can be found in both Lexis (under "Secondary Materials") and Westlaw (under "Secondary Sources").

16. If your research leads you to an older work that does not show signs of recent updating, be sure to check other sources that may contain more recent and relevant law.

17. Outdated annotations are superseded by new series.

lissa K. Stull. The annotation delves into important issues raised by the case and compares the treatment of those issues in other cases. Among some of the topics discussed in the annotation are the reasons Congress enacted EMTALA, the effect of related statutes, the liability imposed on hospitals, and available remedies.

Because cases are so easily obtained online, the publisher stopped printing the cases in A.L.R. beginning with A.L.R.7th and A.L.R. Fed. 3d; therefore, A.L.R. is now strictly a secondary source. These series did, however, include additional features described below.

Annotations follow the same format. They begin with a table of contents, cross-references to other relevant publications, a subject index, and a "Table of Jurisdictions Represented." Next, an introduction identifies the scope of the annotation and provides citations to related A.L.R. annotations. Always review these related annotations; they may lead you to even more relevant annotations. After this introductory material, the annotation continues with the analysis of case law from all jurisdictions that address the issue. A.L.R.7th and A.L.R. Fed. 3d also include a graphical analysis of selected articles, callout boxes of pertinent factors, and jurisdictional headings for substantive setouts.

A.L.R. annotations in print are updated with pocket parts; consult the pocket part to find references to newer information. Online versions of A.L.R. have weekly updates.

There are several ways to locate annotations in A.L.R. If you are researching in print, you will use either the *ALR Index* or the *ALR Digest*.[18] The *ALR Index* has references to annotations in the second through sixth series and the first and second federal series. Conducting research in the *ALR Index* is similar to researching in other indexes. Search for key terms, which will lead to citations to annotations related to those terms.[19] Each index entry includes a brief description of the issue covered by the annotation, as well as its citation.[20] The index also provides cross-references to other terms. A.L.R. indexes are also updated with pocket parts; check them for new material. You should also check the Annotation History Table in the index volumes to see whether an annotation has been supplemented or superseded by a later annotation, rather than just updated in pocket parts. To search for annotations referenc-

---

18. Both the *ALR Digest* and the *ALR Index* are multi-volume works.
19. See Chapter 1, Section III.D, for information on developing a list of terms.
20. Note the series designation when writing annotation citations.

ing specific statutes, use the "Table of Laws, Rules, and Regulations" located in the back of the index. A.L.R. also publishes a one-volume *Quick Index* for both the A.L.R. Federal and the A.L.R. state law series.

If you are having trouble finding relevant annotations using the index, try using the *ALR Digest*. The *ALR Digest* includes references to annotations in A.L.R.'s third through seventh and all three federal series. It separates the law into topics and subtopics and gives short summaries of the annotations that relate to those topics. Beginning with A.L.R.6th, these digest entries have been reclassified to correspond to the West Key Number System;[21] this is also true for the digest references in the supplements to the other A.L.R. editions.

An additional feature found in A.L.R.7th, A.L.R. Fed. 2d, and A.L.R. Fed. 3d is the A.L.R. United States Supreme Court Review. This feature provides a summary of the U.S. Supreme Court decisions from the current term, along with references to related A.L.R. annotations.

A.L.R. is also available on Lexis (under "Secondary Materials") and Westlaw (under "Secondary Sources"). Both allow searching the full text of annotations for key terms. Lexis provides access to the full text of A.L.R. annotations within the second through seventh and all three federal series. Westlaw provides access to the full text of all A.L.R. annotations, including A.L.R. International. Westlaw also provides access to the *A.L.R. Index* and electronic annotations not available in print.

D. Restatements

A *restatement* is an organized and detailed summary of the common law in a specific legal area. Familiar titles include *Restatement of the Law Second, Contracts* and *Restatement of the Law Second, Torts*. Restatements are the result of collaborative efforts by committees of scholars, practitioners, and judges organized by the American Law Institute ("ALI").[22] These committees, led by a scholar called a *reporter*, draft text that explains the common law in rule format (i.e., the restatements are written under outline headings similar to those found in statutes rather than being written in the narrative format found in cases). The committees circulate the drafts for review and comment. A restatement published by ALI includes not only the text of the rules that embody the common law on that topic, but also provides annotations to cases discussing the restatement.

---

21. See Chapter 4.

22. For more information about the American Law Institute, visit its website, www.ali.org.

Table 2-2. Current Restatements of the Law

Restatement of the Law Third, Agency

Restatement of the Law, The Law of American Indians

Restatement of the Law, Charitable Nonprofit Organizations

Restatement of the Law Second, Conflict of Laws

Restatement of the Law Second, Contracts

Restatement of the Law, Employment Law

Restatement of the Law Fourth, The Foreign Relations Law of the United States

Restatement of the Law, The U.S. Law of International Commercial Arbitration

Restatement of the Law Second, Judgments

Restatement of the Law Third, The Law Governing Lawyers

Restatement of the Law, Liability Insurance

Restatement of the Law Second, Property (Landlord and Tenant)

Restatement of the Law Third, Property (Mortgages)

Restatement of the Law Third, Property (Servitudes)

Restatement of the Law Third, Property (Wills and Other Donative Transfers)

Restatement of the Law Third, Restitution and Unjust Enrichment

Restatement of the Law Third, Suretyship and Guaranty

Restatement of the Law Second, Torts

Restatement of the Law Third, Torts: Apportionment of Liability

Restatement of the Law Third, Torts: Liability for Economic Harm

Restatement of the Law Third, Torts: Liability for Physical and Emotional Harm

Restatement of the Law Third, Torts: Products Liability

Restatement of the Law Third, Torts: Intentional Torts to Persons

Restatement of the Law Third, Trusts

Restatement of the Law Third, Unfair Competition

Although some restatements are identified as the second or third series, they are the original works on their subjects.[23] For a list of the current restatements, see Table 2-2. A checklist — but not the text — of the current restatements and their supplements is also available on the American Law Institute's website.[24]

A portion of a restatement may become primary authority in a jurisdiction if a court adopts it in a particular case. After a court has adopted a portion of

---

23. *See e.g. Restatement of the Law Fourth, Foreign Relations Law of the United States; Restatement of the Law Third, The Law Governing Lawyers.*

24. https://www.ali.org/publications/#publication-type-restatements.

a restatement, its accompanying commentary, illustrations, and reporter's notes furnish valuable tools to its interpretation and application. In addition, the researcher may locate and use as persuasive authority cases from other states that have adopted the same section of the restatement.

To find a relevant restatement, search the library catalog for the subject matter, or search for the term "restatement." Within each restatement, use the table of contents, index, or appendix to find pertinent sections. The text of each restatement is followed by the commentary, and occasionally, by illustrations of key points made in the text. Appendix volumes provide citations to cases that have cited the restatement.

An entire restatement is updated only when a later version is published, such as *Restatement of the Law Third, Agency,* published in 2006. Regardless when the restatement you are consulting was published, check the volume's pocket parts (replaced annually), the appendix, or the interim case citations pamphlet (published semi-annually) for new cases citing the restatement section you are viewing. In addition, you may Shepardize or KeyCite a restatement to find cases or other works that have cited it.[25]

The restatements can also be searched in Lexis and Westlaw by entering search terms directly into the universal search box. You can restrict your search to "Secondary Materials" (Lexis) or "Secondary Sources" (Westlaw) or to a specific restatement.[26]

E. Looseleaf Services

A looseleaf service combines both primary and secondary sources under one title. In areas of law like taxation and environmental law, a single title may contain statutes, administrative regulations, annotations to cases and agency opinions, and commentary. The benefit is obvious: all of the material is gathered together so that you do not have to consult multiple sources. Bloomberg BNA, Commerce Clearing House ("C.C.H."), and Research Institute of America ("R.I.A.") are well-known publishers of looseleaf services.

The term *looseleaf* comes from the pages being kept in looseleaf, multi-ring notebooks rather than bound as books. The looseleaf format allows simple and frequent updates, as outdated pages are removed and replaced. A looseleaf service generally fills several volumes, arranged by topic, by statute, or by another system.

---

25. For detailed information on using Shepard's and KeyCite to update legal authorities, see Chapter 9.

26. You can apply these restrictions to the search before or after initially running it.

Looseleaf services typically provide a "How to Use" section, generally near the beginning of the first volume. Review this section before starting your research. Skim through a few volumes to become familiar with the organization of that particular service, paying careful attention to its method and frequency of updating.

If you do not know where to find a particular topic in a looseleaf, begin with the topical index. Often this is the first or last volume of the series. Look up your research terms, and write down the reference numbers given. They will likely be paragraph numbers rather than page numbers. Paragraph numbering facilitates indexing by the looseleaf service, even when it is frequently updated. A "paragraph" can consist of a few sentences, several actual paragraphs, or several pages. The paragraph number may be for the statute, regulations, annotations, or commentary. Turn to each paragraph number referenced in the index under your key terms, and read earlier and later pages around that paragraph number to ensure that you have reviewed all relevant material.

Online sources for looseleaf services include Bloomberg Law, Lexis and Westlaw. On all three services, you can search using Boolean terms and connectors and then use filters to focus the search on secondary materials.

F. Uniform Laws and Model Codes

Uniform laws and model codes are written by organizations that hope to harmonize the statutory laws of the 50 states. Much of the work of writing uniform laws and model codes is done by experts who are law professors, judges, legislators, or experienced attorneys. Statutory language is drafted, comments are solicited, and the language is finalized. The published uniform law or model code includes both the proposed statutory language and explanatory notes from the authors. Once a uniform law or a model code is adopted by a state's legislature, it becomes primary authority in that jurisdiction.

Familiar examples of these secondary sources include the Uniform Commercial Code (drafted by the ALI), the Uniform Testamentary Additions to Trusts Act (drafted by the National Conference of Commissioners on Uniform State Laws (NCCUSL)), and the Model Penal Code (drafted by the ALI). The full text of the Uniform Laws and their annotations can be accessed on Lexis ("Model Acts and Uniform Laws" under "Statutes and Legislation") and Westlaw ("Uniform Laws Annotated" under "Statutes and Court Rules"). Uniform laws enacted by state legislatures are listed at the NCCUSL's website.[27]

---

27. http://www.uniformlaws.org.

G. Legal Periodicals

1. Overview

Legal periodicals include law reviews and bar journals. Legal periodicals publish scholarly and practical articles written by law professors, judges, practitioners, or students. The typical law review article explores a specific legal issue in great detail. Law review authors typically analyze and evaluate the strengths and the weaknesses of laws currently in force, and in many instances, propose changes to those laws. Articles in bar journals are typically written to provide broad overviews of current issues of interest or to outline practical advice about certain areas of the law to members of the practicing bar.

Most law reviews are edited and published by law students. Law review student editors are selected on the basis of their high academic performance or through writing competitions. Because student-edited law reviews are intended for a general legal audience, they cover a broad range of topics. The best known of all is the *Harvard Law Review*. The two general law reviews published in Arkansas are the *Arkansas Law Review* and the *University of Arkansas at Little Rock Law Review*.

Some law reviews have a specialized focus, covering a narrow area of law. Examples include the *Journal of Food Law & Policy* (a student-edited journal published at the University of Arkansas–Fayetteville School of Law), *Arkansas Law Notes* (published by faculty of the University of Arkansas–Fayetteville School of Law), and the *Journal of Appellate Practice and Process* (published by faculty of the UALR Bowen School of Law).

Researchers can benefit from reading articles published in law reviews because the authors often explain the existing law before making their recommendations. The articles tend to be heavily footnoted, providing researchers with rich sources of additional leads to relevant authority. Student-written articles are often labeled "Comments," "Case Notes," "Notes," "Surveys," or "Recent Developments." While not as authoritative as articles written by recognized experts, student articles can provide clear and careful background and analysis of issues of significant interest.

Many bar associations publish their own law journals. Articles in bar journals are not only shorter than typical law review articles (including fewer footnotes), but their focus is more on the practical than the theoretical. The American Bar Association publishes the *ABA Journal*, which addresses issues of national interest. Each state's bar journal, such as *The Arkansas Lawyer*, contains articles of particular interest to attorneys practicing in that state.

2. Finding Tools for Legal Periodicals

There are multiple ways to find articles in legal periodicals. The *Current Law Index* ("CLI") is one of the more popular research tools for legal periodicals, in large part because it offers detailed subject indexing, but also because its electronic version, *LegalTrac*, is so easy to use. Available at computer terminals in many law libraries and updated daily, *LegalTrac* is a cumulative index, eliminating the need to check multiple volumes.

A large number of legal periodicals are searchable in Bloomberg Law, Lexis, and Westlaw databases. Enter your search terms in the universal search box; you can restrict the search initially by content type or specific source, or you can filter results after running the search. Lexis and Westlaw allow you to further restrict a search by segment or field, for instance, by restricting it to articles written by a certain author.

To search for law review articles, Fastcase links to HeinOnline, but you must have a HeinOnline subscription to view the full text. HeinOnline lets subscribers conduct full-text searching of a large number of articles.[28] The original focus of HeinOnline's service was pre-1980 material, often not included in Westlaw or Lexis databases; today, its collection is expanding. A number of law school libraries subscribe to this service and make it free to their students.

Google Scholar gives you another avenue for researching articles in legal periodicals. Enter search terms into Google Scholar's search window, or enter an author, date, or other publication information. Google Scholar's search engine links to other sources, including HeinOnline and JSTOR,[29] a database that stores the text of an article in PDF format.

An online resource for Arkansas legal periodicals, as well as other Arkansas secondary materials, is the *Arkansas Legal Index* ("ARLI"), maintained by the University of Arkansas at Little Rock Bowen School of Law Library.[30] Table 2-3 provides a list of the publications indexed by ARLI.

3. Obtaining an Article Once You Have Its Citation

Once you have the citation to an article using one of the finding tools discussed above, there are multiple ways you can access the full text of the article. Law libraries retain hard copies of various periodicals in bound volumes

---

28. http://home.heinonline.org.
29. www.jstor.org.
30. http://themis.law.ualr.edu:81.

Table 2-3. Publications Indexed by the Arkansas Legal Index (ARLI)

Arkansas Law Notes (1983–present)

Arkansas Law Review (1946–present)

Arkansas Lawyer (1967–present)

University of Arkansas at Little Rock Law Review (1978–present) (formerly *UALR Law Journal*)

ATLA Docket (1982–present) (three-year delay required by publisher)

Legislative Research Reports, Informational Memos, Staff Reports (1950–1986)

Selected CLE materials (1999–present)

Arkansas Bar Association Annual and Midyear Meeting Course Materials (2001–present)

Selected Arkansas treatises and other miscellaneous publications

stored by volume. Online services such as Lexis or Westlaw allow you to retrieve full texts of the article. These services, however, may not have older articles (pre-1980). For older articles, HeinOnline retrieves the full text. Another way to obtain an article's full text is to use an Internet search engine (such as Google) to determine whether the journal publishes online, and if so, to determine whether the journal maintains an online archive of its published articles.

H. Practice Materials

1. Jury Instructions

When cases are submitted to juries for decision, trial judges give the juries guidance on the law and its application, in the form of *jury instructions*. In Arkansas, jury instructions are commonly referred to as the "AMI" (for "Arkansas Model Instructions"). Civil jury instructions are drafted and approved by the Arkansas Supreme Court Committee on Model Jury Instructions–Civil; instructions for criminal cases are prepared by the Arkansas Supreme Court Committee on Model Jury Instructions–Criminal.

Arkansas jury instructions are available from several sources. Both the *Arkansas Model Jury Instructions, Civil* and the *Arkansas Model Jury Instructions, Criminal* are available for free on the Arkansas Judiciary website.[31] The

---

31. https://courts.arkansas.gov/forms-and-publications. See Appendix B for the URLs.

civil instructions are available on Westlaw, and the criminal instructions are available on Lexis. Print sources include *Arkansas Model Jury Instructions, Civil* (Thomson West 2016) (soft-bound with CD-ROM), and *Arkansas Model Jury Instructions, Criminal* (2d ed., LexisNexis 1994–) (looseleaf, or available as an e-book).

Federal jury instructions are also available in print and online sources. Civil and criminal jury instructions for federal district courts in Arkansas are on the Eighth Circuit's website.[32] Both are accessible on Lexis and Westlaw. Print sources include the *Eighth Circuit Manual of Model Jury Instructions–Civil, 2013 ed.* (Thomson West 2013) and the *Eighth Circuit Manual of Model Jury Instructions–Criminal, 2014 ed.* (Thomson West 2013).

2. Form Books and Practice Books

Attorneys frequently are called upon to draft documents needed for routine legal matters. Rather than draft each such document from scratch, they may work from standardized forms. A *form book* provides actual or sample forms or suggested language to insert into a form. A form can be a great shortcut in drafting a legal document, especially one the attorney is drafting for the first time in an unfamiliar area of law. A form is a good starting point, both because it saves the drafter from reinventing the wheel and because its standardized format ensures that necessary provisions are not overlooked. Even so, careful attorneys know not to rely blindly on any form. Forms are designed for general audiences, not for a particular client and that client's situation.

Before using a form, ensure that you understand not only every word it uses, but also that you understand the effect of each provision. Do not fill in the blanks and assume that the form correctly represents your client's needs. Do not hesitate to modify a form when necessary, and unless a particular form is prescribed by statute or by a court, feel free to revise its wording to cut down on legalese.

Arkansas statutes and court rules provide forms for particular situations. For example, Arkansas Code Annotated § 28-39-404 provides the form to use in electing to take against a will. To find statutory forms, search the index of the *Arkansas Code of 1987* for the substantive content of the form, or look under the index topic "Forms." Forms for Arkansas practice are also found in court rules (discussed in Chapter 8) and CLE materials (discussed below in Section H.3).

---

32. www.juryinstructions.ca8.uscourts.gov (pdf format).

Forms are increasingly available through online sources. For example, many standard Arkansas court forms are available through the Administrative Office of the Courts at the *Arkansas Judiciary* website.[33] Arkansas Workers' Compensation Commission forms are available on its website as well.[34] Bloomberg Law, Lexis, and Westlaw also maintain many databases for forms. Forms for federal court practice are available from the websites of the federal district and bankruptcy courts in Arkansas.[35]

Closely related to form books are *practice handbooks*. Practice handbooks are generally written by attorneys with significant experience in the topics they cover. They provide readers with a helpful overview of the topic and generous citations to leading authorities governing the topic. Handbooks often contain forms as well. To find forms in print, search your library's catalog by subject for the general and topical form books in its collection. Several popular Arkansas practice handbook titles are listed in Appendix B.

The Arkansas Bar Association publishes several practice handbooks, covering a variety of topics, including forms.[36] Not all handbooks are regularly updated; note their publication dates and be prepared to update their contents through additional research. The Arkansas Bar Association's flagship handbook, *The Arkansas Formbook*,[37] has been replaced by an online service, ArkBar Docs. ArkBar Docs is an automated document generation program, available to bar association members through subscription.[38]

3. Continuing Legal Education Materials

To maintain their licenses, attorneys in Arkansas are required to obtain 12 continuing legal education ("CLE") credits each year (including an hour of ethics).[39] CLE courses are offered by bar associations, commercial organ-

---

33. https://courts.arkansas.gov/forms-and-publications.

34. www.awcc.state.ar.us/forms.html.

35. http://www.are.uscourts.gov/forms (Eastern District); http://www.arwd.us courts.gov/forms (Western District); and www.arb.uscourts.gov/forms/forms.html (bankruptcy).

36. A complete list can be found at https://www.arkbar.com/for-attorneys/publi cations.

37. While the *Arkansas Form Book* is out of print, law libraries may still have it in their reference collection, but it has not been updated since 2004.

38. See https://www.arkbar.com/arkbardocs/home for more information.

39. Ark. R. Minimum CLE 3(A). Forms and current CLE information are available at the *Arkansas Judiciary* website, https://courts.arkansas.gov/administration /professional-programs/cle.

izations, and other entities, and their topics range from appellate practice to zoning law. A CLE course may be aimed at new lawyers just learning the fundamentals of practice (usually termed a "bridging-the-gap" seminar); however, many CLE courses are intended to offer new insights on specialty areas, hot topics, or emerging issues. A CLE course may be led by practitioners, judges, and law professors. Frequently, the person leading the course prepares handouts that include sample forms, sample documents, and explanations.

The Arkansas Bar Association publishes much of this information in CLE handbooks and practice guides,[40] as do private companies such as the National Business Institute and Lorman Educational Services. Some of the largest national publishers of similar materials are the Practising Law Institute (PLI), the ALI, and the ABA.

CLE material is best located by searching a library catalog by topic. Online researchers can use the ARLI[41] to find Arkansas CLE materials. Bloomberg Law, Lexis and Westlaw also provide access to CLE materials.

---

40. https://www.arkbar.com/for-attorneys/publications/practice-handbooks.

41. http://themis.law.ualr.edu:81; see Table 2-3 for a complete list of publications indexed by the Arkansas Legal Index.

Chapter 3

Constitutions

I. Introduction to Constitutions

Researchers look to constitutions when they are faced with issues that spring from the exercise of or limitations on a government's powers. A government's *constitution* not only describes the structure of that government, but it also spells out the basic relationships between the government and its citizens and among the government's branches.

Each American lives under two constitutions: the Constitution of the United States and the constitution of the state in which that citizen resides, a circumstance creating what James Madison called a "compound republic":

> In the compound republic of America, the power surrendered by the people is first divided between two distinct governments, and then the portion allotted to each subdivided among distinct and separate departments. Hence a double security arises to the rights of the people. The different governments will control each other, at the same time that each will be controlled by itself.[1]

The dual sovereignty of federal and state governments means that each may exercise sole authority in some contexts. For example, domestic relations are generally seen as governed by state law; copyright, on the other hand, is governed by federal law. In some instances, each sovereign may exercise its power. For example, a criminal defendant may violate "the 'peace and dignity' of two sovereigns by breaking the laws of each, [in which case] he or she has committed two distinct offenses, and thus successive prosecutions by the two sovereigns are not barred by the Double Jeopardy Clause of the

---

1. *The Federalist* No. 51, at 323 (James Madison) (Clinton Rossiter ed., 1961).

Fifth Amendment."[2] Where the laws of federal and state governments overlap or are inconsistent, however, federal law controls.[3]

Thus the two constitutions cover somewhat different landscapes. As noted above, the United States Constitution is "the supreme Law of the Land."[4] It establishes the powers of each of the three national branches of government — the legislative, executive, and judicial — while also establishing parameters for the relationships of the states to the federal government and to one another. Guarantees of individual civil liberties are set out in the first ten amendments to the United States Constitution, called "the Bill of Rights."

Under the Tenth Amendment, "[t]he powers not delegated to the United States by the Constitution, nor prohibited by it to the States, are reserved to the States respectively, or to the people." State law thus fills in the gaps; through a state's constitution, the framework of its government is established.

While some of the original 13 states had their own constitutions before the federal constitution was drafted and ratified, the remaining states developed their constitutions as a requirement for achieving statehood. State constitutions are not mere facsimiles of their federal counterpart, however. The nature and length of the constitutional offices differ. Legislative processes vary. Guarantees of individual liberties can differ as well, particularly as many state constitutions were written before the Fourteenth Amendment was ratified.[5]

The United States Supreme Court acknowledges that "a state court is entirely free to read its own State's constitution more broadly than this Court reads the Federal Constitution, or to reject the mode of analysis used by this Court in favor of a different analysis of its corresponding constitutional guarantee."[6]

In accordance with that principle, the Arkansas Supreme Court recognizes that civil rights enumerated in the Arkansas Constitution can provide greater protection for the citizens of the state than they possess by virtue of being citizens of the United States.[7] For example, the Court considered three factors

---

2. *Hale v. State*, 336 Ark. 345, 353, 985 S.W.2d 303, 306–07 (1999).

3. U.S. Const. art. VI, cl. 2 (supremacy clause).

4. *Id.*

5. The Fourteenth Amendment of the United States Constitution makes most of the liberties enumerated in the Bill of Rights applicable to the states.

6. *City of Mesquite v. Aladdin's Castle, Inc.*, 455 U.S. 283, 293 (1982).

7. *E.g., Griffin v. State*, 347 Ark. 788, 792, 67 S.W.3d 582, 584 (2002) ("[W]hile we lack authority to extend the protections of the Fourth Amendment beyond the holdings of the United States Supreme Court, we do have the authority to impose greater restrictions on police activities in our state based upon our own state law than those the Supreme Court holds to be necessary based upon federal constitutional standards").

in holding that a right to privacy is implicitly guaranteed by the Arkansas Constitution.[8] First, the Court considered not only "the history of privacy in Arkansas's constitution but also . . . its privacy jurisprudence in a variety of contexts, including criminal and tort cases"; second, the Court saw significance in "the proliferation of statutory law in Arkansas that protects privacy"; and finally, the Court drew attention to "the textual and structural differences between the Bill of Rights and [Arkansas's] own Declaration of Rights."[9]

Of course, neither Arkansas nor any other state may accord its citizens fewer or less extensive rights than those accorded by the United States Constitution.[10]

II. The Arkansas Constitution

A. Arkansas's Constitutional History

As one constitutional scholar has noted, the "successive versions of a state constitution mirror the political and social changes that have occurred in the state."[11] To date, Arkansas has been governed under five constitutions, all drafted in the nineteenth century, an extraordinary period in the history of both the nation and the state. The first constitution was adopted in 1836, when Arkansas became a state.[12]

When it seceded from the Union and joined the Confederacy in 1861, Arkansas replaced its 1836 Constitution with a new document that differed from its predecessor primarily by its references to the rights of "all free white men."[13] In addition, the 1861 Constitution prohibited passage of any law for the emancipation of slaves.[14] Midway through the Civil War, however, President Abraham Lincoln issued a Proclamation of Amnesty and Reconstruction, encouraging citizens of Confederate states to take oaths of loyalty to the Union

---

8. *See* Robert L. Brown, *Expanded Rights through State Law: The United States Supreme Court Shows State Courts the Way*, 4 J. App. Prac. & Process 499, 517 & n.63 (2002).

9. *Id.*

10. U.S. Const. art. VI, cl. 2; U.S. Const. amend. XIV.

11. G. Alan Tarr, *Understanding State Constitutions* 4 (1998).

12. *See* S. Charles Bolton, Cal Ledbetter, Jr. & Gerald T. Hanson, *Arkansas Becomes a State* 43–50 (1985) (describing creation of the 1836 Constitution).

13. *See* Ark. Const. of 1861 art. 2, § 1 (equal rights); *id.* art. IV, § 2 (vote); *id.* art. IV, § 4 (qualifications for House of Representatives); *id.* art. IV, § 6 (qualifications for Senate).

14. Ark. Const. of 1861 art. 7, § 3.

and to form new state governments with the approval of ten percent of the number of voters in the 1860 presidential election.[15] Twenty-four Arkansas counties responded by electing pro-Union delegates to a constitutional convention. The new constitution was approved in March 1864 by a vote of 12,177 to 266.[16] Although the state's Confederate government continued to operate from its capital at Washington in Hempstead County, the 1864 Constitution declared the 1861 Constitution "null and void . . . and never . . . binding and obligatory upon the people."[17]

Despite adopting the 1864 Constitution, Arkansas, along with other southern states, was required to revise its government when Congress passed the Reconstruction Act in 1867.[18] Thus, in 1868, a constitutional convention drafted a new document that "aimed to destroy white supremacy and to weaken political leaders with Confederate ties."[19] The "Reconstruction" constitution did not, however, resolve issues of the distribution and limits of executive, legislative, and judicial power, nor did it calm political turmoil in the state.

These tensions peaked in the spring of 1874, in a struggle (known as the "Brooks-Baxter War") between political factions supporting different gubernatorial candidates. Elisha Baxter had assumed office when Joseph Brooks, securing a judicial order declaring him the winner, evicted him from the Capitol building. The two camps engaged in a month of skirmishes in which many were killed or wounded. Baxter was eventually restored to office.[20] The dust had hardly settled when yet another constitutional convention was authorized, and on October 13, 1874, the fifth — and current — constitution won voter approval.[21]

---

15. Kay Collett Goss, *The Arkansas State Constitution: A Reference Guide* 4 (1993).

16. *Id.* at 5.

17. Ark. Const. of 1864 pmbl.

18. For an analysis of the legal and political problems engendered by the state's secession from and restoration to the Union, see L. Scott Stafford, *The Arkansas Supreme Court and the Aftermath of the Civil War*, 23 U. Ark. Little Rock L. Rev. 355 (2001).

19. Goss, *supra* note 15, at 6.

20. For the historical and legal details, see Logan Scott Stafford, *Judicial Coup d'Etat: Mandamus, Quo Warranto and the Original Jurisdiction of the Supreme Court of Arkansas*, 20 UALR L.J. 891 (1998).

21. Scanned images of the original copies of the Constitutions of 1836, 1861, 1864, 1868, and 1874 are available from the *Arkansas Constitutions Collection*, Arkansas History Commission, Little Rock, Arkansas, at http://ahc.digital-ar.org (last visited Oct. 30, 2015).

B. Today's Constitution: The Arkansas Constitution of 1874

The Arkansas Constitution of 1874 contains a Preamble and 20 articles, plus multiple amendments. Article 1 declares the state's boundaries and names Little Rock as the seat of government.[22] Article 2 sets out the Declaration of Rights,[23] analogous to the Bill of Rights in the United States Constitution.

Article 3 goes to the heart of democratic government — the vote.[24] Subsequent amendments to this article reflect several twentieth-century social changes in the nation, such as women's suffrage, elimination of the poll tax, the conduct of elections, and voter registration.

Article 4 provides for a three-branched form of government, consisting of the legislative, executive, and judicial departments.[25] Each branch of government is vested with separate powers. Under the classic division of the powers, the legislature makes the laws and appropriates public revenues, the executive administers the laws and expends the appropriations, and the judiciary interprets the laws.

Article 5 details provisions for the legislative department, whose power is vested in the General Assembly, a bicameral legislature made up of the House of Representatives and the Senate.[26] Article 6 describes the executive department, headed by the governor, and it includes several other constitutional officers: the lieutenant governor, the secretary of state, the state treasurer, the state auditor, the attorney general, and the state land commissioner.[27] Under Article 7, judicial power is vested in the Judicial Department, represented by the Arkansas Supreme Court, the Arkansas Court of Appeals, the circuit courts, and the district courts.[28]

---

22. Little Rock has not always been the capital. Between 1819 and 1821, while Arkansas was still a territory, the capital was Arkansas Post. During the Civil War, as Union troops threatened Little Rock, the capital was moved to Washington, in Hempstead County. Researchers interested in the story of Arkansas's capital and other topics of Arkansas history will enjoy reading *The Encyclopedia of Arkansas History & Culture*, an online project of the Butler Center for Arkansas Studies and the Central Arkansas Library System, at www.encyclopediaofarkansas.net (last visited Feb. 28, 2016).

23. Ark. Const. art. 2. Arkansas is not unusual in this regard; state constitutions typically begin with a declaration of rights. *See* Tarr, *supra* note 11, at 11–12.

24. Ark. Const. art. 3.

25. Ark. Const. art. 4, § 1.

26. Ark. Const. art. 5, § 1.

27. Ark. Const. art. 6, § 1; Ark. Const. amend. 63.

28. Ark. Const. art. 7.

The remaining articles deal with a myriad of subjects, from agriculture to education to taxation. Table 3-1 lists the 20 articles of the Arkansas Constitution of 1874.

Table 3-1. Articles of the Arkansas Constitution of 1874

Preamble.

1. Boundaries.
2. Declaration of Rights.
3. Franchise and Elections.
4. Departments.
5. Legislative Department.
6. Executive Department.
7. Judicial Department.
8. Apportionment–Membership in General Assembly.
9. Exemption.
10. Agriculture, Mining and Manufacture.
11. Militia.
12. Municipal and Private Corporations.
13. Counties, County Seats and County Lines.
14. Education.
15. Impeachment and Address.
16. Finance and Taxation.
17. Railroads, Canals and Turnpikes.
18. Judicial Circuits.
19. Miscellaneous Provisions.
20. "Holford" Bonds Not to Be Paid.

C. Changing the Constitution: Amendments to the Arkansas Constitution of 1874

Despite several unsuccessful twentieth-century attempts to totally replace the 1874 Constitution,[29] the document has nonetheless been revised through

---

29. Voters rejected proposed new constitutions in 1918, 1970, and 1980. Goss, *supra* note 15, at 10–14. Amendment 80 — largely replacing the content of Article 7,

the use of constitutional *amendments*. An amendment works to modify one or more provisions of a constitution. An amendment may alter an existing article or amendment by adding, deleting, or replacing specific words or phrases. An amendment may entirely replace an existing article or amendment, or it may simply delete — without replacing — an article or amendment.

To date, the Arkansas Constitution of 1874 has been amended 94 times; several of those amendments have subsequently been repealed or themselves amended. Table 3-2, beginning on the next page, provides a list of the amendments to the Arkansas Constitution.

Proposals for constitutional amendments may travel one of two avenues, each with its own distinct requirements: (1) voter initiative or (2) legislative proposal. The Constitution guarantees to the citizens of Arkansas "the power to propose legislative measures, laws and amendments to the Constitution, and to enact or reject the same at the polls independent of the General Assembly."[30] Under the initiative process, ten percent of the legal voters may propose a constitutional amendment by initiative petition; the number of initiatives considered in a general election is unlimited.[31] Any initiative petition, containing the full text of the proposed amendment, must be filed with the secretary of state at least four months before election day, and the text must be published in a "paper of general circulation" at least 30 days before the election.[32]

The legislative process for amending the constitution works differently, particularly with regard to publication of the proposal. During a regular session of the General Assembly, either chamber may, with a majority vote of its members, propose a constitutional amendment, which the legislative journal

---

the judicial article — was approved by voters in November 2000 and made effective in July 2001. For more information about the Arkansas judicial system, see Chapter 4. *See also* Larry Brady & J.D. Gingerich, *A Practitioner's Guide to Arkansas's New Judicial Article*, 24 U. Ark. Little Rock L. Rev. 715, 715–16 nn.2, 8 (2002); *see also* 2 David Newbern, John J. Watkins & D.P. Marshall, Jr., *Arkansas Civil Practice and Procedure* § 1:2 (5th ed. 2010).

30. Ark. Const. art. 5, § 1, *amended by* Ark. Const. amend. 93; Ark. Const. amend. 7, *amended by* Ark. Const. amend. 93.

31. *Id.* The secretary of state publishes and periodically updates a detailed guide to the initiative process. *E.g.*, Mark Martin, *2015–16 Initiatives and Referenda: Facts and Information for the 2016 General Election* (Nov. 2015), *available at* www.sos .arkansas.gov/elections/pages/initiativereferendums.aspx.

32. *Id.* For an overview of voter-initiated amendments and the initiative process, see Timothy J. Kennedy, *Initiated Constitutional Amendments in Arkansas: Strolling Through the Mine Field*, 9 U. Ark. Little Rock L.J. 1 (1986–87).

**Table 3-2. Amendments to the Arkansas Constitution,
with Dates of Passage**

1. "Holford" Bonds (1885) [adding art. 20].
2. Regulation of Carriers (1899) [amending art. 17, § 10].
3. [repealed]
4. Sureties on Official Bonds (1901) [amending art. 19, § 21].
5. Per Diem and Mileage of General Assembly (1913) [amending art. 5, § 16].
6. Executive Department and Officers (1914) [amending art. 6].
7. Initiative and Referendum (1920) [amending art. 5, § 1].
8. Qualifications of Electors (1920) [amending art. 3, § 1].
9. Supreme Court (1924).
10. Limitation on Legislative and Taxing Power (1924) [amending art. 12, § 4].
11. School Tax (1926) [amending art. 14, § 3].
12. Textile Mills, Tax Exemption (1926).
13. [repealed]
14. Local Acts (1926).
15. Salaries of State Officers (1928).
16. Jury Trial (1928) [amending art. 2, § 7].
17. [repealed]
18. Tax to Aid Industries (1928).
19. Passage of Laws (1934) [amending art. 5].
20. State Bonds (1934) [probably superseded by amend. 65].
21. Criminal Prosecutions — Salaries of Prosecutors (1937).
22. Exemption of Homesteads from Certain State Taxes (1937).
23. Apportionment (1937) [amending art. 8].
24. Probate Courts–Circuit and County Clerks (1938) [amending art. 7, §§ 19, 34, 35].
25. [repealed]
26. Workers' Compensation (1938) [amending art. 5, § 2].
27. Exempting New Manufacturing Establishment from Taxation (1938).
28. Regulating Practice of Law (1938).
29. Filling Vacancies in Office (1938).
30. City Libraries (1940).
31. Police and Firefighters' Retirement Salaries and Pensions (1940).

Table 3-2. Amendments to the Arkansas Constitution, with Dates of Passage, *continued*

32. County or City Hospitals (1942).

33. Boards and Commissions Governing State Institutions (1942).

34. Rights of Labor (1944).

35. Wild Life–Conservation — Arkansas State Game and Fish Commission (1944).

36. Poll Tax Exemption (1944).

37. [repealed]

38. County Libraries (1946).

39. Voter Registration Laws (1948) [amending art. 3, § 2].

40. School District Tax (1948) [amending art. 14, § 3; amend. 11].

41. Election of County Clerks (1952).

42. State Highway Commission (1952).

43. Salaries and Expenses of Judicial Officers (1956) [probably superseding amend. 9, § 2].

44. [repealed]

45. Apportionment (1956) [amending art. 8; amend. 23].

46. Horse Racing and Pari-Mutuel Wagering at Hot Springs (1956).

47. State Ad Valorem Tax Prohibition (1958).

48. [repealed]

49. [repealed]

50. Elections Conducted by Ballot or Voting Machine (1962) [amending art. 3, § 3].

51. Voter Registration (1964).

52. Community Colleges (1964).

53. Free School System (1968) [amending art. 14, § 1].

54. Purchase of Printing, Stationery and Supplies (1974) [repealing art. 19, § 15].

55. Revision of County Government (1974).

56. Constitutional Officers–General Assembly (1976) [repealing art. 19, § 23; amends. 37, 48].

57. Intangible Personal Property (1976) [amending art. 16, § 5].

58. [repealed]

59. Taxation (1980) [amending art. 16].

60. Interest Rate Control (1982) [amending art. 19, § 13].

61. County Road Tax (1982) [repealing amend. 3].

**Table 3-2. Amendments to the Arkansas Constitution,
with Dates of Passage, *continued***

---

62. Local Capital Improvement Bonds (1984) [repealing amends. 13, 17, 25, 49].

63. Four Year Terms for State Constitutional Officers (1984) [probably superseding art. 6, § 1; amend. 6, § 1; amend. 56, § 1].

64. [repealed]

65. Revenue Bonds (1986) [probably superseding art. 16, § 1; amends. 20, 62].

66. Judicial Discipline and Disability Commission (1988).

67. Jurisdiction of Matters Relating to Juveniles and Bastardy (1988) [amending art. 7, § 28].

68. Abortion (1988) [declared unconstitutional in *Unborn Child Amendment Committee v. Ward*, 318 Ark. 165, 883 S.W.2d 817 (1994)].

69. Repeal of Amendment 44 (Protection of States' Rights) (1990).

70. Executive Department and General Assembly Salaries — Restrictions on Expense Reimbursements (1992) [repealing amend. 56, §§ 2, 3].

71. Personal Property Taxes (1992) [amending art. 16, § 5].

72. City and County Library Amendment (1992) [amending amends. 30, 38].

73. Arkansas Term Limitation Amendment (1992) [§ 3 declared unconstitutional in *U.S. Term Limits, Inc. v. Hill*, 316 Ark. 251, 872 S.W.2d 349 (1994); later amended by amend. 76].

74. School Tax — Budget — Approval of Tax Rate (1996) [amending art. 14, § 3, as amended by amends. 11, 40].

75. Environmental Enhancement Funds (1996).

76. Congressional Term Limits Amendment of 1996 (1996) [amending amend. 73, § 3] [declared unconstitutional in *Donovan v. Priest*, 326 Ark. 353, 931 S.W.2d 119 (1996)].

77. Special Judges (1998) [repealing art. 7, §§ 9, 21, 22].

78. City and County Government Redevelopment (2000).

79. Property Tax Relief (2000).

80. Qualifications of Justices and Judges (2001) [repealing art. 7, §§ 1–18, 20–22, 24, 25, 32, 34, 35, 39, 40, 42–45 & 50; amend. 58, § 1; amend. 64, § 1; amend. 77, § 1].

81. Protection of the Secrecy of Individual Votes (2002) [repealing amend. 50, § 3].

82. Obligation Bonds for Economic Development (2004).

83. Marriage (2004).

84. Authorized Bingo or Raffles (2007).

**Table 3-2. Amendments to the Arkansas Constitution,
with Dates of Passage, *continued***

85. Voting and Elections (2008) [amending art. 3, §§ 1, 2; art. 3, §§ 8, 10; repealing art. 3, § 5].

86. General Assembly Sessions (2009) [amending art. 5, §§ 5, 17, 29, 34, 39, 40; amend. 35, § 7].

87. State Lottery Established (2009) [amending art. 19, § 14].

88. Wildlife Conservation and Management (2010).

89. Government Bonds & Loans; Interest Rates & Energy Efficiency Projects (2011) [repealing art. 19, § 13, and interest rate provisions of amends. 30, 38, 62, 65, 78].

90. Bonds for Economic Development (2011) [amending amend. 82].

91. General Obligation Four-Lane Highway Construction and Improvement Bonds (2013).

92. Review and Approval of Administrative Rules (2014) [adding art. 5, § 42].

93. Amendment of Initiative and Referendum Petitions (2014) [amending art. 5, § 1].

94. The Arkansas Elected Officials Ethics, Transparency, and Financial Reform Amendment (2014) [adding art. 19, §§ 28–31; amending art. 5, §§ 29, 30; art. 16, §§ 4, 12; amend. 70, § 1; amend. 73, § 2; amend. 80, § 16(E); repealing art. 5, § 16; art. 19, § 11; amend. 6, § 6; amend. 9, § 2; amend. 15; amend. 43; amend. 70, § 3].

of that chamber will record.[33] At least one newspaper per county must publish the proposed amendment for six months preceding the next general election.[34] Under either avenue, the proposed amendment is approved only if it secures a majority of the popular vote in the general election.[35] No more than three legislative proposals may appear on a ballot.[36]

---

33. Ark. Const. amend. 7, *amended by* Ark. Const. amend. 93.

34. Ark. Const. art. 19, § 22. For an overview of the legislative process and the courts' review of challenged amendments, see Jennifer R. Rovetti, Comment, *Regnat Populus? Amending the Arkansas State Constitution after* Forrester v. Martin, 66 Ark. L. Rev. 429 (2013); Stephen B. Niswanger, Comment, *A Practitioner's Guide to Challenging and Defending Legislatively Proposed Constitutional Amendments in Arkansas*, 17 U. Ark. Little Rock L.J. 765 (1995).

35. Ark. Const. art. 19, § 22. To find amendments referred by the legislature for inclusion on the next general election's ballot, see Martin, *supra* note 31. Alternatively, search reputable websites such as the Public Policy Center of the University of Arkansas's Cooperative Extension Service, at www.uaex.edu/business-communities/voter-education/state-ballot-issues.aspx (last visited Feb. 28, 2016).

36. Ark. Const. art. 19, § 22.

III. Essentials of Constitutional Law Research

Because a state's constitution, by authorizing the fundamental forms and powers of government, is the basic source of *all* the state's laws, and because the state's laws, whether judge-made or enacted, must comply with the dictates of the state constitution to be valid, researchers are wise to consider whether to include state constitutional law in their research.

Researchers encounter two distinct approaches to constitutional law research, either or both of which may apply. The first directly concerns the interpretation and analysis of the constitution itself or its amendments. The second assesses whether other primary law violates constitutional guarantees and limits.

A. Interpretation and Analysis of a Constitutional Provision

Many research topics in constitutional law require interpretation and analysis of a constitutional provision or amendment. When the Arkansas Supreme Court construes an article of or an amendment to the state's constitution, the court examines it in the context of the laws existing at the time of its adoption.[37] Although an amendment modifies the constitution, the court considers that the amendment displaces only such provisions of the existing constitution as are inconsistent.[38] When construing an amendment, the court attempts to harmonize it with all existing provisions of the constitution; the court will not interpret an amendment to conflict with another provision of the constitution unless doing so is absolutely necessary to give effect to the amendment.[39] Use the same research process outlined in Chapter 1, Table 1-3, adapting it to identify the type and nature of the constitutional issue. When conducting research in print sources, look for research terms in the index to the "Constitutions" volume of the *Arkansas Code Annotated* or in the code's general index. Locate references to any constitutional articles or amendments relevant to the issue you are researching.

---

37. *State v. Bostick*, 313 Ark. 596, 598, 856 S.W.2d 12, 13 (1993) (construing a current provision "in context of the law in existence at the time of its adoption").

38. *See Ward Sch. Bus Mfg., Inc. v. Fowler*, 261 Ark. 100, 108, 547 S.W.2d 394, 399 (1977) (Fogleman, J., concurring).

39. *See id.*, 547 S.W.2d at 399.

B. Analysis of the Constitutionality of Other Primary Law

A research topic in constitutional law may require an analysis of whether other state law (e.g., common law, statutes, or administrative regulations) comports with or violates the Arkansas or United States Constitution. In addition to following the research steps outlined in Chapter 1, you may also need to consider researching relevant case law (Chapter 4), statutes (Chapter 5), or administrative law (Chapter 7), depending on the nature of the law at issue.

As a general rule, statutes carry a presumption of constitutionality, and challengers have the burden of showing the statutes "clearly violate the Arkansas Constitution."[40] To put it somewhat differently, if a court can find a way to construe a disputed statute, rule, or regulation as consistent with the Arkansas Constitution, it will do so.[41]

C. Online and Print Sources for Arkansas Constitutional Research

The Arkansas Constitution is available in several online sources. You will find full annotated coverage of the current Arkansas Constitution and its amendments in Lexis and Westlaw, and there is limited coverage in Fastcase and Bloomberg Law. In any of these services, researchers can retrieve a particular article or amendment and its annotations or citing references by entering its citation.

If researchers do not know which specific article or amendment of the constitution is relevant to their issue, they can simply type in a query using the search terms they earlier composed as part of their research planning, and the service retrieves all documents relating to those terms. Clearly, the broader the search terms, the greater the results, but those results contain a lot of irrelevant documents. Experiment with different sorts of queries, using synonyms or analogous concepts, or phrasing the issue more narrowly. This experimentation helps you learn to retrieve a manageable number of relevant sources.

More specifically, in Lexis, researchers can enter a query to search everything, a technique that retrieves links to *all sources* treating those terms (and to limit how much you retrieve, we recommend including the words "Arkansas"

---

40. *Gawenis v. Ark. Oil & Gas Comm'n*, 2015 Ark. 238, at 7, 464 S.W.3d 453, 456.

41. *See, e.g., Otis v. State*, 355 Ark. 590, 611, 142 S.W.3d 615, 627 (2004); *Ark. Health Servs. Comm'n v. Reg'l Care Facilities, Inc.*, 351 Ark. 331, 339, 93 S.W.3d 672, 677 (2002).

and "constitution"). But you also can narrow the universe of potential sources by limiting the search to Arkansas materials. Another route is to select the database "Statutes and Legislation," and within those results, to "Constitutions" before entering the specific query (again, including the key word "Arkansas"). Once the results are displayed, researchers can filter those results by selecting the specific kinds of authorities they're interested in (e.g., cases, statutes, administrative codes and regulations, secondary materials).

In Westlaw, the researcher can similarly enter a query within the main window, retrieving links to *all sources* pertaining to the issue. Researchers can also limit their searches to the "Arkansas Statutes & Court Rules" database and its sub-division "Constitution of the State of Arkansas of 1874."

As for constitutional research in other online services, Bloomberg Law reproduces the current text of the Arkansas Constitution and its amendments, but it is not annotated nor does it contain links to citing references. An unofficial online version of the Arkansas Constitution is available to the public from the General Assembly's website.[42] This version is not annotated. Fastcase links to the General Assembly's website, as do most free online sources.[43]

The official print version of the Arkansas Constitution is set out in the "Constitutions" volume of the official *Arkansas Code of 1987 Annotated*, supplemented annually.[44] The single volume contains not only the current versions of the Arkansas Constitution and its amendments, but also the text of the United States Constitution and its amendments, the four historic Arkansas constitutions (1836, 1861, 1864, and 1868), and miscellaneous other federal materials affecting Arkansas. Provisions of the current United States and Arkansas Constitutions are indexed not only in the "Constitutions" volume, but also in the "General Index" to the code.

An unofficial print version is found in two volumes of *West's Arkansas Code Annotated*, containing not just the Arkansas Constitution and its amendments,

---

42. *See* www.arkleg.state.ar.us/assembly/Summary/ArkansasConstitution1874 .pdf (last visited Feb. 28, 2016).

43. *E.g.,* Cornell University Law School, *Legal Information Institute, Arkansas Legal Materials*, https://www.law.cornell.edu/states/arkansas (last visited Feb. 28, 2016); Findlaw, *Arkansas Legal Research*, http://www.findlaw.com/casecode/arkansas .html (last visited Feb. 28, 2016); Law Library of Congress, *Guide to Law Online: Arkansas*, www.loc.gov/law/help/guide/states/us-ar.php (last visited Feb. 28, 2016).

44. Supplements for sources in print typically come in one of two forms: a "pocket part" inserted into the back cover of a bound hard-cover volume, or a bound paperback publication that is shelved next to the hard-cover volume it supplements. It is not unusual for an increasingly bulky pocket part to be republished as a separately bound supplement.

but also the United States Constitution and its amendments. Depending on the date of your research and the publication date of the bound volume, you may need to check for a supplement to that volume. The current supplement to the second volume often contains recently *proposed* amendments to the Arkansas Constitution. The West publication's "General Index" contains references to current versions of constitutions of both the United States and the State of Arkansas.

D. Online and Print Sources for Federal Constitutional Research

As this book goes to press, the most reliable online resource for the official United States Constitution is FDsys (the Federal Digital System of the U.S. Government Publishing Office).[45] This resource provides the text of the Constitution as well as an index and a table of cases (each in downloadable .pdf format).[46]

As a resource in print, the United States Constitution is published in the same volume of the official *Arkansas Code of 1987 Annotated* and the unofficial *West's Arkansas Code Annotated* in which the Arkansas Constitution is found. It is also available in annotated unofficial print and online versions in *United States Code Service* and *United States Code Annotated*. The official version of the federal constitution is found in the *United States Code*, but it is not annotated.

---

45. *See* http://www.gpo.gov/fdsys/ (last visited Feb 28, 2016). In early 2016, the GPO launched a beta website, https://govinfo.gov/, that is intended to eventually replace FDsys.

46. For more detailed guidance on researching federal constitutional law, consult Mary Garvey Algero, Spencer L. Simons, Suzanne Rowe, Scott Childs & Sarah E. Ricks, *Federal Legal Research* (2d ed. 2015) (Chapter 4).

Chapter 4

Case Law

I. Introduction to Case Law and Court Systems

Analyzing cases is one of the first skills taught in law school, with good reason. Our system of law depends on judicial decision-making. Whether a particular rule is created through legislation or through the common law, a court may eventually be called upon to apply it in resolving a dispute between two or more parties. Understanding how courts have decided similar legal issues in the past allows an attorney to counsel a client about how a rule likely applies in the client's case as well as to advocate for that client if a dispute arises.

The weight of a particular case depends, in part, on which court decided that case. Therefore, this chapter begins with an overview of the Arkansas and federal court systems. Then it explains *reporters*, the books containing published court decisions. Because decisions are still typically cited to reporters, being familiar with reporters is important even when conducting research online. Next, this chapter explains a variety of methods for finding cases, with a focus on Arkansas law. The chapter ends with a discussion of case analysis.

II. Court Systems

Because much legal research includes reading judicial opinions, researchers need to understand the court system of the jurisdiction whose law they are applying. The federal government and most states have a three-level court system, with *trial courts* at the lowest level, an *intermediate court of appeals* at the middle level, and a *court of last resort*, usually denominated the *supreme court*, at the highest level.

Although a case begins its life cycle in a trial court, few trial court opinions are published; in any event, because they are from the lowest-level court in the judicial system, such opinions are not mandatory even if published.[1]

A. Arkansas Trial Courts

In November 2000, voters approved a major overhaul of the Arkansas court system by passing Amendment 80 to the Arkansas Constitution.[2] Before Amendment 80 took effect on July 1, 2001, the state maintained separate trial courts of law and of equity (chancery).[3] Under Amendment 80, however, these two forms of trial courts were merged into a single court of general jurisdiction, called the *circuit court*. Arkansas's 75 counties are divided into 28 judicial circuits.

Although organized as a single court, each circuit court maintains separate divisions for criminal, civil, probate, domestic relations, and juvenile matters. These divisions exist for "purpose[s] of judicial administration and caseload management and [are] not for the purpose of subject-matter jurisdiction."[4] Most cases are tried in the circuit court.

Smaller matters, on the other hand, are typically tried in trial courts of limited jurisdiction known as *district courts*. Amendment 80 aggregated the state's existing hodge-podge of municipal courts, justice of the peace courts, police courts, corporation courts, mayor courts, and courts of common pleas into the district court.[5] District courts handle misdemeanor and preliminary felony cases, as well as civil cases under $5,000, and small claims cases in which parties represent themselves.[6] Each county has at least one district court.[7]

---

1. See Chapter 1, Table 1-2, for the hierarchy of authority in Arkansas legal research. While some federal trial court cases are published, no Arkansas trial court cases are published. For a discussion of the features of published and unpublished appellate cases, see Section III.B, below.

2. For more information about the history of Arkansas's constitutions, see Chapter 3, Part II.A.

3. The history of and the distinctions between Arkansas courts of law and courts of equity are addressed in Morton Gitelman, *The Separation of Law and Equity and the Arkansas Chancery Courts: Historical Anomalies and Political Realities*, 17 U. Ark. Little Rock L.J. 215 (1995).

4. Ark. Sup. Ct. Admin. Or. 14, ¶ 1, https://courts.arkansas.gov/rules-and-administrative-orders/administrative-orders.

5. *See* Ark. Const. amend. 80, § 19(B).

6. The development of Arkansas district courts is well documented in Vic Fleming, *Municipal Gone District: Jurisdiction in New Court of First Resort*, 24 U. Ark. Little Rock L. Rev. 277 (2002).

7. Ark. Const. amend. 80, § 7(C).

Amendment 80 also provided for the phasing out of city courts.[8] City courts handled minor cases involving violations of a city's bylaws or ordinances. City courts were consolidated with district courts by legislative action, effective January 1, 2012.[9]

The *Arkansas Judiciary* website contains a helpful diagram of the structure of the state's court system, as well as information about the state's circuit and district courts.[10]

B. Arkansas Appellate Courts

An appeal from a decision of an Arkansas circuit court may be taken to either the Arkansas Supreme Court or the Arkansas Court of Appeals, depending on the nature of the case and issues. These two courts have a unique relationship, as reflected by the court rules governing appellate jurisdiction. Unless a case's subject matter falls into one of the eight classes of cases decided by the Arkansas Supreme Court, the case is appealed directly to the Arkansas Court of Appeals.[11] Among the eight classes of cases which are appealed directly to the supreme court are cases with questions concerning Arkansas's Constitution, death penalty and life imprisonment, elections, and the discipline and regulation of attorneys and judges.[12]

The courts' division of labor, including decisions to transfer cases from one court to the other, is predicated in part upon the size of each court and, consequently, its ability to handle a given number of cases.[13]

When the Arkansas Court of Appeals was created in 1979, its six judges sat in panels of three to decide cases. For the first several years of the court of appeals' existence, the Arkansas Supreme Court took jurisdiction over 17 categories of appeals, in order to more or less equally divide the appellate docket

---

8. City courts will remain until such time as they are abolished by the governing body of the city or by the Arkansas General Assembly. Ark. Const. amend. 80, § 19(B)(2).

9. Ark. Code Ann. § 16-17-1202 (2006).

10. View or download the diagram from the Arkansas judiciary website, www .courts.arkansas.gov, by clicking the "Courts" tab. Access current information on circuit courts and district courts in Arkansas at the same location.

11. *See* Ark. Sup. Ct. R. 1-2(a).

12. *See id.*

13. *See* Ark. Sup. Ct. R. 1-2(g) ("[C]ases may be assigned and transferred between the courts by Supreme Court order to achieve a fair allocation of the appellate workload . . . .").

between the two courts. The court of appeals has subsequently increased in size, now numbering 12 judges, who continue to sit in panels of three.

In contrast, the Arkansas Supreme Court is composed of seven justices — one chief justice and six associate justices — who today sit *en banc* to decide each case that comes before the court.[14] As the court of appeals has increased in size, the supreme court has reduced the number and kinds of cases it deals with.[15]

While it is not obligated to do so, the Arkansas Supreme Court may also accept an appeal that raises an issue of first impression or in which it finds strong policy concerns. For example, the supreme court will probably entertain questions involving substantial public interest, changing trends in the law, or questions about the interpretation of a statute.[16]

Should the appellant send his case to the wrong court, this error is not fatal. Instead, the courts simply transfer the case where it belongs.[17] Even if a case has properly been placed before the court of appeals, when it involves a major public interest issue or a weighty legal principle, the court of appeals may certify the case to the supreme court. The supreme court, however, may not agree and may send it back.[18]

The courts' division of labor does not mean that the supreme court never reviews a decision of the court of appeals. The supreme court may grant a *petition for review* in one of three instances: (1) it determines that the case should have come to it in the first instance; (2) it determines that the court of appeals should have certified the question to it; or (3) the court of appeals is deadlocked in a tie vote.[19]

C. Other States' Courts

Most states have a three-tier court system like that of Arkansas. A few states do not have an intermediate appellate court. Another difference in some court

---

14. At times in its past, the Arkansas Supreme Court has sat in divisions for certain types of appeals. *See In re Supreme Court Procedure for Sitting in Divisions,* 260 Ark. 380 (1976); *see also* Ark. Code Ann. § 16-11-103 (2006) (permitting the supreme court to sit in two divisions).

15. For an interesting discussion of the development of the Arkansas Court of Appeals and the apportionment of the appellate workload between that court and the Arkansas Supreme Court, see John J. Watkins, *Division of Labor Between Arkansas's Appellate Courts,* 17 U. Ark. Little Rock L.J. 177 (1995).

16. *See* Ark. Sup. Ct. R. 1-2(b).

17. Ark. Sup. Ct. R. 1-2(f).

18. *See* Ark. Sup. Ct. R. 1-2(d).

19. *See* Ark. Sup. Ct. R. 1-2(e); Ark. Sup. Ct. R. 2-4(c).

systems is that the "supreme" court is not the highest court. In New York, for example, the trial courts are called supreme courts and the highest court is the Court of Appeals. Two other states, Massachusetts and Maine, call their highest court the Supreme Judicial Court.

D. Federal Courts

In the federal system, the trial courts are called *United States District Courts*. The federal system has 94 district courts, with each district representing a particular state or portion of a state. A state with a relatively small population may not be subdivided into smaller geographic regions. The state of Kansas, for example, comprises the entire federal District of Kansas. States with larger populations are subdivided into geographical districts, such as the Northern and Southern Districts of Iowa.

Arkansas is subdivided into the Eastern and Western Districts. The main courthouse for the Eastern District is located in Little Rock.[20] Other Eastern District courthouses are in Batesville, Helena, Jonesboro, and Pine Bluff. The main courthouse for the Western District is in Fort Smith, and additional courthouses for that district are located in El Dorado, Fayetteville, Harrison, Hot Springs, and Texarkana.[21]

The main office for the federal bankruptcy court for both the Eastern and Western Districts is in Little Rock. The bankruptcy court's website is particularly important to attorneys, as this court uses only electronic filing.[22]

The 13 intermediate appellate courts in the federal system are called *United States Circuit Courts of Appeals*. Arkansas is located within the *Eighth Circuit*. Therefore, appeals from federal cases in the United States District Courts for the Eastern or Western Districts of Arkansas go to the United States Court of Appeals for the Eighth Circuit. The Eighth Circuit encompasses Arkansas, Iowa, Minnesota, Missouri, Nebraska, North Dakota, and South Dakota.[23]

The highest appellate court in federal jurisdiction is the *Supreme Court of the United States*.[24] The Supreme Court decides cases concerning the Constitution of the United States and other federal law. In general, parties wishing to have their cases reviewed by the Supreme Court must file a petition for a

---

20. The website for the Eastern District is www.are.uscourts.gov.
21. The website for the Western District is www.arwd.uscourts.gov.
22. The address is www.arb.uscourts.gov.
23. The Eighth Circuit's website is www.ca8.uscourts.gov.
24. The United States Supreme Court's website is www.supremecourt.gov.

writ of certiorari, which means the Court exercises its discretion whether to accept the case.[25] The Supreme Court typically limits its grants of certiorari to (1) significant conflicts among the decisions of federal circuit courts; (2) important issues of first impression in determining or applying federal law; or (3) the highest state courts' treatment of federal questions or existing Supreme Court precedent.[26]

While the Supreme Court is the final authority on federal issues, it is not the final authority on state issues. That authority rests with the highest appellate court in each state, which in Arkansas is the Arkansas Supreme Court.

III. Cases and Reporters

When appellate courts decide cases, they write opinions that summarize the facts of the case and existing law and that explain how they have resolved the case and why. Courts provide this information, in part, because they know their opinions serve purposes beyond just explaining to the opposing parties how the case has been resolved and why. A judicial opinion in the United States not only resolves the dispute before the court, but also may make new law, provide readers with interpretation of the law to consult for future analogous cases, and educate readers on the law. In order for this precedent-based, common-law system to function, judges, attorneys, and potential litigants must have a way to access these opinions in order to read them. This access is accomplished through a series of books called *reporters*, which contain the collection of case opinions decided and designated for publication by the various courts.

A. Official and Unofficial Reporters

Cases are published in both official and unofficial reporters, in print and online. *Official reporters* are typically published by state governments.[27] Historically, a significant lag time occurred between when a court rendered a decision and when that decision was published in the official reporters of that

---

25. Sup. Ct. R. 10.

26. *Id.* For more detailed information about federal courts, see Mary Garvey Algero, Spencer L. Simons, Suzanne E. Rowe, Scott Childs & Sarah E. Ricks, *Federal Legal Research* § 8.II.A (2d ed. 2015).

27. Refer to the jurisdictional tables in *ALWD* Appendix 1 or *Bluebook* Table T1 to determine a jurisdiction's official reporter.

court. To remedy this situation, the West Publishing Company devised a system of *unofficial reporters* that covers all of the federal and state courts in the American legal system. This system is called the National Reporter System. These unofficial reporters proved accurate and timely. Often, a court's written decision or opinion in a case is published in *both* an official reporter and an unofficial West reporter. Sometimes, a court's decision appears in print only in a West reporter; this occurs when a state government stops publishing its own reports.

1. Arkansas Cases

In 2009, Arkansas became the first state to designate an online version of its appellate court cases as official.[28] The *Arkansas Judiciary* website contains the text of all Arkansas Supreme Court and Arkansas Court of Appeals cases issued after February 14, 2009. Effective July 1, 2009, these online versions of Arkansas appellate cases became the *official* publications of the courts. The website also contains the unofficial full text of published cases of the Arkansas Supreme Court dating back to 1837 and of the Arkansas Court of Appeals dating back to 1981.[29]

Prior to their moving online, decisions of the Arkansas Supreme Court were officially reported in *Arkansas Reports*, and those of the Arkansas Court of Appeals were officially reported in *Arkansas Appellate Reports*. The two official reporters were published consecutively in the same bound volume (e.g., Volume 353 of *Arkansas Reports* is bound into the same book as Volume 28 of *Arkansas Appellate Reports*).[30]

The decisions of both courts are unofficially reported in West's *South Western Reporter*, which also contains cases from courts in Kentucky, Missouri,

---

28. As of this writing, Illinois and Nebraska have followed suit; other states are at various stages of investigation.

29. These cases are virtually all searchable and browsable, arranged in folders by *Arkansas Reports* volume number and within the volume folder, alphabetically. As of this writing, unofficial cases (pre-2009) cannot be retrieved by searching for the case citation. The court is in the process of inputting this data, so in the future it will be possible to retrieve unofficial cases by citation. Because the cases are scanned in from the old *Arkansas Reports* volumes, the text within very old cases may not be searchable.

30. Between 1979 and early 1981, cases from the then-new court of appeals were published along with supreme court cases in *Arkansas Reports*. The first volume of *Arkansas Appellate Reports* begins with an opinion decided on February 25, 1981.

Table 4-1. Official and Unofficial Reporters for Arkansas and Federal Cases

Court	Reporter Name	Reporter Abbreviation
Arkansas Supreme Court	*Arkansas Judiciary* (official, 2009–present)	Ark.
	Arkansas Reports (official, pre–2009)	Ark.
	South Western Reporter (first, second, third series) (unofficial)	S.W. S.W.2d S.W.3d
Arkansas Court of Appeals	*Arkansas Judiciary* (official, 2009–present)	Ark. App.
	Arkansas Appellate Reports (official, pre–2009; in same bound volume with *Arkansas Reports*)	Ark. App.
	South Western Reporter (first, second, third series) (unofficial)	S.W. S.W.2d S.W.3d
Arkansas Circuit Courts (trial courts)	The opinions of Arkansas trial courts are not reported.	
United States Supreme Court	*United States Reports* (official)	U.S.
	Supreme Court Reporter (unofficial)	S. Ct.
	United States Supreme Court Reports, Lawyers' Edition (first, second series) (unofficial)	L. Ed. L. Ed. 2d
	United States Law Week (unofficial; contains material in addition to judicial opinions)	U.S.L.W.
Eighth Circuit Court of Appeals	*Federal Reporter* (first, second, third series) (unofficial but sole reporter)	F. F.2d F.3d
	Federal Appendix (unofficial) (selected unpublished cases)	F. App'x
United States District Courts for Eastern & Western Districts of Arkansas	*Federal Supplement* (first, second, third series) (unofficial but sole reporter; selected cases)	F. Supp. F. Supp. 2d F. Supp. 3d
	Federal Rules Decisions (unofficial but sole reporter; selected cases 1941–present concerning Federal Rules of Civil and Criminal Procedure not otherwise published in *Federal Supplement*)	F.R.D.

Tennessee, and Texas.[31] Table 4-1 sets out the official and unofficial reporters for cases from Arkansas state and federal courts, and each reporter's citation abbreviations.

2. West's National Reporter System

The National Reporter System divides the 50 states into seven regions. Each region has a separate reporter that contains judicial opinions from the states' highest courts and intermediate courts of appeal. The seven regions are Atlantic, North Eastern, North Western, Pacific, Southern, South Eastern, and South Western.

Each reporter in the National Reporter System has been issued in more than one series. Each series covers a specific time span. When locating a specific opinion, whether in print or online, ascertain the correct series. For example, *South Western Reporter* is now in its third series. The first series covers decisions between the years 1886 and 1927. The second series covers the years 1927 to 1999. The third series began in 1999 and includes current decisions.

South Western Reporter publishes decisions from five states: Arkansas, Kentucky, Missouri, Tennessee and Texas. Some novice researchers wrongly believe that because these states are grouped together, Arkansas courts consider their decisions as more persuasive than decisions from other jurisdictions. The grouping of states is geographic; the important thing to remember is that courts afford no additional weight to cases from these jurisdictions because of the coincidence of their being published in the same regional reporter.

The National Reporter System covers federal cases as well. The *Supreme Court Reporter* publishes United States Supreme Court cases; the *Federal Reporter* publishes United States Circuit Courts of Appeal cases; and the *Federal Supplement* and the *Federal Rules Decisions* publish United States District Court cases.[32]

The West reporter volumes contain many helpful tables and reader's aids. Features found in current reporter volumes can include (a) a list of the judges serving during the period in which the reported cases were decided; (b) an

---

31. While the Arkansas Supreme Court has removed the distinction between published and unpublished cases, not all cases will appear in the *South Western Reporter* due to the sheer volume of cases. According to the publisher, the decision of which cases to print is based in part on whether the case creates new law, contains a new interpretation of the law, or has national applicability. (Even if not included in the *South Western Reporter*, all written opinions are included in electronic format on Westlaw.)

32. See Table 4-1 for a complete list of reporters, along with their abbreviations.

alphabetical table of cases reported in that volume (alphabetized by both the appellant's and appellee's name); (c) a section called Words and Phrases that lists cases in that volume of the reporter that define particular legal terms; (d) a table of statutes construed, which lists all statutes, rules, and constitutional provisions discussed in the volume and the cases that discuss them; and (e) a subject index called the Key Number Digest (for that reporter volume).

B. Published and Unpublished Opinions

Prior to 2009, not all Arkansas appellate cases were published. When a court's opinion added nothing new to the body of existing precedent in its jurisdiction, the court could decline to officially publish it. Even when a case is "unpublished," however, researchers may find it in an unofficial online database. Such a case bears a conspicuous notation that it is "not designated for publication." Arkansas researchers are less likely to encounter unpublished opinions from the Arkansas Supreme Court prior to 2009; under the then-existing court rule, "[a]ll signed opinions of the Supreme Court shall be designated for publication."[33]

As for the Arkansas Court of Appeals, only those opinions which resolved novel or unusual questions were designated for publication.[34] Before 2009, it was *prohibited* to cite unpublished cases from the Arkansas Court of Appeals. Beginning in July 2009, however, all opinions of the Arkansas Supreme Court and Arkansas Court of Appeals are published and may be cited as precedent.[35]

Similarly, the Federal Rules of Appellate Procedure permit the citation of unpublished federal opinions, even though local rules may restrict their being given precedential value:

> A court may not prohibit or restrict the citation of federal judicial opinions, orders, judgments, or other written dispositions that have

---

33. Ark. Sup. Ct. R. 5-2(a).

34. Ark. Sup. Ct. R. 5-2(c).

35. *See In Re: Arkansas Supreme Court & Court of Appeals Rule 5-2*, No. 09-540, at 2–3 (May 28, 2009):

> The amended rule . . . abandons the distinction between published and unpublished opinions and makes every Supreme Court and Court of Appeals opinion issued after July 1, 2009, precedent. . . . In light of our adoption of publication of the official reports of all Arkansas appellate decisions in electronic format, we shall no longer distinguish between "published" and "unpublished" opinions. The official electronic publication and reporting of all decisions eliminates the basis for this distinction.

been: (i) designated as "unpublished," "not for publication," "non-precedential," "not precedent," or the like; and (ii) issued on or after January 1, 2007.[36]

At any rate, it is undesirable to rely on the holding of an unpublished case when the law is also addressed in published cases. If such a case seems to be the most analogous authority, it is wiser to look instead to published sources cited *within* the unpublished case.

Table 4-2 lists commercial databases and free online sources containing cases from the Arkansas Supreme Court and the Arkansas Court of Appeals. Online resources typically make both published and unpublished opinions available to researchers.

Table 4-2. Online Sources for Arkansas Judicial Opinions

	Court (Coverage)	Provider, Web Address
Commercial	Arkansas Supreme Court and Court of Appeals (all)	Bloomberg Law, www.bloomberglaw.com
	Arkansas Supreme Court and Court of Appeals (all)	Fastcase, www.fastcase.com *or* www.arkbar.com (for Arkansas bar member access, log in, then click "Fastcase")
	Arkansas Supreme Court and Court of Appeals (all)	LexisNexis, www.Lexisadvance.com
	Arkansas Supreme Court and Court of Appeals (all)	Westlaw, www.Westlawnext.com
Public (Free)	Arkansas Supreme Court (all)	Arkansas Judiciary, https://courts.arkansas.gov/opinions-and-disciplinary-decisions
	Arkansas Court of Appeals (all)	Arkansas Judiciary, https://courts.arkansas.gov/opinions-and-disciplinary-decisions
	Arkansas Supreme Court and Court of Appeals (1950–present)	Google Scholar, www.scholar.google.com

---

36. Fed. R. App. 32.1. For an interesting analysis of the effect of unpublished case law, see J. Thomas Sullivan, *Unpublished Opinions and No Citation Rules in Trial Courts*, 47 Ariz. L. Rev. 419 (2005).

C. Anatomy of a Reported Case[37]

A case decision printed in a regional reporter contains the exact language of the court's opinion. Additionally, the publisher includes supplemental information to aid researchers in learning about the case, locating its relevant parts, and finding similar cases. Some of these research aids are gleaned from the court record of the case, while others are written by the publisher's editorial staff. This discussion explains the information and enhancements in the *South Western Reporter*. Most reporters provide these items, perhaps in a different order. Other West reporters and Westlaw have nearly identical publisher enhancements and information. To best understand the following discussion, examine a case in a volume of the *South Western Reporter* or on Westlaw. Alternatively, refer to the case excerpt in Figure 4-1 for examples of the concepts explained below.

- *Parallel citation.* The reporter provides the case's citation for every official or unofficial reporter in which the case is printed.
- *Parties and procedural designations.* All parties are listed with their procedural designations. In general, the losing party who appeals is called the *appellant* and the opposing party is called the *appellee*.[38]
- *Court.* Immediately after the listing of the parties, the reporter lists the court that decided the case.
- *Docket number.* When filed in the appellate court, each case receives a *docket number*, a unique identification number assigned by the court clerk.
- *Dates.* Each case indicates the date of the court's decision. Some cases may also include the date that the case was argued and submitted to the court, or a date that a higher appellate court denied further review or hearing. For citation purposes, usually only the year that the case was decided is necessary.
- *Synopsis.* One of the most helpful research aids added by the publisher is a synopsis of the case (also known as a "syllabus"). A synopsis summarizes key facts, procedure, legal points, and disposition. Reading a synopsis quickly tells you whether a case is on point. You cannot rely exclusively on a synopsis; at least skim each case to determine whether it is impor-

---

37. This section is drawn from *Oregon Legal Research* by Suzanne E. Rowe and is used with permission.

38. In other jurisdictions, the terms *petitioner* may be used for an appellant and *respondent* for an appellee, particularly where appellate review is discretionary.

Figure 4-1. Sample Case from *South Western Reporter*

WHITE v. SHEPARD

Ark. **333**

Cite as 459 S.W.3d 333 (Ark.App. 2015)

These briefing deficiencies should not be considered an exhaustive list; we encourage appellant to review our rules of appellate procedure to ensure that any subsequent brief comports with our requirements.

Dismissed without prejudice; appellee's motion to dismiss appeal moot.

Glover and Hoofman, JJ., agree.

2015 Ark. App. 223

Richard WHITE, Appellant

v.

Karen SHEPARD, Appellee

No. CV–14–157

Court of Appeals of Arkansas, DIVISION II.

Opinion Delivered April 8, 2015

Background: Wife filed complaint for divorce from bed and board, and filed motion for summary judgment seeking to enforce mediated property settlement agreement. Husband filed counterclaim for absolute divorce. The Circuit Court, Carroll County, Gary Arnold, J., granted wife's motion for summary judgment, dismissed husband's counterclaim, and granted divorce which prohibited husband from suing for absolute divorce. Husband appealed.

Holdings: The Court of Appeals, Rita W. Gruber, J., held that:

(1) husband was entitled to grant of counterclaim for absolute divorce as a matter of law;

(2) genuine issues of material fact as to whether husband refused to comply with memorandum of understanding

and mediated settlement agreement precluded summary judgment; and

(3) genuine issues of material fact as to whether property and debts were marital or nonmarital precluded summary judgment.

Reversed and remanded.

1. Divorce ⬅11.5

Husband was entitled to grant of counterclaim for absolute divorce as a matter of law in light of the parties' agreement that they had lived separate and apart for 18 months without cohabitation. Ark. Code Ann. § 9-12-301.

2. Judgment ⬅181(20)

Genuine issues of material fact as to whether husband refused to comply with memorandum of understanding and mediated settlement agreement precluded summary judgment for wife on that issue in divorce action.

3. Judgment ⬅181(20)

Genuine issues of material fact as to whether property and debts not listed in mediated property settlement agreement were marital or nonmarital precluded summary judgment in divorce action. Ark. Code Ann. § 9-12-315.

APPEAL FROM THE CARROLL COUNTY CIRCUIT COURT, WESTERN DISTRICT [NO. DR–2012–43 WD], HONORABLE GARY ARNOLD, JUDGE

Parker Law Firm, by: Tim S. Parker, for appellant.

Kristine Bradt Kendrick, Rogers, for appellee.

RITA W. GRUBER, Judge

₁On July 24, 2012, Karen Shepard (now appellee) filed a complaint for absolute ditant for your research. Moreover, never cite a synopsis, even when it gives an excellent summary of the case. The synopsis was not written by a judge, but by the publisher, and it is therefore not authoritative.

- *Disposition.* The disposition of the case is the court's decision to affirm, reverse, remand, or vacate the decision below. If the appellate court agrees with only part of the lower court's opinion, the appellate court may affirm in part and reverse in part.

- *Headnotes, Topics, and Key Numbers.* A *headnote* is a sentence or short paragraph that summarizes a single point of law in a case. Most cases have several headnotes. The text of the headnote may come directly from the text of the opinion, or it may be an editor's paraphrase of the text. In West reporters, each headnote has a *topic*, such as "Parent and Child," and a *key number*, such as "3.3(8)." Section IV.B.2 of this chapter discusses how to use these headnotes to find additional cases on the same subject.

- *Attorneys.* The attorneys representing each of the parties, the attorneys' law firms, and the cities in which they practice are listed.

- *Authoring Judge and Text of Opinion.* The name of the judge who wrote the opinion immediately precedes its text. Some cases list the judges who heard the case and note those judges who concurred with or dissented to the majority opinion. Certain abbreviations may follow a judge's name: "C.J." for chief justice or chief judge and "J." for any other judge or justice. The terms "Special Judge" or "Special Justice" indicate judges sitting by special designation.[39]

Let's examine more closely the structure and operation of headnotes. At the beginning of each headnote, immediately before the topic and key number, is a number identifying it in sequence with the other headnotes in that case. Within the text of the opinion, the same sequential numbers appear in bold brackets[40] at the point in the decision supporting the headnote. Thus, to quickly find the text of the opinion supporting the second headnote, skim through the case until you locate the bold, bracketed [2] in the decision.

Opinions also merit a closer look. If the judges who heard the case do not agree on the outcome or the reasons for the outcome, the case may have several opinions. The opinion supported by a majority of the judges is the *major-*

---

39. For example, an attorney or retired judge invited to hear an appeal sits by special designation.

40. In some reporters, the numbers are printed in bold but not bracketed.

ity opinion, which is controlling and functions as precedent that represents the court's holding. An opinion written to agree with the outcome but not the reasoning of the majority is a *concurring opinion*. An opinion written by a judge who disagrees with the outcome supported by the majority opinion is a *dissenting opinion*. While only the majority opinion is binding precedent, the other opinions provide valuable insights and may be cited as persuasive authority. If there is no majority on both the outcome and the reasoning, the case is decided by the opinion garnering the most support, a *plurality opinion*.

D. Case Summaries

Case summaries are helpful tools to keep abreast of recent Arkansas Supreme Court and Arkansas Court of Appeals decisions. Case summaries are available from the following sources:

- Arkansas Bar Association — The Arkansas Bar Association website posts weekly reviews of significant Arkansas decisions, organized by topic, such as criminal law, family law, and criminal procedure;[41] these reviews are available only to members of the bar.
- Fastcase[42] — Fastcase provides summaries of cases with Arkansas Bar Association reviews, even when accessed by users who are not Arkansas bar members.
- The Administrative Office of the Courts publishes a monthly newsletter, "Appellate Updates," on the Arkansas judiciary website.[43]
- *Arkansas Court Bulletin* is a pay service that summarizes Arkansas cases.[44]

IV. Finding Cases

Although cases are published in the order in which they are issued, no researcher would attempt to find them that way. Fortunately, there are many efficient and effective ways to find cases. Some are more efficient and effective than others.

---

41. The address is www.arkbar.com.
42. The address is www.fastcase.com, or www.arkbar.com for Arkansas Bar members.
43. Go to www.courts.arkansas.gov, and then click "Forms and Publications."
44. For more information, see https://www.courtbulletin.com.

When a researcher already has a case's *citation*, finding it is easy, whether by walking to the library shelf on which that particular reporter volume is located or by retrieving it online. (Remember that citations to cases are often found in the secondary sources consulted at the beginning of research.) But case research is rarely so effortless. Instead, a researcher usually locates cases according to the subjects they address. In print-based research, the most efficient way to find cases is with a *digest*. If electronic databases are employed for online legal research, researchers may use a *terms-and-connectors* (also known as "Boolean") query, a *natural-language* search, or an online subject-based search.

Whether you search for cases online or in print, the method is similar. Start by developing a research vocabulary. Brainstorm the issue; think of synonyms, antonyms, and related phrases that might lead you to relevant cases. This brainstorming is especially important when researching an area of law with which you are not already familiar. Then, as described below, use those terms to search for cases. Use updating tools to verify that the cases you have found are still good law and to find additional authorities.[45]

A. Finding a Case When You Know Its Citation

A case citation allows anyone who sees it to find that specific case. The citation consists of the volume number of the reporter, the reporter series, and the page number on which the case begins. For example, *Spears v. State* is published at 905 S.W.2d 913, i.e., volume 905 of the *South Western Reporter, Second Series*, beginning at page 913. Table 4-3 analyzes the elements of a case citation. In the law library, simply find the second series of the *South Western Reporter*, remove volume 905 from the shelf, and turn to page 913. If you're searching online, type the citation in the appropriate box and immediately retrieve the case.

Table 4-3. Analyzing a Case Citation

Volume	Reporter Abbreviation	Page number
905	S.W.2d	913

---

45. The final step of updating requires the use of citators, explained in Chapter 9.

Cases are often published in two or more reporters. When you don't have access to one of those reporters, or when the specific volume you need is missing from the shelf, you can use the *parallel citation* to locate the case. The parallel citation gives the location of the same case in a different set of books. There are several ways to find a parallel citation:

- Electronic legal research sources usually display parallel citations at the beginning of the document; similarly, you can find parallel citations by using the system's electronic updating features.
- The *Arkansas Blue and White Book* contains parallel reference tables that allow a researcher to find the *South Western Reporter* citation if he has the Arkansas citation, or to find the Arkansas citation if he has the *South Western Reporter* citation. This pamphlet is a subset of the *National Reporter Blue Book* system, which includes tables of parallel citations for all reported state cases.
- West reporters include Parallel Citation Tables in the beginning of the reporters, often on blue pages.
- Advance sheets published for West reporters also include a table of parallel citations for cases.
- The *Arkansas Digest* Table of Cases contains parallel citations; the pocket parts to the *Arkansas Digest* sometime have more current information than the *Arkansas Blue and White Book*.

B. Finding Cases Using Print Digests

1. Benefits of Digests

An effective way to search for these case authorities is to use a *digest*. Despite the many options for finding cases electronically, digest systems are often a more effective way of doing legal research. Digest research employs conceptual research — researching issues by topic — rather than looking for keywords as in computerized searching. Utilizing key word searching can cause you to miss important cases unless you use the exact terms the court used in deciding a case.

West publishes many different digests, corresponding not only to series in the company's National Reporter System[46] (such as regional digests for various state reporters or the *Federal Practice Digest* for reporters containing federal cases) but also to larger compilations, such as the massive *Decennial*

---

46. See Section III.A.2 for further details on West's National Reporter system.

Digest (which references state and federal cases from all jurisdictions), and smaller compilations, such as those of individual states and specialized areas of the law (e.g., the *Bankruptcy Digest* and the *Military Justice Digest*). Despite these geographic and specialty divisions, the West digest system is used consistently in each. In other words, once you learn how to use one digest, you can use any of them.

Begin work in the narrowest digest that represents the jurisdiction or specialty area in which the legal problem is set. In other words, for an Arkansas state-law problem, start with the *Arkansas Digest*.

The *Arkansas Digest* indexes judicial decisions from Arkansas appellate courts and federal cases originating in Arkansas, covering the years 1820 to the present. The *Arkansas Digest* indexes not only cases decided by the Arkansas Supreme Court and the Arkansas Court of Appeals, but also decisions of the federal courts sitting in Arkansas and decisions from the Eighth Circuit Court of Appeals and the United States Supreme Court that originated in Arkansas. Each volume is supplemented annually with its own cumulative pocket part. A cumulative pamphlet is published every January, supplementing the previous year's pocket parts for all the volumes.

2. Headnotes

Headnotes are the product of a given reporter's editorial staff, even when the text of the headnote is identical to the language used in the opinion. Thus, in states where case decisions are published in more than one reporter, the number and text of the headnotes likely differ in some respects, as each reporter has its own editorial staff creating those headnotes.

The West digest system is based on headnotes from reported decisions. A West attorney editor picks out important parts of the case and summarizes them at the beginning of the published opinion. These summaries of points of law are called *headnotes*. Although it is tempting to cite or quote headnotes as "the law," resist that temptation. Headnotes are summaries that are written by the publisher rather than by the court. They have no precedential value. And headnotes are sometimes wrong. In rare instances, they sometimes even flatly contradict what the court has said in the written opinion.[47] Because

---

47. *See* Ronald D. Rotunda, *Constitutionalizing Judicial Ethics: Judicial Elections after* Republican Party of Minnesota v. White, Caperton, and Citizens United, 64 Ark. L. Rev. 1, 35 (2011):

I emphasize this point because, oddly enough, the West headnotes claim that there was only a plurality on this issue. I realize that headnotes are not

only the opinion itself is authoritative, do not rely on headnotes when analyzing cases, and do not cite them in legal documents.

Instead of quoting a headnote as authority, use the headnote to locate language within the opinion itself that you can summarize, restate, or quote. When used in this way, headnotes are an indispensable research tool. Get the case, read it, and use language directly from the case (instead of indirectly from the headnote). See Section III.C for further discussion of headnotes.

3. Organization of the Digest

What makes these headnotes indispensable is that, once they are written for publication with the case, they are then organized into categories that researchers can use to locate the legal authority that they need. The West system, for example, organizes headnotes into seven major categories: Persons, Property, Contracts, Torts, Crimes, Remedies and Government.

Within these broad categories, the West system uses more than 400 *topics* to categorize the thousands of cases decided each year. The topics themselves are also broad, and thousands of cases can fall within each topic. For this reason, West further subdivides topics using *key numbers* that correlate to specific legal issues. As of this writing, West uses 106,000 classifiable key numbers.

Some topics, such as "Election of Remedies," utilize relatively few key numbers, while other more complex topics, such as "Evidence," have hundreds of key numbers.[48]

4. Ways to Use the Digest

Digests furnish several ways to find applicable case law. You can start with a case you've already found and use the digest to find other cases catalogued by the same topics and key numbers, or you can go straight to the digest on its own, using its Descriptive-Word Index, its Topic Analysis, its *Words and Phrases*, or its Table of Cases. Each of these techniques is explained in detail below.

---

part of the opinion, and that a lawyer should not rely on headnotes to determine what the Court held anymore than an English major should rely on *Cliff's Notes* to understand what *Hamlet* really means. Still, we are often in a hurry and often we just want the shortened version of a long opinion. In this case, the shortened version, in the form of headnotes, is wrong.[fn165]

[fn165] One does not find this claim in the summary in the official United States Reports. 536 U.S. 765. Nor do the headnotes of the Lawyer's Edition make this assertion. 153 L. Ed. 2d 694.

48. A list of West's main topics is set out in the preface of every digest.

a. Beginning with Topics and Key Numbers from a Known Case

Sometimes you have already found a case on point in another primary or secondary authority, such as an annotated statute or a legal encyclopedia, but you are not entirely comfortable about its scope or about certain aspects of its contents. If you begin a research project knowing one case on point, however, you can retrieve that case in a West reporter or on Westlaw and identify its relevant headnotes. Note the topic and key number given for each relevant headnote. A digest lists topics alphabetically; select a digest volume containing one of the relevant topics. Within each topic, key numbers are arranged numerically. Under the key number, all the headnotes of cases with that topic and key number are listed. Repeat this step for each relevant topic and key number in the case that was your starting point. Update the search to find the most recent cases on point. See Chapter 9 for information on updating cases.

b. Beginning with the Descriptive-Word Index

Most digest research begins with the Descriptive-Word Index, which translates research terms into the topics and key numbers used by the digest to index cases.

To begin, use an organized method of brainstorming to generate a list of research terms that describe the situation you are analyzing. Create a list of search terms using the TARP method or journalistic approach outlined in Chapter 1, including synonyms. Then look up each term in the Descriptive-Word Index (contained in several volumes at the end of the digest), writing the topic and key number for each. (Record both the topic and key number. Many topics employ the same numbers, so a key number without its topic is not helpful.) Check each volume's pocket part for the most recent information. Figure 4-2 shows an excerpt from the Descriptive-Word Index in the *Arkansas Digest*. Note that some topics are abbreviated in the Descriptive-Word Index. A list of topics and their abbreviations appears at the front of each index volume.

Using the topics and key numbers you recorded from the Descriptive-Word Index, select a digest volume containing one of those topics. Each topic begins with a list of "Subjects Included" as well as "Subjects Excluded and Covered by Other Topics." These lists help you decide whether that topic is likely to index cases relevant to your research. The list of excluded subjects may refer to relevant topics elsewhere in the digest. Following these lists is the key number outline of the topic, under the heading "Analysis," as shown in Figure 4-3. Longer topics have a short summary outline and a detailed outline. Many topics follow a general litigation organization, discussing elements, defenses,

Figure 4-2. Descriptive-Word Index

COVENANTS

References are to Digest Topics and Key Numbers

COVENANTS—Cont'd
ASSESSMENTS and taxes—Cont'd
Covenants against incumbrances—Cont'd

Breach, **Covenants** ☞ 96(6)

Real covenants imposing burdens, **Covenants** ☞ 68

Warranty of title, breach of, **Covenants** ☞ 100(3)

ASSIGNMENTS. See heading **ASSIGNMENTS, COVENANTS.**

ATTORNEY fees in action for breach, **Covenants** ☞ 132(2)

BENEFITS, real covenants conferring, **Covenants** ☞ 61

BREACH,

Generally, **Covenants** ☞ 92-102

Actions for breach. See subheading ACTIONS for breach, under this heading.

Against incumbrances,

Generally, **Covenants** ☞ 96

Easements, **Covenants** ☞ 96(7)

Judgments, **Covenants** ☞ 96(5)

Leases, **Covenants** ☞ 96(3)

Mortgages, **Covenants** ☞ 96(4)

Restrictions as to use of property, **Covenants** ☞ 96(8)

Taxes and assessments, **Covenants** ☞ 96(6)

Demand for performance, **Covenants** ☞ 86

Further assurance, **Covenants** ☞ 98

Notice to defend title, **Covenants** ☞ 87-90

Quiet enjoyment, **Covenants** ☞ 97

Restrictive covenants. See heading **RESTRICTIVE COVENANTS AND CONDITIONS,** generally.

Right to convey, **Covenants** ☞ 95

Seisin, **Covenants** ☞ 94

Sufficiency of performance, **Covenants** ☞ 91

Title, covenants of, **Covenants** ☞ 93

Use of property, covenants as to. See heading **RESTRICTIVE COVENANTS AND CONDITIONS,** generally.

Warranty,

Generally, **Covenants** ☞ 99-102

Eviction, **Covenants** ☞ 102

Liens, **Covenants** ☞ 100(2)

Mortgages, **Covenants** ☞ 100(2)

Paramount title or right, **Covenants** ☞ 101

Taxes and assessments, **Covenants** ☞ 100(3)

COVENANTS—Cont'd

BUILDINGS. See heading **RESTRICTIVE COVENANTS AND CONDITIONS, BUILDINGS.**

BURDEN of proof, **Covenants** ☞ 118

CHANGED circumstances,
Ground for release or discharge of real covenants, **Covenants** ☞ 72.1

CHARGES,
Real covenants creating, **Covenants** ☞ 70

COLLATERAL covenants, **Covenants** ☞ 24

COMPETITION,
Assignability, **Assign** ☞ 19
Breach, **Contracts** ☞ 312(4)
Confidential information,
Preventing disclosure, **Contracts** ☞ 118
Consideration, **Contracts** ☞ 65(2)
Construction and operation, **Contracts** ☞ 202(2)
Customer lists,
Preventing disclosure, **Contracts** ☞ 118
Effect of illegality,
Generally, **Contracts** ☞ 135-140
Blue penciling, **Contracts** ☞ 137(4)
Enforcement of contract, **Contracts** ☞ 138(1)
Partial illegality, **Contracts** ☞ 137(4)
Relief of parties, **Contracts** ☞ 138
Injunctions, **Inj** ☞ 61
Trade secrets,
Preventing disclosure, **Contracts** ☞ 118
Validity, **Monop** ☞ 12(4)
Generally, **Contracts** ☞ 114-118
Burden of proof, **Contracts** ☞ 141(1)
Duration of restraint, **Contracts** ☞ 117
Evidence, **Contracts** ☞ 141
Extent of restraint, **Contracts** ☞ 117
Fairness, **Contracts** ☞ 116-118
General or partial restraints, **Contracts** ☞ 117
Geographical limitations, **Contracts** ☞ 117
Legitimate business interests, **Contracts** ☞ 116(2)
Nature of business, **Contracts** ☞ 117(1)
Presumptions, **Contracts** ☞ 141(1)
Questions for jury, **Contracts** ☞ 142
Reasonableness of restraint, **Contracts** ☞ 117
Restriction necessary for protection, **Contracts** ☞ 116(2)
Scope of restraint, **Contracts** ☞ 117
Territorial limitations, **Contracts** ☞ 117
Time limitations, **Contracts** ☞ 117

pleadings, and evidence in that order. Skim the Analysis outline to ensure that you found in the Descriptive-Word Index all the relevant key numbers within that topic.

Next, turn to each relevant key number and review the case headnotes listed there. Write the citation for each case you plan to read. (At this point, citations need not be complete or conform to any system of citation. One party name, the volume, reporter, and the initial page number provide sufficient information to retrieve a case.)

To find more recent topics, key numbers, and case headnotes, check for a *pocket-part supplement.* If there are too many pages to fit in a pocket part, the digest volume is accompanied by a soft-bound supplement. These supplements are in turn updated by cumulative supplementary pamphlets containing updates for all topics.[49] For more current cases using West tools, go to Westlaw, explained later in this chapter.[50]

Reviewing headnotes and recording citations to possibly relevant cases constitute time-consuming but critical work. To analyze accurately a client's situation, you need to read every relevant case, as the cost of missing a key case is high. However, be selective in deciding what cases to read first; when a topic and key number contain many headnotes, or when you are working under tight deadlines, first read the cases that are binding authority in your jurisdiction. Within that subset, read the most recent cases. If the facts in a digest headnote are similar to facts in your client's case, read that case, too.

For example, suppose your client has entered into an employment contract that restricts her from working for a competitor for a period of two years (remember Ms. Goshen from Chapter 1?). To determine whether a two-year restraint on employment is enforceable, you could look up the term "covenant not to compete" in the Descriptive-Word Index (remembering to also check its pocket parts). There you'd find a reference to the Topic "Contracts," and for the subtopic "validity" (i.e., enforceability), the key numbers 114 to 118.[51]

---

49. You may find coverage after the cumulative supplements by going to a particular reporter's most recent volumes and advance sheets and using the digest contained in each. A table at the beginning of each digest volume indicates which reporter volumes it indexes. Updating requires you to check the digest sections of subsequent reporters.

50. Only Westlaw allows you to continue research using West topics and key numbers. See Section IV.C for performing research in Westlaw and other databases.

51. See Figure 4-2 for the full digest index page.

Figure 4-3. Digest Topic Analysis

CONTRACTS

I. REQUISITES AND VALIDITY.—Continued.

(F) LEGALITY OF OBJECT AND OF CONSIDERATION.—Continued.

    ◦⟶116. —— In general.—Continued.

        (3). Combinations and agreements to control prices and prevent competition in general.

        (4). Contracts for purchase of entire output.

        (5). Grant of exclusive privileges.

        (6). Exclusive agencies.

        (7). Use and sale of patented inventions.

    117. —— General or partial restraint.

        (.5). In general.

        (1). Nature of business to which contract relates.

        (2). Limitations as to time and place in general.

        (3). Extent of territory embraced in general.

        (4). Entire state or larger territory.

        (5). Particular cities or towns and small districts.

        (6). Particular premises.

        (7). Restrictions unlimited as to place.

        (8). Restrictions unlimited or indefinite as to time.

        (9). Restrictions unlimited as to place and time.

    118. —— Preventing disclosure of trade secrets.

    119. Prevention of competition in bids or proposals.

    120. Procuring or making fictitious bids or proposals.

    121. Control of corporation.

    122. Prohibited traffic or transactions.

    123. Injury to public service in general.

        (1). In general.

        (2). Contracts with railroad companies.

    124. Affecting election or appointment to office.

    125. Affecting emoluments of office.

    126. Influencing legislation.

    127. Ousting jurisdiction or limiting powers of court.

        (1). In general.

        (2). Agreement to refer or arbitrate disputes in general.

        (4). Agreement as to place of bringing suit; forum selection clauses.

    128. Compounding offenses.

        (1). In general.

        (2). Guilt or innocence of accused.

        (3). Offenses that may be compounded.

        (4). Compensation for loss or civil liability.

    129. Obstructing or perverting administration of justice.

        (.5). In general.

        (1). Agreements relating to actions and other proceedings in general.

        (2). Contracts with witnesses.

COVENANTS
   COMPETITION
     Validity
       Generally, **Contracts 114–118**

Because the digest arranges its topics alphabetically, look for the digest volume containing the topic "Contracts." The key numbers correspond to subtopics in the law of contracts. For example, under "Contracts" key number 117(2), "Limitations as to time and place in general," you'll find headnotes from and citations to cases that address those points of law. Figure 4-4 is a page from the Arkansas Digest showing some of the cases listed under Contracts key number 117(2). Cases are listed by jurisdiction, beginning with federal, and then by date, in reverse chronological order. On the following pages of the digest are cases from the Arkansas Supreme Court and the Arkansas Court of Appeals.

Table 4-4 contains examples of Arkansas cases indexed under "Contracts" key number 117(2).[52]

The example in Table 4-4 vividly illustrates why careful researchers do not rely on the content of headnotes alone in selecting case law for their legal analysis. The *Dawson* case upheld a five-year restraint, but the older *Brown* case declared that a period of five years was unreasonable. While it is possible the Arkansas Supreme Court could have changed its rule in the 30 years that elapsed between those cases, the more likely explanation is that something very significant in the facts of those two cases accounts for the different outcomes.

This example also demonstrates that, while headnotes are important tools for indexing and finding case law on a particular topic, they cannot substitute for reading the cases themselves and discovering the basis for the courts' reasoning. Neither can a headnote indicate to the researcher whether the case is still "good law." To make that determination, the researcher must update the case with a citator, as explained in Chapter 9.

c. Beginning with the Topic Analysis

After researching a specific area of law many times, you may be very familiar with the topics under which cases in that area are indexed. If so, you can begin your research using the Analysis outline that appears at the beginning

---

52. Note that these entries follow the publisher's citation format rather than formats conforming to national standards as represented by the *ALWD Guide* or the *Bluebook*.

Figure 4-4. *Arkansas Digest*

CONTRACTS ☞117(2)

For references to other topics, see Descriptive-Word Index

Ark.App. 2003. The covenant not to compete executed by corporate sales agent for cellular telephone service provider, which applied to corporate sales agent's "key employees," was not overly broad; the term "key employee" was more restrictive than "employee" and indicated a reasonable desire to restrain competition only as to important personnel from corporate sales agent who possessed key information.

Statco Wireless, LLC v. Southwestern Bell Wireless, LLC, 95 S.W.3d 13, 80 Ark. App. 284.

The covenant not to compete executed by corporate sales agent for cellular telephone service provider, which prohibited agent's stockholders from selling or promoting a competitor's service, was not overly broad.

Statco Wireless, LLC v. Southwestern Bell Wireless, LLC, 95 S.W.3d 13, 80 Ark. App. 284.

Ark.App. 1991. Covenant not to compete which precluded former employee from selling insurance product that former employer did not sell was overly broad and void.

Federated Mut. Ins. Co. v. Bennett, 818 S.W.2d 596, 36 Ark. App. 99.

☞117(2). Limitations as to time and place in general.

C.A.8 (Ark.) 2007. Under Michigan law, non-compete covenant, prohibiting lumberyard operator from providing insulation installation services for two years if operator terminated contract with insulation manufacturer, forbade competitive conduct, and thus operated in restraint of trade, such that manufacturer's business interest justifying covenant was required to be greater than merely preventing competition.

Guardian Fiberglass, Inc. v. Whit Davis Lumber Co., 509 F.3d 512.

C.A.8 (Ark.) 2004. Under Arkansas law, in determining the enforceability of a covenant not to compete, the restraint must be reasonable in geographical limitation and duration, must protect a legitimate interest, must be no greater than reasonably necessary to protect the legiti-

mate interest, and should not injure the public's interest.

Hardesty Co., Inc. v. Williams, 368 F.3d 1029.

C.A.8 (Ark.) 1988. Under Arkansas law, provision in employment contract between general agent and manager and insurance company, reducing by one-half the posttermination compensation otherwise due agent if, within two years after termination of agreement, agent went to work for competitor within 200 miles of agency office he occupied at time of termination, was enforceable covenant not to compete; geographic restriction was not overbroad, time limitation was reasonable, and covenant protected valid business interests as agent had been given special training and been made privy to confidential business information, including customer lists.

Owens v. Penn Mut. Life Ins. Co., 851 F.2d 1053, rehearing denied.

E.D.Ark. 2006. Under Arkansas law, a noncompetition clause of an agent appointment agreement between an insurance agent and an insurer was valid and enforceable, despite claim that it was overbroad in its geographical restriction and in that it would prohibit the agent from advertising for one year, because an advertisement could be seen by the insurer's policyholders and therefore would be a prohibited solicitation of them; the contract did not prohibit the agent from advertising, and left the agent free to solicit, accept, and service the insurance business of 93% of the potential customers in the district at issue.

Sensabaugh v. Farmers Ins. Exchange, 420 F.Supp.2d 980.

E.D.Ark. 1966. Under Arkansas law, restrictions on competitive activity by employee for as long as five years are looked upon with extreme disfavor whereas under Texas law, such a period is not disfavored.

Credit Bureau Management Co. v. Huie, 254 F.Supp. 547.

Postemployment, noncompetition agreement which restrained manager of collection agency in Arkansas from doing similar work for competitor for five years was effective to prohibit such work for two years under Arkansas law which was based on strong public policy against long-

† **This Case was not selected for publication in the National Reporter System**

Table 4-4. Selected Arkansas Cases in *Contracts 117(2)*

Ark. 1999. There is nothing inherently unreasonable about a five-year duration in a covenant not to compete.

Dawson v. Temps Plus, Inc., 987 S.W.2d 722, 337 Ark. 247.

Ark. 1977. In determining whether time limitation in restrictive covenant not to compete is reasonable, each case must be determined on its own facts.

Borden, Inc. v. Huey, 547 S.W.2d 760, 261 Ark. 313.

Ark. 1966. A five-year restraint provision in contract of employment is unreasonable.

Brown v. Devine, 402 S.W.2d 669, 240 Ark. 838.

Source: *Arkansas Digest*. Reprinted with permission of Thomson Reuters.

of each relevant topic.[53] Scan the list of key number subtopics, and then review the headnotes under each key number that appears to be on point. As always, remember to check the pocket parts, supplementary pamphlets, and reporter advance sheets for more recent cases under the topics and key numbers you are searching.

d. *Beginning with* Words and Phrases

Courts are often called upon to define terms at issue in a case. While a dictionary like *Black's Law Dictionary* provides a general definition of a term, the *Words and Phrases* volume of the digest[54] directs you to a case defining the term for a particular jurisdiction. Judicial definitions are especially helpful when an important term in a statute is vague.

The *Words and Phrases* volume of the *Arkansas Digest* collects and alphabetically indexes these judicial definitions, citing the cases from which they came and indicating the digest topic and key number for which the definition is relevant. Where multiple case sources for these definitions exist, the cases are arranged in reverse chronological order. *Words and Phrases* is updated yearly with a cumulative pocket part.

For example, imagine that a research project involves a challenge to circumstantial evidence presented at trial. *Words and Phrases* shows that Arkansas courts have defined the term "circumstantial evidence" six times. The first time was in 1951, when the Arkansas Supreme Court ruled that " 'circumstantial evidence' consists of a number of disconnected and independent

---

53. See Figure 4-3.

54. West also produces a multi-volume set, *Words and Phrases*, containing court definitions from federal and state jurisdictions combined.

facts, coming from several witnesses and different sources, each of which is consistent and which converges towards the facts at issue as a common center, tending to the same conclusion."[55]

The phrase was defined again in 1993:

> "Circumstantial evidence" may constitute substantial evidence, and in order for circumstantial evidence to be sufficient to sustain conviction, it must exclude every other reasonable hypothesis consistent with innocence; whether evidence excludes every other reasonable hypothesis is for finder of fact to determine and it is only when circumstantial evidence leaves jury solely to speculation and conjecture that it is insufficient as matter of law.[56]

Five more definitions for this phrase appear in the 2016 cumulative supplement, beginning with Arkansas Supreme Court cases. In the first two entries, *Words and Phrases* states, "'Circumstantial evidence' is evidence of circumstances from which a fact may be inferred."[57] The third entry states, "'Circumstantial evidence' is evidence that allows a fact to be established by inference from other facts in the case."[58] The next two entries are Arkansas Court of Appeals cases: "'Circumstantial evidence' sufficient to support a jury verdict may constitute substantial evidence, but it must be consistent with the defendant's guilt and inconsistent with any other reasonable conclusion";[59] and "'Circumstantial evidence' does not directly prove the existence of a fact, but gives rise to a logical inference that it exists."[60]

Even though *Words and Phrases* referred to these seven cases, a wise researcher won't stop there. *Words and Phrases* is not primary authority. Retrieve, read, and update each case in order to determine its usefulness. In this example, the seven cases were decided at different times and by different

---

55. *Words and Phrases* (citing *Hearnsberger v. McGaughey*, 218 Ark. 663, 670, 239 S.W.2d 17, 21 (1951)).

56. *Words and Phrases* (citing *Tiller v. State*, 42 Ark. App. 64, 69, 854 S.W.2d 730, 733 (1993)).

57. *Words and Phrases* (citing *Chatmon v. State*, 2015 Ark. 28, at 9, 467 S.W.3d 731, 736, and *Jackson v. State*, 363 Ark. 311, 315, 214 S.W.3d 232, 235–36 (2005)).

58. *Words and Phrases* (citing *Mills v. State*, 351 Ark. 523, 529, 95 S.W.3d 796, 799 (2003)).

59. *Words and Phrases* (citing *Blair v. State*, 103 Ark. App. 322, 326, 288 S.W.3d 713, 716 (2008)).

60. *Words and Phrases* (citing *Reed v. Smith Steel, Inc.*, 70 Ark. App. 110, 119, 78 S.W.3d 118, 125 (2002)).

Table 4-5. Sample Entries from the *Arkansas Digest* Table of Cases

---

Brown v. Department of Human Services, Ark, 956 SW2d 866, 330 Ark 764. — Admin Law 669.1; Infants 133.

Brown; Dermott Special School Dist. v., Ark, 485 SW2d 204, 253 Ark 222. — Schools 106.4(2).

Brown v. Devine, Ark, 402 SW2d 669, 240 Ark 838. — Contracts 117(1), 117(2).

Brown; DeWitt v., CA8 (Ark), 669 F2d 516. — App & E 930(1), 1001(1); Evid 12; Fed Civ Proc 2142.1; Fed Cts 431, 644, 757; Health 620, 665, 823(7), 832; Neglig 1657.

Brown; De Yampert v., Ark, 28 Ark 166. — Paymt 18; Ven & Pur 265(2).

Devilemont's Heirs v. U S, USArk, 54 US 261, 13 How 261, 14 LEd 183. — Pub Lands 207.

De Villemont's Heirs v. U. S., DArk, FedCasNo 3,839, Hempst 389, affd Devilemont's Heirs v. U S, 54 US 261, 13 How 261, 14 LEd 138. — Pub Lands 203.

Devine; Brown v., Ark, 402 SW2d 669, 240 Ark 838. — Contracts 117(1), 117(2).

DeViney v. State, Ark, 772 SW2d 607, 299 Ark 471. — Crim Law 1069(1), 1081(4.1), 1106(3).

Deviney v. State, ArkApp, 685 SW2d 179, 14 ArkApp 70. — Crim Law 438(1), 438(6), 438(7), 552(1), 552(3), 552(4), 741(6), 1153(1); Homic 1146.

Source: *Arkansas Digest*. Reprinted with permission of Thomson Reuters.

courts. Their facts and issues differ; some of the cases were appeals from criminal trials, while others were from civil cases. Once you know the content and history of each case, you can predict whether and how it may apply to the client's facts.

e. *Beginning with the Table of Cases*

The Table of Cases lists all the cases indexed in a particular digest series. Each case is listed twice, once by the primary plaintiff's name and once by the primary defendant's name (see Table 4-5; note that *Brown v. Devine* is listed twice, once by appellant Brown's name and once by appellee Devine's name). The table is helpful when you do not know the citation to a relevant case but do know one or both party names. This situation may occur (1) because a colleague recommended the case, (2) because you used it in previous research, or (3) because the only citation you have is to an official reporter that does not use West's topics and key numbers. Each entry features the abbreviated name of the court deciding the case, the unofficial and official reporters' volumes, the case's initial page, and the West digest topics and key numbers for the points of law it contains. After consulting the Table of Cases, read the case in a reporter or continue working in the digest using the listed topics and key numbers to find more related cases.

C. Finding Cases Online

Court opinions are available from many resources, and the resources are constantly improving. An appellate court website typically posts a decision the day it is issued or within a very short time thereafter. In Arkansas, the Arkansas Judiciary website[61] posts Arkansas Supreme Court cases every Thursday and Arkansas Court of Appeals cases every Wednesday when these courts are in session.

You can also find cases online if you have access to commercial databases such as Lexis, Westlaw, and Bloomberg, available by paid subscription.[62] Attorneys who are members of the Arkansas Bar Association receive free access to Fastcase. All of these services publish judicial opinions shortly after they are released. But most case law research does not involve reading recent cases. Instead, you are apt to be searching for a particular rule, or a court's interpretation of that rule, or the application of a rule to the facts of a specific dispute that resembles your client's case. This means that you will more often than not use an online database to find *all* the relevant case law applicable to the problem before you.

It's easy to be overwhelmed by the large number of results uncovered through an electronic search for cases. Like a researcher entering a physical law library, an online researcher should determine what types of sources will most likely lead to the information sought and consult those sources first. The online researcher uses filters to narrow results, keeping in mind that the goal is rarely to read everything ever written on a subject in every jurisdiction, but instead to locate current information relevant to the issue on which the researcher is working.

Platforms like Lexis and Westlaw provide efficient tools for saving and organizing research. You can save documents in electronic folders and annotate or highlight relevant passages. You can share folders with others working

---

61. The address is www.court.arkansas.gov. You can also subscribe on the website to receive weekly notifications when new cases are posted.

62. See Table 4-2 for a list of online providers of judicial opinions.

on the same project. The platforms also keep track of your prior searches as a safeguard to prevent duplication or backtracking.

1. Introduction to Full-Text Searching

The major advantage of online searching is that it allows researchers to navigate quickly through a huge volume of cases. Most typically this is done through full-text searching — in other words, searching directly in the text of reported cases for search terms.

In its broadest form, full-text searching essentially bypasses indexes or digests. Traditionally, the researcher would select a database corresponding to a particular jurisdiction, and then search within that database for cases that contained specific terms or phrases. This is still how some simpler search engines work. Fastcase, Lexis, Westlaw, and Bloomberg Law, however, have developed more sophisticated search mechanisms that allow searching across various databases, to retrieve materials from multiple jurisdictions or materials addressing similar issues, all accomplished with one search.

The ability to search the full text of cases is both an advantage and disadvantage of online research. Online searching is helpful when you are looking for a unique term of art or for cases involving an unusual factual situation. If you are searching for general or commonly used terms, however, or an unfamiliar area of law, a full-text search may retrieve many more cases or authorities than you can reasonably read or analyze for a single issue, including many that are irrelevant. For this reason, becoming proficient in constructing and refining online searches is essential.

This section explains how to use (a) *terms and connectors* or (b) *natural language* queries to uncover relevant case law. Each has benefits and drawbacks. Terms-and-connectors searching gives the researcher more control over the query, but constructing that query requires extra effort. Natural-language searching is more intuitive, but it cedes control of the query to the computer.

a. Terms and Connectors

Most legal search engines offer a number of ways to limit or shape search results. These limitations include *connectors*, i.e., symbols that combine research terms, as well as choices to limit a search result by court, date, and other parameters.

In terms-and-connectors (Boolean) searching, the researcher selects key terms and combines them with connecting or limiting phrases, such as "and," "or," "/10" or "w/10" ("within 10 words"). Other often-used connectors are "/s" or "w/s" (retrieving words within the same sentence), and "/p" or "w/p" (within the same paragraph). Synonymous terms can be placed in parentheses, expanding the search to look for any of the alternatives. For instance, in a suit involving medical professionals, using the alternative terms (doctor or physician) tells the search engine to find documents containing either term.

Searches can combine multiple connectors. For example, a search for cases involving the admission of evidence under the "excited utterance" exception to the hearsay rule might look like this:

"excited utterance" /p exception /p hearsay

This search retrieves only cases using the precise phrase "excited utterance" in the same paragraph as the words "exception" and "hearsay." Searching with terms and connectors allows a tightly focused search, but you need to choose connectors with care. If you searched instead for

"excited utterance" and exception and hearsay

you would retrieve all cases where the three terms appear anywhere within an opinion—which could include cases analyzing other hearsay exceptions in depth and mentioning excited utterances only in passing.

Connectors are not uniform among different online providers; variations exist even among different services provided by the same company. For this reason, it is essential to familiarize yourself with the available connectors when you begin using a new provider. Table 4-6 compares the connectors available in Bloomberg, Fastcase, Lexis, and Westlaw.

Sometimes a search needs to account for variations of a word. For instance, a search for the word "admissible" in a database returns only cases containing that particular word. Think about the words that appellate judges writing opinions might choose. They might say that the evidence was "admissible," or that it was "admitted," or even talk about the "admissibility" of the evidence.

Wildcards are provided by each of the major online legal research providers to help you deal with this situation. Wildcards allow you to expand a search by locating variants of a word. Wildcards can substitute for one letter or for multiple letters; some can be used only as root expanders (e.g., wom*n finds both woman and women; child! finds child and children). The particular characters used vary with the provider you are using. Table 4-7 compares the wildcards available in Bloomberg, Fastcase, Lexis, and Westlaw.

Table 4-6. Search Connectors in Bloomberg, Fastcase, Lexis, and Westlaw (with alternative connectors)

Form of search connector	Bloomberg	Fastcase	Lexis	Westlaw
Both terms	AND	AND &	AND and &	AND &
Either term	OR	OR	OR or	OR [space]
Exact phrase [phrase]	"[phrase]"	"[phrase]"	"[phrase]"	"[phrase]"
Terms in proximity to each other within specified number (#)		w/#	w/# /#	/#
Terms in variable proximity			near/#	
Two or more terms in same paragraph	P/ /P /PARA		W/p /p	/p
First term precedes second in same paragraph			PRE/#	+p
First term precedes second by specified number (#)	N/# /# W/#		PRE/# onear/#	+n
Two or more terms in same sentence	S/ /S /SENT		W/s /s	/s
First term precedes second in same sentence				+s
Terms in same segment or field			W/SEG W/seg	Specify field
Excludes term	NOT ANDNOT BUTNOT	NOT	AND NOT	BUT NOT %
Excludes term within specified number (#)			NOT w/#	

Table 4-6. Search Connectors in Bloomberg, Fastcase, Lexis, and Westlaw (with alternative connectors), *continued*

Form of search connector	Bloomberg	Fastcase	Lexis	Westlaw
Excludes term in same paragraph			NOT W/P	
Excludes term in same sentence			NOT W/S	
Excludes term in same segment or field			NOT W/SEG NOT W/ seg	
Term appears at least specified number (#) of times			ATLEAST atleast	
Term appears in all capital letters			ALLCAPS allcaps	
Term contains capital letter anywhere			CAPS caps	
Term contains no capital letters			NOCAPS nocaps	

b. *Natural Language*

Many legal search engines allow natural-language searching — that is, queries written in plain English. These searches rely on complex (and proprietary) algorithms to generate results that appear to closely match your search. The power of the algorithm can affect the results of your search. While some free or low-cost legal research providers have very simple search engines for natural-language searches, the results at least get you started with a few relevant cases. On the other end of the scale, Lexis and Westlaw are so powerful that natural-language searches are very effective, particularly with the filtering tools they make available. For example, searching in Westlaw for our excited utterance example above ("excited utterance" /p exception /p hearsay) returns 115 cases when filtered to only Arkansas cases; using a natural lan-

**Table 4-7. Wildcards in Bloomberg, Fastcase, Lexis, and Westlaw
(with alternative wildcards)**

Wildcard	Bloomberg	Fastcase	Lexis	Westlaw
Variable character within term	*	?	?	*
Variable adjacent characters within term	* *	??	??	* *
Two or more letters follow term's root	!	*	! *	!

guage search ("Is 'excited utterance' an exception to the hearsay rule?") returns 112 cases.

2. Searching with Free and Low-Cost Providers

There are many free or low-cost resources for case law. Sometimes a simple search in the search engine you normally use (e.g., Google, Yahoo!) can be a "quick and dirty" way to jumpstart case law research. This kind of search won't return a comprehensive result, and you're likely to retrieve many more irrelevant results than relevant ones. However, if a quick search leads to even one or two cases on point, those cases can help you expand or refine research terms for little or no cost. If you are looking for a particular decision and know the parties' names, a quick search using the names as search terms can be an easy way to locate the slip opinion for no cost. This is not, however, a substitute for methodical research using an established provider.

A better — and free — starting point is Google Scholar,[63] which allows you to retrieve state appellate and supreme court decisions from 1950 to the present, federal court decisions from 1923 to the present, and United States Supreme Court decisions from 1791 to the present. You can narrow searches by jurisdiction and further limit them by date. The search box also provides the option of using a drop-down menu to focus on key words or phrases. When you click the link to a specific decision within the search result, the page containing the full text of the document has a link called "How cited"; this link is

---

63. The address is www.scholar.google.com.

not a substitute for KeyCiting or Shepardizing,[64] but it will indicate how that decision has been treated.

A number of low-cost online services also provide access to case law, including Casemaker, Fastcase (discussed more fully below), Loislaw, and VersusLaw. The competition among them — and between the low-cost and premium providers in general — has encouraged them to develop user-friendly interfaces and premium features that mimic the validation and subsequent citation functions of citators. (Their results are computer-generated, however, and not analyzed by legal editors.) These services' search mechanisms typically employ simple terms-and-connectors searching. Some also support natural-language searching. No low-cost provider presently provides access to the range or depth of legal materials available on Lexis or Westlaw; for example, unpublished opinions are typically not retrievable. However, they provide a viable alternative to the premium providers for researching case law. Their coverage is constantly evolving.

3. Searching with Fastcase, Lexis, Westlaw, or Bloomberg Law

Fastcase, Lexis, Westlaw, and Bloomberg Law provide multiple ways to research cases. All feature a universal search bar in which to enter a case by citation, by party name(s), or through full-text searching. All allow you to search databases containing solely Arkansas authorities. Lexis and Westlaw provide topical searching, and Bloomberg provides searches by practice area. Because the features of these programs are constantly being updated, become familiar with the features of each program by taking advantage of the excellent tutorials provided by each.[65] What follows is a basic description of these services.

a. Fastcase

Fastcase[66] contains case law from all state and federal courts. Federal court coverage goes back to the beginning of the reported cases. State coverage varies; some states' case law goes back only to 1950. For states whose bar associa-

---

64. Citators are discussed in Chapter 9.

65. Lexis and Westlaw provide certifications to researchers who complete their trainings.

66. More detail is provided here about Fastcase, since many Arkansas attorneys will have free access to Fastcase through their bar membership. Fastcase does not, however, have all the features provided in the premium Lexis and Westlaw databases, and it does not contain a true citator.

tions have adopted Fastcase as a member benefit, coverage typically goes back to the beginning of the reported cases in that state. Arkansas Supreme Court cases go back to 1886 and Arkansas Court of Appeals cases to 1979.

Fastcase provides a universal search bar where you can type in a case citation, a natural-language search, or a terms-and-connectors search.[67] It remembers the specific jurisdiction(s) you choose, and it automatically populates the jurisdiction selection the next time you begin a search. You can limit a search by date, but only to within a certain beginning and ending month.

Fastcase contains many features found in more expensive online legal research tools, such as the ability to filter results by jurisdiction. Other features include a "favorites" folder, a list of recent searches, and the ability to email research to yourself or someone else. There are options to jump to the next case or the next incident of your search term, as well as the ability to search within the results list for additional terms. The "Forecite" function analyzes the results list and identifies any additional decisions that may be relevant to your research topic, even though they lack one or more of your search terms.

You can review results in multiple ways. By default, results are sorted by relevance, but they can also be sorted by case name, date, or Authority Check results.[68] Results can also be displayed in an interactive timeline instead of a list. On the timeline, each case is represented by a circle; hovering over any of the circles in the timeline displays information about that case, including the name of the case and the most relevant passage from the case. In the results list, there is an option to add alerts. Adding an alert asks the service to send an email update when Fastcase adds new documents germane to your search.

All cases and statutes cited in a case are hyperlinked. Arkansas cases display internal pagination for both the *South Western Reporter* and the official reporters, both in print and online.[69] For cases reviewed in the Arkansas Bar Association case summaries,[70] look for those summaries at the beginning of the case.

---

67. See Tables 4-6 and 4-7 for specific information about connectors and wildcards used by Fastcase.

68. Authority Check is Fastcase's pseudo-citator; for more information on Authority Check, see Chapter 9.

69. See Section III.A for an explanation of official reporters in Arkansas.

70. See Section III.D for an explanation of case summaries.

b. Lexis

Lexis is a premium legal research service that contains all American primary law and many secondary sources.[71] It also includes access to Shepard's Citations,[72] incorporating Shepard's analysis into your search results.

Use the universal search bar on Lexis to search for cases by citation or by party name(s). Alternatively, enter terms for a full-text search, then limit your search with restrictions available from drop-down menus under the universal search bar.

You can conduct natural-language or terms-and-connectors searches.[73] Search results display materials from all content categories (e.g., cases, statutes, secondary sources), and by using the content links, you can narrow those results to a specific type of content. You can add more filters to further narrow or limit the results list, or you can search only for specific "segments" of a decision, such as the judge who authored the opinion, the attorneys who appeared, or the parties.

Lexis does not have an equivalent to the indexing provided by the West topic/key number system (discussed next). However, Lexis's own legal topic hierarchy indexes case law, allowing topical browsing. Most topics have multiple subtopics; look for the most specific subtopics relevant to your research task.

c. Westlaw

Westlaw is a premium legal research service that contains all primary law and many secondary sources; case law is indexed by West key numbers, discussed above in Section IV.C. Its citator is called KeyCite,[74] and KeyCite results are incorporated into your search results.

Westlaw features a universal search bar that encourages natural-language searching. This type of search is good for browsing background information and related content, but it returns a large number of results unless you have limited its output by the use of filters, such as limiting results by jurisdiction or by a topic-specific database.

---

71. This discussion focuses on Lexis Advance. Some users may still have access to Lexis.com, but that service is in the process of being phased out.

72. See Chapter 9 for a discussion of Shepard's Citations.

73. See Tables 4-6 and 4-7 for specific information about connectors and wildcards used by Lexis.

74. See Chapter 9 for a discussion of KeyCite.

Full-text searching can use terms and connectors or natural language.[75] Results are presented in an overview showing selected examples of each type of authority in the result. Narrow the search by selecting specific sources or searching within results.

As an alternative to full-text searching, search by topic using the West topic/key number system, which permits you to browse in a manner similar to the process used in a printed digest.[76] Once you locate relevant topic/key numbers, retrieve cases indexed under those numbers. In addition to the topic/key number search, Westlaw also provides a browsable topic search where you can select practice areas.

d. Bloomberg Law

Bloomberg Law is a premium legal research service that contains all state and federal primary law, including cases, statutes, and regulations, as well as a number of secondary sources including selected books, treatises, and legal periodicals. It permits both natural-language and terms-and-connectors searching.[77] Searches can be limited by content type, jurisdiction, and practice area. It prominently features databases focusing on transactional and business materials, as well as litigation dockets. It employs a limited citator service (BCite).[78]

V. Reading and Analyzing Case Opinions[79]

Once you locate a case, you must read it, understand it, and analyze its potential relevance to the problem you are researching. An attorney, judge, or client who has asked you to do the research will not be satisfied if you report back with a stack of cases you have not yet analyzed.

Do not expect reading a case opinion to be easy. Understanding an opinion takes more mental work than typically dedicated to a few pages of reading. It is perfectly normal for beginning lawyers to read complex decisions at the rate of ten pages per hour. While you are reading, refer to a law dictionary for

---

75. See Tables 4-6 and 4-7 for specific information about connectors and wildcards used by Westlaw.

76. See Section IV.B for a full discussion of digests.

77. See Tables 4-6 and 4-7 for specific information about connectors and wildcards used by Bloomberg.

78. See Chapter 9 for more information about BCite.

79. This section is drawn from *Oregon Legal Research* by Suzanne E. Rowe and is used with permission.

definitions of unfamiliar terms. Early efforts are more productive if you have a basic understanding of civil procedure terms and the fundamental aspects of case analysis. The final section of this chapter lists strategies for reading case opinions.

A. A Thimbleful of Civil Procedure

Civil litigation begins when the *plaintiff*—the person who believes he or she was harmed—files a complaint against the *defendant*—the person charged with some sort of wrongdoing. Plaintiffs or defendants do not have to be persons; they can be entities, such as corporations or other organizations. The *complaint* names the parties to the lawsuit, states the facts giving rise to the suit, makes reference to applicable law, and asks for relief. Courts vary considerably in how much information is required at this stage of litigation. In general, the complaint must be at least specific enough to put the defendant on notice of the legal concerns at issue and to allow the preparation of a defense. Some states (but not Arkansas) require a greater level of detail.

The defendant has a limited amount of time in which to file a response to this complaint. In Arkansas, the defendant must file a response within 30 days of being served with the complaint.[80] If the defendant does nothing within the prescribed time, the plaintiff can ask the court for a *default judgment*, which grants the plaintiff the relief sought in the complaint. The most common form of response to the complaint is the *answer*. In the answer, the defendant admits to undisputed allegations of the complaint, denies disputed allegations, and raises available affirmative defenses.

Throughout the litigation, parties submit a variety of documents and briefs to the court for its consideration. Either party may file a pre-trial *motion* asking the court to make some sort of decision or take some action. For example, a party may *move* the court for additional time to respond to a discovery request. Another example is a motion for summary judgment, where a party asks the court to decide in that party's favor without the need for a trial.

When the trial judge grants a motion that conclusively ends a case (a *dispositive motion*), the losing party is entitled to appeal that *order* to a higher court in the jurisdiction. In deciding an appeal from an order granting a motion, the appellate court determines whether the trial judge was correct in issuing the order at that stage of the litigation. If the appellate court concludes that the trial judge committed no error, it *affirms* the order. If not, it *reverses*

---

80. Ark. R. Civ. P. 12(a)(1).

the order granting the motion. If the reversal means that the case will go forward, the appellate court *remands* the case to the trial court.

Even at trial, the court may consider a motion made by either party. For example, during the trial, the plaintiff is the first to present evidence. After all of the plaintiff's witnesses have testified, but before the defendant's witnesses are called, the defendant may move for a *directed verdict*, arguing that the plaintiff cannot win based on the evidence presented and asking for an immediate decision in favor of the defendant. An order granting that dispositive motion is appealable.

Many reported case decisions review orders granting dispositive motions. These cases apply an appellate *standard of review*, depending on the motion that is the subject of the appeal. The standard of review indicates the level of deference that the appellate court accords to the action of the lower court. While standards of review are beyond the scope of this book, understanding the procedural posture of the case is crucial to understanding the court's holding. For example, in an appeal of an order granting summary judgment in a products liability case, the appellate court could hold that the factual evidence submitted in support of the motion for summary judgment was insufficient or genuinely in dispute; in that situation, the appellate court would reverse the decision of the trial court. This opinion may have little relevance in another products liability case, no matter how factually similar, if the second case required a jury to find facts in order to render a final verdict, because the two cases are in different procedural postures; different standards of review apply. The relevant rules of civil procedure and appellate procedure govern your analysis.

B. Analyzing the Substance of Case Opinions

It can be difficult to determine whether a case is relevant to your research problem. If the case addresses the same issues, it concerns legally significant facts similar to those in your client's situation, and the court applies applicable law to those facts, then the case is relevant. *Legally significant facts* are those that affect the court's decision. Some attorneys call these outcome-determinative facts or key facts. Which facts are legally significant depends on the applicability of the law to those facts. The height of the defendant in a contract dispute is unlikely to be legally significant, but that fact may be critical in a criminal case where the only eyewitness testified that the thief was about five feet tall.

Rarely will your research reveal a case with facts that are exactly the same as those in your client's situation. Rather, several cases may involve facts that are similar to your client's situation but not exactly the same. Your job is to determine whether the facts are similar enough for a court to apply the law in the same way and reach the same conclusion. If a court's ruling is favorable to your client's position, highlight the similarities between that case and your client's situation. If, from your client's perspective, the court reached an unfavorable conclusion, you may argue that the case is distinguishable from yours based on its facts, or you may be able to demonstrate that its reasoning is faulty.[81] You have an ethical duty to ensure that the court knows about any mandatory case directly on point, even if the outcome of that case is adverse to the outcome you are seeking for your client.

You are also unlikely to find a single case that addresses all aspects of your client's situation. Most legal claims are based on rules that have several elements or factors. *Elements* are required parts of a claim while *factors* are important considerations, but not all are necessarily required. For example, the elements of a negligence claim are:

- the existence of a duty on the defendant's part to conform to a specific standard of conduct that protects the plaintiff;
- the defendant's breach of that duty;
- an injury to the plaintiff that the defendant's breach of duty actually and proximately caused; and
- resulting damages to the plaintiff or his property.[82]

If a court decides that any one of these elements is not met, it need not discuss the others, as without all four required elements present, the case will fail.

In a different type of case, a court may look at a group of factors. The court weighs the factors, determining their collective impact in resolving the dispute. In a divorce case, for instance, in determining whether to make an unequal distribution of property, a court looks at the following factors:

- the marriage's length;
- the parties' ages, health, and station in life;

---

81. This discussion assumes that you are preparing an argument to the court in which you advocate on your client's behalf. When preparing an objective inter-office memorandum, it is important to remain as even-handed as possible in your description and analysis of applicable authorities, so that the client and other attorneys working on the case can make the best judgments possible as to likely case outcomes and the best way to proceed.

82. *Cross v. W. Waste Indus.*, 2015 Ark. App. 476, at 7, 469 S.W.3d 820, 825 (citing *Chambers v. Stern*, 347 Ark. 395, 64 S.W.3d 737 (2002)).

- their occupations;
- the amounts and sources of income;
- the parties' vocational skills;
- their employability;
- each party's estate, liabilities, and needs and each party's opportunity for further acquisition of capital assets and income;
- each party's contributions in acquisition, preservation, or appreciation of marital property, including services as a homemaker; and
- the federal income tax consequences for the court's division of property.[83]

A court may decide that some factors are so overwhelming that others have little impact on the outcome, and it addresses those other factors only briefly, if at all. In these circumstances, if the other factors are important to your case, you will have to find additional cases to support an argument that they merit more consideration.

Once you determine that a case is relevant to some portion of your analysis, you must decide how heavily it will weigh. Two important points need to be considered here. One is the concept of *binding precedent*; the other is the difference between the *holding* of the case and *dictum* within that case.

Courts are required to follow only the *holdings* of prior cases, that is, the court's ultimate decisions on the matters of law at issue in the cases. A statement or observation included in the opinion is not binding; it is referred to as *dictum*. For example, a court in a property dispute may hold that the land belongs to X. In reaching that decision, the court may note that had the facts been slightly different, it would have decided the land belongs to Y. That observation is not binding on future courts, though it may be cited as persuasive authority.

The holding of an appellate opinion on an issue or principle of law is *binding precedent* with respect to the same issue in later cases presented to lower courts in the same jurisdiction. Thus, the lower courts must follow the holdings of higher courts in the same jurisdiction, ensuring consistency in the application of the law. Arkansas trial courts faced with issues of state law must follow the decisions of the Arkansas Court of Appeals and the Arkansas Supreme Court, but not those of the courts of any other state. The Arkansas Court of Appeals must follow the decisions of the Arkansas Supreme Court, but not the decisions of lower Arkansas courts.

---

83. *Farrell v. Farrell*, 2013 Ark. App. 23, at 6–7, 425 S.W.3d 824, 829–30 (citing Ark. Code Ann. § 9-12-315).

The concept of binding precedent is related to the doctrine of *stare decisis*, which means to "stand by things decided."[84] Under the doctrine of *stare decisis*, courts generally follow their own previous decisions instead of re-opening an issue for a possible different outcome. If a court decides not to follow its own precedent, that decision is typically based on subsequently enacted legislation or societal changes outdating the law of the earlier cases.

Finally, in determining whether an earlier decision is binding precedent, you must determine whether that earlier decision has been reversed, overruled, or modified in a way that substantially affects the holding in question. To do this, legal researchers use citator services such as Shepard's or KeyCite.

After finding cases that have similar facts, discuss the same legal issue, and bind the court hearing your client's case, the next step is to *synthesize* the cases in order to formulate a complete picture of the legal rule. Synthesis is much more than a mere summary of the various cases. Sometimes a court states the rule fully; if it does not, the synthesis of cases combines all their reasoning to formulate a coherent rule that accounts for all their outcomes. You can then use the analysis and facts of various cases to explain the law, decide how the rule applies to your client's facts, and determine the likely conclusion.

C. Strategies for Reading Case Opinions

As you begin reading opinions, the following strategies may help you understand them more quickly and more thoroughly.

- Review the synopsis (and summary of holdings, if available) to determine whether the case seems to be on point. If so, skim the headnotes to find the most relevant portion(s) of the opinion. Remember that one opinion may discuss several issues of law, only one or two of which may interest you. Go to the portion of the opinion identified by the relevant headnote and decide whether it is important for your project.
- If so, skim the entire decision to get a feeling for what happened and why, focusing on the portion of the opinion identified by the relevant headnote.
- Now read the opinion more slowly and carefully, giving extra scrutiny to the parts that are plainly the most relevant to your legal issue. Browsing text online or highlighting text in printed pages is insufficient to achieve thorough comprehension of judicial opinions.

---

84. *The Law Dictionary*, http://thelawdictionary.org/stare-decisis/ (defining "stare decisis").

- At the end of each paragraph or page, consider what you have read. If you cannot summarize it, try reading the material again. Look up unfamiliar or confusing words or phrases.
- The next time you read the case, take notes. The notes may be in the form of a formal *case brief* or they may be scribbles that only you can understand. Regardless of the form, taking notes helps you identify, parse, and comprehend the essential concepts of the case.

Chapter 5

Statutes and Ordinances

I. Introduction to Statutory Law

The legislative branch of government produces primary authority in the form of *enacted law*, also known as *statutory law*. Legislative bodies include the United States Congress; state legislatures, such as the Arkansas General Assembly; and on the local level, bodies such as county quorum courts, municipal boards, and city councils. Because the body of statutory law has increased enormously in recent years, also consider the possibilities that either federal or state statutes may govern the legal issue, and that one or more statutes may affect the resolution of that issue.

In drafting *statutes*, a legislative body defines and describes the law so that the statutes apply only to the persons, entities, conditions, and conduct that fall within their intended scope. As Congress or a state legislature passes bills during its legislative session, the new acts (sometimes referred to as *slip laws*) are collected chronologically into publications known as *session laws*.[1] As it is extremely difficult to research or locate laws arranged only by their dates of passage, enacted law is typically compiled or *codified* according to subject matter.

Technically speaking, a *compilation* is an unofficial form of collection and publication of statutory laws by subject. *Codification*, in contrast, entails a legislature's positive *enactment* of its laws in a particular published form and arrangement.[2] In addition to bringing together all laws on the same subject matter, the process of codification also edits the statutory law, removing repealed or

---

1. Chapter 6 discusses how to research legislation and legislative history, which is a record of the steps taken by the legislature in considering and passing the legislation.

2. The respective advantages, disadvantages, and effects of compilation versus codification are explored in Morell Eugene Mullins, *An Academic Perspective on Codification and the* Arkansas Code of 1987 Annotated, 11 U. Ark. Little Rock L.J. 285 (1989).

expired provisions, incorporating amendments into an original statute's language, or making technical corrections.

Because the process of codification sometimes distributes the provisions of a single piece of enacted legislation into several different statutes, be alert to the danger of reading any statute or legislative act in isolation.[3] It is common to find several statutes in sequence, all related, but separately setting out the purpose of the legislation, definitions of terms, active subject matter, and exceptions.

Not only is there an official code of statutes for each jurisdiction, but unofficial versions are also available to researchers in both print and online forms. Unlike other kinds of primary authority, the appearance, format, and organization of statutes varies widely from jurisdiction to jurisdiction and from publisher to publisher.[4] Even so, most codes have certain features in common.

A jurisdiction's official statutory code usually appears in a multi-volume set, divided into separate *titles* according to subject matter and then subdivided into smaller units such as *chapters* and *sections*.[5] Subdivisions are arranged numerically. In the *Arkansas Code of 1987 Annotated*, a researcher may find common sections in each chapter or subchapter, such as definitions, legislative intent, applicability, or effective date.

The code is usually *annotated*, which means that the text of each statute is supplemented with additional information.[6] Some of this information is historical, including references to the original *act number* or *public law number* and any subsequent amending or repealing legislation.[7] Some of it provides

---

3. An effective legal researcher will review a statute in the context of its codification. It is a common but misguided practice of laypersons to continue to refer to an older act even after that law is amended, instead of referring to the statute's location in the Arkansas Code.

4. Although the enacted law will read the same from publisher to publisher, certain portions may be different. For example, the caption is editorial (and usually copyrighted) rather than enacted. Similarly, publishers will annotate the statutes differently.

5. The features of the official and unofficial versions of the *Arkansas Code of 1987 Annotated* are described in Section II.D.

6. Arkansas's official code is annotated. The text of each statute is accompanied by generous annotations including material such as legislative history, cross-references, and notes of cases. See Section V.C.1 for further discussion of annotations in the *Arkansas Code of 1987 Annotated*.

7. When a bill is approved by both houses of the Arkansas General Assembly and signed into law by the governor, it is assigned a chronological act number along with its year of enactment (*e.g.*, Act 2216 of 2005). Similarly, newly enacted federal legislation is assigned a number corresponding to the session of Congress and the chrono-

cross-references to related statutes or administrative regulations. A statute's annotated material may also include citations to secondary sources that analyze the statute. Finally, whenever a statute has been the subject of litigation, you will find citations to and brief summaries of cases that have interpreted and applied the statute.

II. Arkansas Statutes

A. Historic Compilations of Arkansas Statutes

The enacted laws of the State of Arkansas have been published in various compilations over the years, from the first collection, entitled *Revised Statutes of the State of Arkansas*, published in 1836, to miscellaneous "digests" of statutory law published in the 19th century, to the maroon-covered volumes of the *Arkansas Statutes Annotated*, published in 1947. The current code, which is the first codification of Arkansas law, is the *Arkansas Code of 1987 Annotated*, and is published in red volumes.

Present-day researchers working with older cases and periodicals occasionally encounter citations to statutes appearing in some of these historic compilations. In fact, many of these laws remain in effect today, although they have been re-arranged, and more importantly, re-numbered for the current code, as described in Section II.B below.[8] Table 5-1 lists the historic statutory publications preceding the current code, in reverse chronological order.

B. Creation of the *Arkansas Code of 1987 Annotated*

In 1983, the gargantuan task of codifying Arkansas statutes was given to the Arkansas Statute Revision Commission (subsequently renamed the

---

logical order of the act (e.g., the first act of the 108th Congress is known as Pub. L. 108-1). The cumulative body of laws enacted by a particular session of the General Assembly or Congress is known as its *session laws*. For more information about state and federal legislation, see Section VI.A and Chapter 6.

8. To locate historic statutes that are still in effect, refer to the charts set out in the "Tables" volumes of the official *Arkansas Code of 1987 Annotated*. Two kinds of conversion tables are provided: (1) "parallel reference" tables, which match obsolete statutory citations to their current locations in the code (e.g., Ark. Stat. Ann. § 43-2025, now codified as Ark. Code Ann. § 16-43-301), and (2) "acts disposition" tables, which match act numbers with their corresponding code sections (e.g., Act 1260 of 1997, now codified as Ark. Code Ann. §§ 22-7-301 to 22-7-306). To go the other direction, i.e., to find the former statutory citation for a current code section, consult the history note printed after that section.

Table 5-1. Historical Statutes of Arkansas

Arkansas Statutes Annotated of 1947

Pope's Digest of 1937

Crawford and Moses' Digest of 1921

Kirby and Castle's Digest of 1916 (unofficial)

Kirby's Digest of 1904

Sandels and Hills Digest of 1894

Mansfield's Digest of 1884

Gantt's Digest of 1874

Digest of 1869

Gould's Digest of 1858

English's Digest of 1848

Revised Statutes of the State of Arkansas 1838

Arkansas Code Revision Commission). The Commission and its staff worked in concert with the publisher for almost four years to collect, read, analyze, group, classify, and edit more than 33,000 acts created over 150 years of legislative activity.[9] In the process, the Commission also uncovered "[o]ver 200 laws or parts of laws . . . which should have been compiled in the digests and compilations over the years but for some reason were not."[10] Once it had reviewed all the existing statutory laws, the Commission prepared the new code and submitted it to the Arkansas legislature for official adoption.

In 1987, the Arkansas General Assembly enacted the code, declaring its intent to codify, revise, modernize, and reenact the statutory law of Arkansas.[11] This code, titled the *Arkansas Code of 1987 Annotated,* is the official body of statutory law in effect today. In adopting the code, the legislature took the fi-

---

9. For a detailed account of the codification process, see Vincent C. Henderson, II, *The Creation of the Arkansas Code of 1987 Annotated*, 11 U. Ark. Little Rock L.J. 21 (1988).

10. *Id.* at 47.

11. Ark. Code Ann. § 1-2-101(a) (2008). Eagle-eyed readers may have noticed that the citation beginning this footnote is dated 2008, even though the code's official name is the *Arkansas Code of 1987 Annotated*. It's no mistake. Each time a bound volume of the code is replaced with a new edition, the citation indicates the publication date of the replacement volume. For more information on replacement volumes, see Section III.C. See Appendix A for a discussion of the essentials of citations to statutes.

nal step of repealing all prior versions of Arkansas statutory law, with limited exceptions.[12]

C. Organization of the *Arkansas Code of 1987 Annotated*

The Arkansas Statute Revision Commission organized the new code into 28 *titles*, each reflecting a broad category of statutory law, some of which cover two or more volumes.[13] Titles were deliberately drawn broadly in order "to make reclassification of the statutes less complicated and to give researchers of the code larger targets to hit when doing research in the code, thus decreasing the need for extensive intertitle cross-referencing."[14] Table 5-2 lists the 28 titles of the *Arkansas Code of 1987 Annotated*. Note that the title number does not necessarily relate directly to the volume number where the title is found.

Although the 28 titles of the *Arkansas Code of 1987 Annotated* originally were published in 35 volumes, almost three subsequent decades of legislative activity and judicial interpretation have expanded that number of volumes, as pocket part supplements became too fat to fit between volume covers. Several titles originally once fitting in a single volume have been subdivided into two or more separate volumes. As of this writing, only one volume from the original 1987 publication of the *Arkansas Code of 1987 Annotated* has not been replaced: Volume 12, containing part of Title 14. Every other volume has been replaced and/or subdivided.[15]

---

12. *See* Ark. Code Ann. § 1-2-103(a) (2008). Under section 1-2-103(a), all enacted law in effect on December 31, 1987, was repealed unless a provision met one of the following exceptions:

(1) Expressly continued by specific provision of this Code;
(2) Omitted improperly or erroneously as a consequence of compilation, revision, or both, of the laws enacted prior to this Code, including, without limitation, any omissions that may have occurred during the compilation, revision, or both, of the laws comprising this Code; or
(3) Omitted, changed, or modified by the Arkansas Code Revision Commission, or its predecessors, in a manner not authorized by the laws or the constitutions of Arkansas in effect at the time of the omission, change, or modification.

13. Title 16, for example, encompasses four volumes.

14. Henderson, *supra* note 9, at 28.

15. When a volume is replaced, the Code Revision Commission staff integrates the supplement into the respective code sections amended, and the entire volume is edited for grammatical style and correction of typographical errors.

Table 5-2. Titles and Volumes of the *Arkansas Code*
of 1987 Annotated

Title	Description	Volume(s)
1	General Provisions	1
2	Agriculture	1
3	Alcoholic Beverages	1
4	Business and Commercial Law	2A, 2B, 2C
5	Criminal Offenses	3A, 3B
6	Education	4A, 4B, 5
7	Elections	6
8	Environmental Law	6, 6A
9	Family Law	6B
10	General Assembly	7A, 7B
11	Labor and Industrial Relations	7
12	Law Enforcement, Emergency Management, and Military Affairs	8A, 8B
13	Libraries, Archives, and Cultural Resources	8B
14	Local Government	9, 10, 11A, 11B, 12
15	Natural Resources and Economic Development	13A, 13B
16	Practice, Procedure, and Courts	14A, 14B, 15, 16
17	Professions, Occupations, and Businesses	17A, 17B, 17C
18	Property	18
19	Public Finance	19A, 19B
20	Public Health and Welfare	20A, 20B
21	Public Officers and Employees	21
22	Public Property	21
23	Public Utilities and Regulated Industries	22, 23A, 23B, 24A, 24B
24	Retirement and Pensions	25A

Table 5-2. Titles and Volumes of the *Arkansas Code*
of 1987 Annotated, continued

Title	Description	Volume(s)
25	State Government	25A, 25B
26	Taxation	26A, 26B, 27A, 27B
27	Transportation	28A, 28B
28	Wills, Estates, and Fiduciary Relationships	29
	Constitutions	unnumbered
	General Index	unnumbered
	Tables/Commentaries	unnumbered
	Court Rules	unnumbered

Each title is subdivided into chapters, subchapters, and sections.[16] An analysis at the beginning of each title, chapter, and subchapter previews its scope and content by listing the names of its subdivisions. Scanning these subdivisions helps a researcher find general provisions applicable to a set of statutes and to see the relationships of statutes to one another. For example, Title 5 addresses Criminal Offenses. The title's analysis at the beginning of the title lists the six subtitles into which criminal statutes are divided:

- General provisions
- Offenses against the person
- Offenses involving families, dependents, etc.
- Offenses against property
- Offenses against the administration of government
- Offenses against public health, safety, or welfare.

Each subtitle is divided into chapters. Subtitle 2 of Title 5, for example, has eight chapters: Homicide; Kidnapping and Related Offenses; Robbery; Assault and Battery; Sexual Offenses; Voyeurism Offenses; Death Threats; and Human Trafficking Act of 2013.[17] Each chapter is divided into sections. For example,

---

16. A few of the very large titles are subdivided into subtitles.
17. The analysis shows one chapter, *Slander*, as repealed.

the chapter on Kidnapping and Related Offenses is divided into six sections;[18] Definitions; Kidnapping; False Imprisonment in the First Degree; False Imprisonment in the Second Degree; Vehicular Piracy; and Permanent Detention or Restraint. Immediately following the text of each statute are *annotations* written by the publisher and Commission staff that provide important information about the statute to researchers.[19]

Legislators may change Arkansas statutory law only through legislation that amends, creates, or repeals sections of the Arkansas Code.[20] Therefore, a legislative act will contain a reference to a code section, strike through repealed language, and underline new language.[21] An act will identify temporary language or language that does not amend a statute as "Not To Be Codified."

The Commission, which is staffed by the Bureau of Legislative Research, has a duty to maintain the integrity of the code, and has limited authority to make changes to legislation in the process of codifying newly enacted statutes. Therefore, a researcher will see that statutes are not always codified exactly as written in the legislation. Arkansas law requires legislation to follow as closely as possible "the plan, scheme, style, format, arrangement, and classification" of the code so that the code as amended "will compose a harmonious entity."[22] The Commission may make changes such as the following in order to preserve the organization and style of the code:

- Correct spelling, punctuation, grammatical, capitalization, word usage, and typographical errors;

---

18. The chapter sections are listed in the chapter level analysis.

19. See Section V.C.1 for further discussion of annotations.

20. Arkansas Code Ann. § 1-2-116(a)(2008) states:

All acts enacted after December 31, 1987, of a general and permanent nature shall be enacted as amendments to this Code. No local, private, or temporary acts or provisions and no provisions appropriating funds shall be enacted as amendments to this Code. If the subject matter of any law is already generally embodied in one of the titles of this Code or can be appropriately classified therein, that new law shall be enacted as an amendment to that title of the Code. If it is not possible to classify the subject matter of a new law in an existing title, a new title shall be enacted containing the new law as a chapter or chapters, each chapter to contain a proper designation and descriptive name or heading . . . .

21. See Chapter 6 for additional information on reading and researching legislation.

22. Ark. Bureau of Legislative Research, *Legislative Drafting Manual* (2010), www .arkleg.state.ar.us/bureau/legal/Publications/2010 Legislative Drafting Manual.pdf.

- Correct internal references;
- Number, renumber, re-designate, and rearrange chapters, subchapters, sections, subsections, and subdivisions; and
- Alphabetize definition lists.[23]

However, the Commission cannot "change the substance or meaning of any provision of the Arkansas Code or any act of the General Assembly."[24]

D. Official and Unofficial Versions of the *Arkansas Code of 1987 Annotated*

The official print version of the *Arkansas Code of 1987 Annotated* is an annotated set of volumes, presently published by LexisNexis. An unofficial print version of the statutes, published by West, has been in existence since 2004. The statutory content of *West's Arkansas Code Annotated* conforms to the text of the statutes contained in the *Arkansas Code of 1987 Annotated*, although the editorial materials are somewhat different. The West print version uses the official code's classification and numbering system, but West editors have prepared their own analyses, cross-references, case notes (called "Notes of Decision"), and index. In addition, the editorial materials following each statute make reference to West's Topics and Key Numbers.[25] The Notes of Decisions are identical to West's headnotes from the cases interpreting or applying the statute.[26]

---

23. Ark. Code Ann. § 1-2-303(d)(1) (2008). There are exceptions to the Code's style and organization. Code style may not apply to *uniform laws* and *model acts*, which are laws that are enacted by a legislature based on laws approved by the National Conference of Commissioners on Uniform State Laws, or certain interstate compacts. *See Legislative Drafting Manual* § 3, *supra* note 22.

24. Ark. Code Ann. § 1-2-303(d)(1) (2008). The Arkansas Supreme Court has ruled on three occasions that the Commission exceeded its authority. *Ortho-McNeil-Janssen Pharm., Inc. v. State*, 2014 Ark. 124, at 15, 432 S.W.3d 563, 573 (in subdividing a sentence into separate provisions, Commission "substantively altered" statute and "rendered its meaning ambiguous"); *Harrell v. State*, 2012 Ark. 421, at 5, 2012 WL 5462868, at *2–3 (Commission erroneously changed meaning of statute when it rearranged wording of provision); *Porter v. Ark. Dep't of Health & Human Servs.*, 374 Ark. 177, 182, 286 S.W.3d 686, 691 (2008) (Commission erred in removing the word "not" immediately before the word "pregnant").

25. See Chapter 4 for a discussion of the West Digest System's Topics and Key Numbers.

26. See Chapter 4 for a discussion of West case headnotes.

Fastcase, Lexis, and Westlaw provide electronic sources for the *Arkansas Code of 1987 Annotated*.[27] Lexis provides a free online source for researchers on the Arkansas legislature's website.[28] This free source is provided by Lexis specifically for the Arkansas General Assembly, but it is not official, and the statutes are not annotated, except for a statute's history. It does not provide the more extensive search features of the Lexis online version for subscribers.

The most complete electronic sources for the code are Westlaw and Lexis, each of which has all the editorial enhancements that these two publishers make available in their print versions. Because Lexis is the publisher of the official code (in print), it provides an electronic version of the official *Arkansas Code of 1987 Annotated*. Westlaw provides researchers access to the unofficial print version *West's Arkansas Code of 1987* or an electronic version of the official *Arkansas Code of 1987 Annotated*. In both Westlaw and Lexis, searches can be run in annotated or non-annotated versions of the code; Fastcase does not provide annotations, but does provide a list of cases that have cited to the code section you retrieve. An advantage of using any of these electronic versions is that Westlaw and Lexis can quickly incorporate new legislation into their existing statutory databases. The act number of the new legislation will be reflected in the historical notes immediately following the text of the statute.

For example, in passing Act 2216 of 2005, the Arkansas General Assembly not only amended Ark. Code Ann. §§ 5-27-201 and 5-27-202 (first and second degree offenses, respectively, of endangering the welfare of an incompetent person), it created a new section, Ark. Code Ann. § 5-27-207, setting out a third degree of the offense. Westlaw published the amendments and new sections online before they appeared in the pocket parts of the print volume. Lexis placed the amendments online after the official print version. Therefore, there is a time lag of approximately six months between the date of enactment and the official Lexis print publication and the (unofficial) online publication. Fastcase updates its electronic version after the official version is published. Each time that statutes are created or amended, both Westlaw and Lexis provide the researcher with hyperlinks to the text of the legislation.

---

27. Even though Lexis publishes the *Arkansas Code of 1987 Annotated*, only that print version is official. All electronic versions of the Code, including the version on Lexis, are unofficial.

28. The Arkansas General Assembly website is found at www.arkleg.state.ar.us. Scroll down the left pane to find "Arkansas Law," and "Search/View Arkansas Code and the Constitution of 1874."

III. Federal Statutes

The official text of federal statutes appears in the 51 titles of the *United States Code* ("U.S.C."). Within each title, individual statutes are assigned section numbers. For example, the federal statute granting appellate jurisdiction to federal appellate courts is 28 U.S.C. § 1291. Title 28 is devoted to courts and judicial matters, and 1291 is the section number assigned to this statute.

The U.S.C. is updated infrequently and does not include annotations, so it is of limited value in research. The sources you are more likely to use are the *United States Code Service* ("U.S.C.S."), published by LexisNexis, and the *United States Code Annotated* ("U.S.C.A."), published by West, both of which are available in print and online versions. Both U.S.C.S. and U.S.C.A. contain the text of federal statutes, references to related research sources, and annotations that refer you to cases interpreting or applying each federal statute. In addition, both sources direct you to federal regulations and executive orders that may be relevant to the statute being researched.[29]

Federal statutes and other statutory research aids are also available online, both on the Internet and through the subscriber databases. Free Internet sources of federal statutory law include a version of the U.S.C. maintained by the Office of the Law Revision Counsel,[30] searchable by Boolean terms and connectors. For recent legislation, a good site is Congress.gov, the legislative service maintained by the Library of Congress.[31]

Subscriber databases include Fastcase, Lexis, and Westlaw. Fastcase gives its subscribers access to the U.S.C., and includes links to cases which have cited the code section. Lexis materials include the U.S.C.S., the U.S.C.S. Table of Contents, the U.S.C.S. Popular Names Table, the U.S. Statutes at Large, all enacted Public Laws, and a U.S.C.S. archive for statutes no longer in effect.

Westlaw contains the General Index for U.S.C.A., which you can browse, as well as conversion tables that connect U.S.C.A. sections to sections of the Revised Statutes of 1878, the U.S. Statutes at Large, acts of Congress prior to 1957, executive orders, proclamations, and reorganization plans. Other useful databases for federal statutory research on Westlaw include databases for the U.S.C.A. Popular Names Table, U.S. Public Laws, U.S. Statutes at Large,

---

29. For more information about administrative regulations and executive orders, see Chapter 7.

30. The address is http://uscode.house.gov.

31. The address is http://congress.gov.

and separate databases for certain statutory schemes, including the Internal Revenue Code and the USA Patriot Act.

IV. Local Government Ordinances

Local governments in Arkansas have limited legislative powers. The Arkansas Constitution prohibits them from passing "any laws contrary to the general laws of the state" and sets limits on their ability to tax real and personal property.[32] The laws passed by these local governmental bodies are called *ordinances.*

County governments, acting through their quorum courts, are authorized to exercise local legislative power over a number of matters, including the power to levy taxes; appropriate public funds for the county's expenses; and to define and enforce non-felony crimes.[33] County governments must enact ordinances to provide for the following "necessary services" for their citizens:

- The administration of justice through the several courts of record of the county;
- Law enforcement protection services and the custody of persons accused or convicted of crimes;
- Real and personal property tax administration, including assessments, collection, and custody of tax proceeds;
- Court and public records management, as provided by law, including registration, recording, and custody of public records; and
- All other services prescribed by state law for performance by each of the elected county officers or departments of county government.[34]

The *Arkansas Code of 1987 Annotated* also spells out the specific legislative powers that may be exercised by the state's municipalities. They are granted the "power to make and publish bylaws and ordinances, not inconsistent with the laws of this state, which, as to them, shall seem necessary to provide for the safety, preserve the health, promote the prosperity, and improve the morals, order, comfort, and convenience of such corporations and the inhabitants thereof."[35] Municipalities are affirmatively charged with the duty not only to

---

32. Ark. Const. art. 12, § 4.
33. Ark. Code Ann. § 14-14-801(b) (2013).
34. Ark. Code Ann. § 14-14-802(a) (2013).
35. Ark. Code Ann. § 14-55-102 (1998).

provide their citizens with police and fire protection, but to safeguard public morals, specifically to "[s]uppress riots, gambling, and indecent and disorderly conduct; and . . . [p]unish all lewd and lascivious behavior in the streets and other public places."[36] Additional authorized legislative activity for Arkansas municipalities includes the passage of ordinances relating to building, zoning, health, electrical, or plumbing codes.[37]

Each local government is obligated to record its bylaws and ordinances.[38] County ordinances must be compiled into a published code every five years.[39] Unfortunately for researchers, no centralized source of local government law is available in Arkansas. Print copies of a municipality's ordinances or code may be available in local law libraries, but if not, you may need to contact officials of the local government in question.

A large number of Arkansas cities and counties now make their ordinances available online, some on their official websites and others via miscellaneous legal publishers such as the Municipal Code Corporation[40] or American Legal Publishing Corporation.[41] Be aware that not all codes published on the Internet by the various legal publishers are the most current codes. The publisher may keep the old codes on the website after the county or municipality begins publishing the ordinances on their own websites. It is, therefore, best to search first on the city or county website and follow the link provided.

Updating your research on local government law will be critical. As is true for researching state and federal law, the most recent ordinances available in print may not necessarily have been updated immediately on a website. Similarly, whether the print version in a library or other collection is the most recent is dependent on local government personnel and resources. Remember, too, that state law only requires a county to publish its code every five years.[42] Therefore, contact the city or county clerk to determine whether the ordinance found is still good law.

---

36. Ark. Code Ann. § 14-55-103 (1998).

37. Ark. Code Ann. § 14-55-207 (1998).

38. Ark. Code Ann. § 14-14-903 (2013); Ark. Code Ann. § 14-55-205 (1998).

39. Ark. Code Ann. § 14-14-903(d).

40. The Municipal Code Corporation publishes the print versions of several codes of ordinances, and it also makes these codes available online at www.municode.com.

41. The American Legal Publishing Corporation website address is www.amlegal.com.

42. Ark. Code Ann. § 14-55-207 (1998).

V. The Process of Researching Statutory Law

This section discusses the most common processes used in researching statutory law. There are several approaches to statutory research, and you will choose an approach based on the information you have at hand and your level of familiarity with the issue. You may already know the *popular name* of the statute (e.g., the "No Child Left Behind Act"). You may already have a citation to a specific title or chapter that generally governs the topic (e.g., Title VII). You may already know the class of statutes to which the issue pertains (e.g., criminal homicide).

Remember that your issue will determine whether you need to research state or federal statutes, local ordinances, or a combination.[43] But you may be unsure where to begin. Table 5-3 outlines the additional steps needed for statutory research when you do not have a popular name, citation, or other information to give you a head start.

A. Researching with a Citation or Popular Name

Depending on your experience with the subject being researched, you may begin your research already knowing a statute's section number or its popular name. When you start with a section number, you need only to scan the spines of the volumes to the find the one containing the reference,[44] or if you are researching online, to enter the abbreviation of the code and the section number into a search box.

A popular name may be a short descriptive title assigned by the legislative body, or it may be a name by which the statute is frequently referred to by the media or general public (*e.g.*, "HIPAA," or the "Health Insurance Portability and Accountability Act"). To find a statute by its popular name, look it up in the index to the code. You may also find that the code lists popular names in a reference table. For example, the U.S.C. lists popular names and their statutory citations in the table, "Acts Cited by Popular Name." Popular name tables are also available in statutory databases of Westlaw and Lexis.[45]

---

43. Refer to Chapter 1 for a discussion of how to identify your issue and determine the appropriate jurisdiction for your research.

44. Always check the pocket part of the volume to update your research. See Chapter 9 for more information about updating the law.

45. Fastcase does not provide a popular names table.

**Table 5-3. Additional Steps for Researching
Statutory Law by Subject**

1. Determine the relevant jurisdiction whose statutory sources of law will govern the issue.

2. Develop a comprehensive list of search terms, using the TARP or journalistic method discussed in Chapter 1, or any other method that will help you to describe the subject governed by a statute.

3. Use an appropriate statutory index (print or online) to locate references and cross-references to relevant statutes.

4. Locate, read, and analyze each relevant statute's sections, including those in any supplemental materials. Remember that definitions, applicability, or legislative intent relating to your statute may be stated in a different section of the title where your statute is codified.

5. Check the effective date of the statute for its applicability to your issue. Research older enactments if necessary.

6. Use an annotated version of the statute to locate cases that have interpreted and/or applied the statute.

7. Read and analyze cases interpreting or applying the statute.

8. Update sources, as described in Chapter 9.

B. Researching with Key Terms

If you do not already have a citation or popular name as a starting point, you will need to develop a comprehensive list of search terms, using the TARP or journalistic method discussed in Chapter 1, or any other method that will help you to describe the subject governed by a statute.

Most researchers looking for statutes will begin by finding their search terms in a code's print or online index. Because codes are statutes organized by subject (rather than chronologically as they are enacted), statutory indexes are arranged topically. Statutory indexes use terms drawn from words and phrases in the statutes themselves, judicial opinions interpreting the statutes, and common legal terminology. They commonly contain extensive cross-referencing to related topics and statutes. Print sources of statutes generally provide you with several volumes of general indexes. Individual volumes of the code may have their own indexes in the back. Lexis and Westlaw also provide indexes for statutory research.

To assist your understanding of statutory enactments on a particular topic, you may also wish to browse a code's table of contents to get a sense of the breadth and depth of the statutory scheme.

C. Reading and Analyzing Statutes

1. Reading Statutes in Context

After you have located the statutes relevant to your research topic and issue, read and analyze each relevant section, including those in supplemental materials. An effective legal researcher will avoid reading the statute in isolation, but will become familiar with the contents and organization of the title where the relevant statute is found and all legal research tools available in print or online. Remember that definitions, applicability, or legislative intent relating to your statute may be stated in a different section of the title where your statute is codified. Read a statute more than once to reach a good understanding of the statute's meaning and relevance to the issue being researched.

Check the effective date of the statute for its applicability to your issue. You may need to research older enactments if the law has changed since the issue arose, or you may need to update the statute for recent changes.

2. Using Annotations

The publisher and the Commission add annotations to the code with a host of information that a researcher can use to analyze statutes. Typically, annotations follow a statute. However, the Commission staff may also include information at the beginning of a chapter, such as emergency clauses and language directed in legislation as "not to be codified." Reading the annotations to the statute will help you determine how the statute has changed over time, how courts have interpreted and applied the statute, and how other legal scholars have analyzed the statute. Annotations may consist of various legal research aids, such as:

- "Historical Notes" — citations to its enacting legislation and any amendments;
- "Cross-references" — references to related statutes in other parts of the code;
- "Research References" or "Library References" — materials citing or discussing the statute such as *American Law Reports*, legal encyclopedias, and law review articles;
- "Case Notes" or "Notes of Decisions" — brief descriptions of court decisions that interpret or apply the statute. Read and analyze the cases

for yourself, as a publisher's summary may not include specific information relevant to the researcher's issue, or may not be updated;

- "A.C.R.C. Notes" — notes added by the Commission staff such as effective dates, full citations to federal materials, corrective information, and information about what was amended in the section by recent legislation.

3. Interpreting Statutory Language

The language of statutes is sometimes subject to interpretation. Arkansas courts have consistently held that the plain meaning of a statute is the first line of interpretation.[46] As the Arkansas Supreme Court explains,

> The basic rule of statutory construction is to give effect to the intent of the legislature. Where the language of a statute is plain and unambiguous, we determine legislative intent from the ordinary meaning of the language used. In considering the meaning of a statute, we construe it just as it reads, giving the words their ordinary and usually accepted meaning in common language. We construe the statute so that no word is left void, superfluous or insignificant, and we give meaning and effect to every word in the statute, if possible.[47]

However, when there is ambiguity, courts have developed canons of statutory construction to aid in their interpretation of statutes.[48] Depending on the type of statute, a court may narrowly construe the statute or liberally construe it. For example, statutes that disturb vested rights or create new obligations, such as criminal liability, are strictly (or narrowly) construed.[49] Remedial

---

46. *Pope v. Overton*, 2011 Ark. 11, at 10, 376 S.W.3d 400, 407.

47. *Id.*, 376 S.W.3d at 407.

48. For an overview of federal canons of statutory interpretation, see National Conference of State Legislatures, *The Rehnquist Court's Canons of Statutory Construction*, www.ncsl.org/documents/lsss/2013PDS/Rehnquist_Court_Canons_citations .pdf (last visited Feb. 17, 2016). For a discussion of how Arkansas courts approach statutory construction, see Michael W. Mullane, *Statutory Interpretation in Arkansas: How Arkansas Courts Interpret Statutes: A Rational Approach*, 2005 Ark. L. Notes 405; Michael W. Mullane, *Statutory Interpretation in Arkansas: How Should a Statute Be Read? When Is It Subject to Interpretation? What Our Courts Say and What They Do*, 2004 Ark. L. Notes 85.

49. "The strict rule of construction does not apply to remedial statutes which do not disturb vested rights, or create new obligations, but only supply a new or more appropriate remedy to enforce an existing right or obligation." *Bean v. Office of Child Support Enforcement*, 340 Ark. 286, 297, 9 S.W.3d 520, 526 (2000).

statutes are liberally construed, that is, read broadly to accomplish the statute's purpose.[50]

An additional source of statutory interpretation is agency rules and regulations. State and federal agencies enforce statutes and use their expertise to interpret them through rules, regulations, and advisory opinions.

---

50. *Id.*, 9 S.W.3d at 526 ("The cardinal principle for construing remedial legislation is for the courts to give appropriate regard to the spirit which promoted its enactment, the mischief sought to be abolished, and the remedy proposed."). However, "even a liberal interpretation must be consistent with the basic intent of the statute." *Whetstone v. Daniel,* 217 Ark. 899, 901, 233 S.W.2d 625, 626 (1950).

Chapter 6

Legislation and Legislative History

I. Introduction to the Legislative Process

This chapter discusses the legislative process in Arkansas and briefly describes its counterpart in the federal government. *Legislative process* refers to the means by which an idea is transformed into a legislative proposal (a *bill*), which in turn is debated, discussed, and negotiated until ultimately being enacted into law by the legislature.

Of course, a bill may fail to persuade at any stage of the process. A proposal may fail to win a sponsor. A bill that has been introduced may not survive the intense scrutiny it receives in legislative committee hearings. A bill that is approved by a legislative committee may fail to win a majority vote in both houses of the legislature. Finally, some bills enacted by the legislature meet their doom via gubernatorial *veto* (although they may be resurrected by a legislative override).

When a bill succeeds in passing all these hurdles, however, it becomes an *act* of the legislature. Following its gubernatorial approval and signature, each act is deemed a *slip law*. In Arkansas, slip laws are not only published in print, but they are also made available on the website of the Arkansas General Assembly.[1] At the conclusion of a legislative session, all the slip laws from that session are published as *session laws* in the LexisNexis publication *Acts of Arkansas*.

II. The Arkansas General Assembly

The legislative body in Arkansas government is the Arkansas General Assembly. The General Assembly has two chambers, the House of Representatives, with 100 members, and the Senate, with 35 members. A member of the House is elected to a two-year term,[2] and a Senator is elected to a term of four

---

1. The address is www.arkleg.state.ar.us.
2. Ark. Const. amend. 73, § 2(a).

years.[3] Their terms are *limited*, meaning that a member of the Arkansas General Assembly cannot serve more than 16 years as a representative, a senator, or, in combined terms, as both.[4]

The General Assembly meets in three types of sessions: *regular sessions, fiscal sessions*, and *extraordinary sessions*.[5] The 60-day regular session convenes every two years.[6] That session's length may be extended an additional 15 days by a two-thirds vote of the legislators; any greater extension must be approved by a three-fourths vote of the legislators.[7]

In a regular session, the General Assembly considers non-appropriation bills and appropriation bills,[8] as well as resolutions. The General Assembly meets in biennial 30-day fiscal sessions to consider only appropriation bills.[9] A fiscal session may be extended for an additional 15 days, but only one such extension is permitted, and that extension requires a three-fourths vote.[10] A legislator is permitted to file a non-appropriation bill in a fiscal session, but only after obtaining approval of the bill's introduction by a two-thirds majority of the legislature.[11]

By a two-thirds majority vote of each house, the General Assembly may change the years in which regular and fiscal sessions occur.[12] When the General Assembly is not in session, it continues its work through interim committees and the Arkansas Legislative Council.[13]

---

3. Ark. Const. amend. 73, § 2(b).

4. *See* Ark. Const. amend. 73, § 2(c).

5. A synonym for extraordinary session is *special session*.

6. Ark. Const. art. 5, §§ 5(b), 17(a); Ark. Code Ann. § 10-2-101 (Supp. 2015).

7. Ark. Const. art. 5, § 17(a).

8. Bills introduced in the Arkansas legislature are classified as either appropriation bills or non-appropriation bills. Appropriation bills provide for the funding of state government and the withdrawal of those funds from the State Treasury. Ark. Const. art 5, § 29. Non-appropriation bills are all other bills, including those that amend the Arkansas Code or are resolutions.

9. Ark. Const. art. 5, § 5(c).

10. Ark. Const. art. 5, § 17(b).

11. *Id*.

12. Ark. Const. art. 5, § 5(d). A regular session normally begins the second Monday in January in odd-numbered years, and a fiscal session normally begins the second Monday in February in even-numbered years. *See* Ark. Const. art. 5, § 5(b), (c). Proposed bills may be introduced in either chamber until the last three days of a regular or fiscal session. Ark. Const. art. 5, § 34.

13. Ark. Code Ann. § 10-3-203 (2012). The General Assembly maintains a list of legislative committees and a calendar of their meetings on its website, www.arkleg .state.ar.us.

Unlike regular and fiscal sessions, extraordinary sessions are not regular occurrences. The governor is empowered to proclaim the need for a special session to address one or more specific issues.[14] Once those issues have been addressed, the legislature may remain in session up to 15 additional days, but only with a two-thirds vote of approval from both houses.[15]

III. How an Arkansas Bill Becomes Law

Whatever the source of a proposal for new legislation, the procedure for enacting that proposal into law follows a series of formal steps. To begin, only a member of the Arkansas General Assembly may introduce a bill for consideration. In preparing a bill for introduction, the representative or senator is likely to contact the Bureau of Legislative Research for assistance in researching and drafting the proposal. Staffers in the Bureau help to ensure that the language of the proposed bill satisfies the statutory standard of clarity: "No bill shall be considered and no law enacted unless the bill or law is written in clear, unambiguous language."[16]

The Bureau's attorneys enter all bills into the General Assembly's computerized bill-drafting system.[17] The bill-drafting system provides useful tracking information for each new draft of a bill through its enactment. The system assigns a tracking notation using the draft number and the drafter's initials. The draft bill's header indicates the session type and date, the names of its sponsor(s) and co-sponsor (if any), the title, and any subtitle. A bill title must summarize the content of the bill and indicate whether it contains an *emergency clause*.[18]

---

14. Ark. Const. art. 6, § 19.

15. *Id.*

16. Ark. Code Ann. § 1-2-121 (2008).

17. Ark. Bureau of Legislative Research, *Legislative Drafting Manual* § 1.1 (2010), www.arkleg.state.ar.us/bureau/legal/Publications/2010%20Legislative%20Draft ing%20Manual.pdf. See Table 6-1 for a chart indicating all the parts of a bill.

18. An act of the General Assembly becomes effective on the 91st day after the end of the session unless it contains a valid emergency clause directing an earlier effective date. *See Stroud v. Cagle*, 87 Ark. App. 95, 99, 189 S.W.3d 76, 79 (2004) (citing Ark. Const. amend. 7). Passed in 1920, Amendment 7 provides a right of the people to petition for the referendum against Acts of the General Assembly. A petition for referendum must be filed not later than 90 days after the final adjournment of the session (*sine die adjournment*) in which the Act was passed. Ark. Const. art. 5, § 1.

As a bill is drafted and revised, the date of each new draft appears in a footer.[19]

When a bill is in proper final form, it is prepared for filing through the bill-drafting system. The sponsoring legislator signs the original and submits it to the bill clerk in his or her chamber. The clerk assigns a *bill number* to each bill for tracking purposes. Bills are numbered sequentially in each chamber: House bills begin with 1001 and Senate bills begin with 1. After its filing, the bill is twice read aloud in the originating chamber and then assigned to the appropriate House or Senate committee for discussion. If a bill is amended after its filing, the dates that any amendments were *engrossed* into the bill are noted in its header.[20]

The legislative committee recommends one of three actions for a bill: "Do Pass"; "Do Pass as Amended" (if it has been amended by the committee); or "Do Not Pass." Only bills with a "Do Pass" or "Do Pass as Amended" recommendation return to the legislative chamber for further action. After additional debate, if desired, and possible amendment by the chamber, the bill is read again and put to a vote. If approved, it is sent to the other chamber for consideration. If the second chamber amends the bill in order to secure its passage there, the amended bill must be reconsidered by the original chamber — and approved as amended by a majority vote — in order to advance. It then returns to the second chamber, where it goes through a similar process of discussion, debate, and vote.

While a simple majority suffices for passage of most legislation,[21] tax increases require a three-fourths vote of approval.[22] Appropriation bills and bills proposing new taxes must be approved by a two-thirds vote.[23] The only exception to the two-thirds requirement is for appropriation and taxation bills "to

---

19. *Legislative Drafting Manual, supra* note 17, § 2.1(i). The manual contains detailed descriptions of every part of a bill, and it displays samples of bills and resolutions in the appendices.

20. A header's indication of an engrossed amendment appears in Figure 6-1. On the line immediately above the words "A Bill" is the notation "As Engrossed: H4/1/09." That notation signifies that an amendment to the bill passed the House and was included in the text of the bill by the House on April 1, 2009. If more than one amendment is engrossed into a bill, the notation includes all of them. Amended text is displayed in italics, as seen in the second page of Figure 6-1, lines 14–18. The full text of an amendment appears on the bill's page in the General Assembly's website.

21. Ark. Const. art. 5, § 37.

22. Ark. Const. art. 5, § 38.

23. Ark. Const. art. 5, § 31.

raise means for the payment of the just debts of the State, for defraying the necessary expenses of government, to sustain common schools, [and] to repel invasion and suppress insurrection."[24] Such bills require a simple majority vote.

Once both chambers of the General Assembly have approved a bill (or its amended version), it is sent to the governor for final action. If the governor approves the bill, he or she signs it into law. If the governor does not approve the bill, two courses of action are possible. The governor may *veto* the bill, in which case it will not become law unless a majority of each chamber subsequently votes to override the veto.[25] Alternatively, the governor may elect to let the bill become law without his or her signature, an action known as the *pocket veto.* In other words, if no action is taken on the bill within five days after the General Assembly presents it to the governor, it becomes law without the gubernatorial endorsement. Should the legislature adjourn before the governor takes action, the bill may effectively be vetoed if filed with the governor's objections in the office of the secretary of state within 20 days of the legislature's adjournment.[26]

When a bill becomes an act, ascertain its effective date to determine whether it governs a specific situation. An act becomes effective in one of three ways: (1) as stated in an emergency clause;[27] (2) on a date specified in the act; or (3) if there is no stated effective date or emergency clause, on the 91st day after the General Assembly adjourns *sine die.*[28] Note that an act might designate

---

24. *Id.*

25. Ark. Const. art. 6, § 15.

26. *Id.* It is for this reason that the General Assembly recesses after all bills presented for a vote have been voted upon. The legislature then reassembles to take action — if needed — to override a veto.

27. *See Legislative Drafting Manual, supra* note 17, § 6.5. An emergency clause provides either a specific date or indicates that the act becomes immediately effective upon one of the following: (1) the date of the governor's approval; (2) if the bill is neither approved nor vetoed by the governor, the day after the period for the governor's veto expires under Ark. Const. art. 6, § 15; or (3) the date the General Assembly overrides the governor's veto. An emergency clause must meet constitutional requirements of Ark. Const. art. 5, § 1 and be adopted by a two-thirds vote of each chamber. The Arkansas Supreme Court has interpreted Ark. Const. art. 5, § 1 as requiring an emergency clause to state a "grave problem," and to show a need for a prompt response to the circumstances that generated the emergency. *ACW, Inc. v. Weiss*, 329 Ark. 302, 307, 947 S.W.2d 770, 772 (1997).

28. *Sine die* means that the session is adjourned until the next legislative session begins. The 91st day is derived from the 90-day period following enactment of legislation within which the public may file for a referendum. Ark. Const. art. 5, § 1. See *supra* note 18 for additional explanation of *sine die* adjournment.

Table 6-1. Parts of a Bill

Markup Language	Appears at very top of bill. Strikethrough indicates deletion from existing code section; underlining indicates new text.
Session Identifier	Appears at top left of bill and indicates General Assembly number, date, and type of session.
Sponsor Name(s)	Appears below Session Identifier and indicates bill's primary sponsor (listed first) and each co-sponsor.
Amendment Notation	Appears directly above words "A Bill" and states "As Engrossed" followed by date the amendment was engrossed into the bill.
Bill Number	Appears at top right of bill and indicates chamber of origin.
Title	Appears under caption, indicated with words "For An Act To Be Entitled." If bill contains emergency clause, the words "And to declare an emergency" appear at end of title.
Subtitle	Appears just below title—a shorter version that chamber uses for its reference. When bill contains an emergency clause, words to that effect must appear in its subtitle.
Enacting Clause	Sets out words "Be It Enacted By The General Assembly of the State of Arkansas," required by Ark. Const. art. 5, § 1(b).
Body	Following enacting clause are bill's sections, each containing a number and introductory language alerting reader to Arkansas Code section being amended, repealed, or created.
Bar Code	Appears at bottom left of bill when Bureau of Legislative Research runs bill for introduction.
Document ID Number	Appears at lower left of bill and indicates date, time of day, draft number, and initials of drafter at time bill was run for introduction.
Successive Page Header	Following bill's first page, each additional page has header with engrossing information and bill number.
Emergency Clause	When applicable, appears as last section of bill.
Bill Sponsor Signature	At end of bill, displays electronic indication of bill sponsor's signature.
Approval by Governor	Notation following bill sponsor's signature that says "Approved" and date that governor signed bill into law.

Figure 6-1. Sample Bill

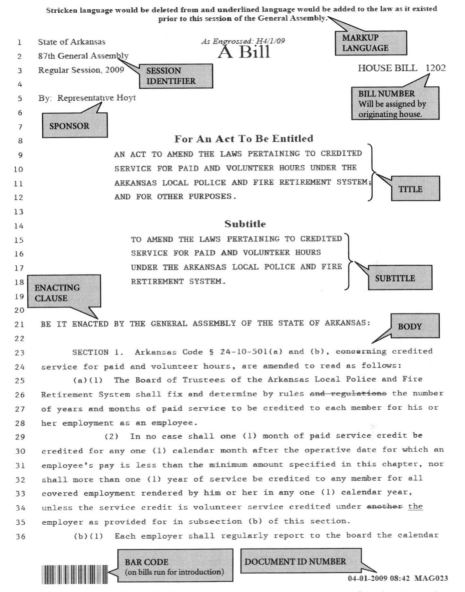

Sample Bill – Amendatory – Simple

Stricken language would be deleted from and underlined language would be added to the law as it existed prior to this session of the General Assembly.

1	State of Arkansas
2	87th General Assembly
3	Regular Session, 2009

As Engrossed: H4/1/09
A Bill

MARKUP LANGUAGE

SESSION IDENTIFIER

HOUSE BILL 1202

4	
5	By: Representative Hoyt
6	
7	
8	

BILL NUMBER
Will be assigned by originating house.

SPONSOR

For An Act To Be Entitled

9 AN ACT TO AMEND THE LAWS PERTAINING TO CREDITED
10 SERVICE FOR PAID AND VOLUNTEER HOURS UNDER THE
11 ARKANSAS LOCAL POLICE AND FIRE RETIREMENT SYSTEM;
12 AND FOR OTHER PURPOSES.

TITLE

13

Subtitle

15 TO AMEND THE LAWS PERTAINING TO CREDITED
16 SERVICE FOR PAID AND VOLUNTEER HOURS
17 UNDER THE ARKANSAS LOCAL POLICE AND FIRE
18 RETIREMENT SYSTEM.

SUBTITLE

ENACTING CLAUSE

19
20

21 BE IT ENACTED BY THE GENERAL ASSEMBLY OF THE STATE OF ARKANSAS:

BODY

22

23 SECTION 1. Arkansas Code § 24-10-501(a) and (b), concerning credited
24 service for paid and volunteer hours, are amended to read as follows:
25 (a)(1) The Board of Trustees of the Arkansas Local Police and Fire
26 Retirement System shall fix and determine by rules ~~and regulations~~ the number
27 of years and months of paid service to be credited to each member for his or
28 her employment as an employee.
29 (2) In no case shall one (1) month of paid service credit be
30 credited for any one (1) calendar month after the operative date for which an
31 employee's pay is less than the minimum amount specified in this chapter, nor
32 shall more than one (1) year of service be credited to any member for all
33 covered employment rendered by him or her in any one (1) calendar year,
34 unless the service credit is volunteer service credited under ~~another~~ the
35 employer as provided for in subsection (b) of this section.
36 (b)(1) Each employer shall regularly report to the board the calendar

BAR CODE
(on bills run for introduction)

DOCUMENT ID NUMBER

04-01-2009 08:42 MAG023

Source: *Legislative Drafting Manual*. Reprinted with permission of the Arkansas Bureau of Legislative Research.

Figure 6-1. Sample Bill, *continued*

As Engrossed: H4/1/09   HB1202

1   months of covered employment by each of its members that the employer wishes

2   to be credited to the member as volunteer service.

3   (2)   The board shall credit the member with the volunteer

4   service, ~~but in no case shall one (1) month of volunteer service be credited~~

5   ~~for any one (1) calendar month for which a month of paid service can be~~

6   ~~granted by the same employer, nor shall more than one (1) year of service be~~

7   ~~credited for all covered employment rendered by him or her in any one (1)~~

8   ~~calendar year with the same employer.~~

9   (3) (A) ~~Beginning January 1, 1999~~ Beginning January 1, 2010, the

10   board may credit a member both with volunteer service and with paid service

11   when the member earns the service credit simultaneously ~~under different~~

12   ~~employers~~,.

13   (B) ~~except that he or she shall be~~ For purposes of

14   subdivision (b)(3)(A) of this section:

15   (i) A member is limited to earning volunteer service with

16   only one (1) covered employer at a time; and

17   (ii) A member shall not earn volunteer service if the

18   member is entitled to paid service for the same work.

19

20

21

22   /s/ Hoyt

23

24

25

26

27

28

29

30

31

32

33

34

35

36

04-01-2009 08:42   MAG023

the expiration date of a statute and the effective date of its replacement. When this situation occurs, the Code Revision Commission[29] codifies both versions of the statute, each with its respective expiration and effective date.

IV. Arkansas Legislative Resolutions

A legislature uses a resolution as a mechanism to express its opinion, to establish or change a legislative rule, or to propose a constitutional amendment. Although a resolution is introduced during a legislative session, it does not have the force and effect of law. The four categories of resolutions are set out in Table 6-2. At the beginning of each legislative session, each chamber adopts a simple resolution setting out the rules of the chamber for the session. Joint rules for the session are expressed in a joint resolution. You may search for resolutions on the General Assembly's website under "Search Bills and Resolutions."

Table 6-2. Types of Arkansas Legislative Resolutions

Type	Designation	Description
Simple	HR or SR	Typically a statement of recognition of an individual, an act, or event; introduced in only one chamber.
Concurrent	HCR or SCR	Introduced in one chamber and concurred in by the other chamber; must be signed by governor to become effective.*
Joint	HJR or SJR	Adopted by both chambers. A constitutional amendment may only be proposed by the legislature through a joint resolution.**
Memorial	HMR or SMR HCMR or SCMR	Memorializes a person's life or contributions; may be simple or concurrent.

* Ark. Const. art. 6, § 16.
** Ark. Code Ann. § 7-9-201 (2011).

---

29. The Code Revision Commission is responsible for codifying acts of the Arkansas General Assembly. Ark. Code Ann. § 1-2-303 (2008). Refer to Chapter 5 of this text for a full discussion of the statutes of Arkansas.

V. Finding and Tracking Current Arkansas Legislation

A. Online Sources for Current Arkansas Legislation

Online free sources on the Internet and commercial databases are the best avenues for tracking current legislation during a legislative session. The Arkansas General Assembly's own website[30] provides the full text of pending legislation, including amendments and fiscal impact statements, and identifies whether a bill has become an act or has died in committee. The website also provides calendars and agendas for committee meetings and biographical and contact information for representatives and senators. Click "Bills and Resolutions" to access current proposed legislation and personalized bill tracking; "Committees" for calendars, agendas, and committee memberships; and "Legislators" for information about members of the General Assembly and the bills they sponsor.

The House of Representatives of the General Assembly provides live streaming video of its meetings during a session and archives those videos.[31] House committee meetings held during a legislative session are also live-streamed and archived.

The personalized bill-tracking system on the General Assembly's website allows a researcher to set up an individualized ongoing search for the progress of one or more particular bills. The personalized bill-tracking system provides researchers with emails and web tracking updating the status of a bill through each step of the legislative process.

Digest Web is a web-based service marketed primarily to lobbyists but available by subscription to any interested researcher. Its standard features include a bill-tracking system, full-text searching, analysis of legislation, detailed voting records, and voting analysis, schedules and agendas for legislative committees. *Digest Web* operates in several states, including Arkansas.[32]

Lexis provides current legislation in its commercial databases through the "Arkansas Advance Legislative Service" database. The service is located by browsing sources to find Arkansas and selecting the category "Statutes and

---

30. The General Assembly changes its website for each regular session. The address www.arkleg.state.ar.us will take you to the most recent web page. When bookmarking the web address, be sure that the session date is *not* included in the bookmark. A web page for a previous session will have a redirect link to the current session page.

31. On the General Assembly website, www.arkleg.state.ar.us, go to the "House" tab. Video archives begin with the 2010 Fiscal Session.

32. The Arkansas website is www.ardigest.net.

Legislation." Bill information is listed in reverse date order, but Boolean searching is available. Lexis databases also include bill tracking reports and the full text of bills.[33]

On Westlaw, conduct searches for pending bills by selecting the database for State Materials/Arkansas, then Arkansas Proposed & Enacted Legislation. Westlaw also includes bill tracking and legislative calendars under the "Tools & Resources" side bar. The "Tools & Resources" side bar also provides bill tracking, bill summaries, committee schedules, and historical information. Westlaw's "Arkansas Proposed & Enacted Legislation" database includes "Enacted Legislation" and "Proposed Legislation." A researcher may use a Boolean search, or narrow the search by including the document fields: date, citation, sponsor, summary, text, title, or topic.

Interest groups increasingly track the status of pending and proposed legislation. For example, the Arkansas chapter of the ACLU tracks legislation at its website.[34] Similarly, information on current legislation of interest to county government is maintained at the website of the Association of Arkansas Counties.[35] The Arkansas Municipal League has developed a website[36] for keeping up with the activities of the General Assembly, called *Legislative Action Center*.

B. Print Sources for Current Arkansas Legislation

While online sources provide for easy bill tracking during a legislative session, for those who prefer to use a print resource, the *Arkansas Daily Legislative Digest* is published every day during legislative sessions. This looseleaf service provides summaries of the current status of bills and resolutions that have been introduced in the House and Senate. Much as the General Assembly's website does, the *Arkansas Legislative Digest* gives its readers detailed information about members of the legislature and the current and scheduled activities of legislative committees. It indexes proposed legislation by several categories: author, bill number, subject of bill, and act number.

When the General Assembly is not in official session, the *Arkansas Legislative Digest* publishes a weekly looseleaf, the *Interim Legislative Reporting Service*.

---

33. On Lexis, "Full Text Bills" also contains resolutions and executive orders. Researchers using Lexis.com should consult the ARBILL database.

34. *See American Civil Liberties Union of Arkansas*, www.acluarkansas.org (last visited Dec. 3, 2015).

35. The address is www.arcounties.org.

36. The address is www.arml.org.

This publication keeps readers up to date with administrative appointments, attorney general opinions, election results, and interim study proposals or resolutions.

VI. Publication of Arkansas Slip Laws and Session Laws

A. Online Sources for Arkansas Slip Laws and Session Laws

As each Arkansas legislative session progresses, unofficial electronic versions of the session's slip laws are made available on the General Assembly's website, www.arkleg.state.ar.us. The full text of bills and acts dating back to 1987 is also available on the General Assembly's website, under the links "Search Bills" or "Search Acts." The researcher can then select the appropriate session year and enter search criteria such as the bill or act number or key words and phrases.

Following each legislative session, the Bureau also provides an unofficial but useful resource that summarizes all enacted legislation and any proposed constitutional amendments approved during the session. The *Summary of General Legislation* and the *Summary of Fiscal Legislation* are found on the General Assembly's website within six weeks following the session. These publications contain summaries of acts organized by subject matter as well as cross-references to bill and act numbers.

Other online sources provide access to slip laws and session laws. Fastcase contains a link to the "Search Acts" location of the General Assembly website in the Arkansas database under "Arkansas Acts." Lexis and Westlaw provide access to current legislation in ways similar to that described above for other online sources. Lexis provides slip laws and session laws through the "Arkansas Advance Legislative Service." On Westlaw, slip laws and session laws are available in the "Arkansas Proposed & Enacted Legislation" database.

B. Print Sources for Arkansas Slip Laws and Session Laws

LexisNexis and West publish print versions of the slip laws. LexisNexis collects slip laws in *Advance Legislative Service*, a set of inches-thick soft-cover "pamphlets" (a misnomer if ever there was one). The pamphlets are published by LexisNexis exactly as the publisher receives the acts, without corrections or editing. To assist the researcher in determining which sections of the state's official code (*Arkansas Code of 1987 Annotated*) are affected by the passage of the new acts, each *Advance Legislative Service* pamphlet includes a cumulative table of statutory sections that were repealed, amended, transferred, or added; a summary of the legislative session's acts; and a cumulative index.

West publishes slip laws in soft-cover volumes titled *West's Arkansas Legislative Service*. The West slip laws publication similarly summarizes current legislation and includes cumulative tables and an index. Issues of the West slip laws are published more frequently than the LexisNexis *Advance Legislative Service*.

The multi-volume *Acts of Arkansas* is the official compilation of session laws. It is published in a multi-volume, hard-cover set, the volumes titled by year, legislative session, and act numbers. The contents of each volume are arranged sequentially by act number, with each volume containing a subject matter index. A complete chronological summary of the session appears in the first volume of each set. A full index to the session laws is in the last volume of each set. Session laws for an extraordinary session are published in the last volume of the set for the regular session following that extraordinary session. For example, the First Extraordinary Session of 2008 is published at the end of the 2009 Regular Session volume of *Acts of Arkansas*.

VII. Arkansas Legislative History

When a court is called upon to ascertain what the legislature intended when enacting a statute, it examines many things: "the history of the statutes involved, as well as the contemporaneous conditions at time of their enactment, the consequences of interpretations, and all other matters of common knowledge within the court's jurisdiction."[37] Therefore, because the legislative process that produces a statute may be relevant to its interpretation, researchers may find it necessary to study the *legislative history* of a piece of enacted law.

A. Online Sources for Arkansas Legislative History

The Arkansas General Assembly's increasing use of technology has resulted in a record of the outlines of legislative history as the progress of each bill is recorded on the legislature's website. If you are researching legislation enacted in the most recent regular or fiscal legislative session, you may follow the same steps discussed in Sections V.A and VI.A above for bill tracking. For older legislative sessions, go to the General Assembly's website and click "Search Bills and Resolutions" or "Search Acts." Use the year, act, or bill number,

---

37. *S.W. Bell Tel. Co. v. Ark. Pub. Serv. Comm'n*, 69 Ark. App. 323, 329, 13 S.W.3d 197, 201 (2000).

or the sponsor's name, or other key terms and criteria as search terms. When your search result is displayed, click the title of the bill or act to retrieve the full text, or click the link showing the bill number to retrieve the bill's full history.

On the page containing the full history of the bill are details of the bill's progression, set out in reverse chronological order, including its date of introduction, the dates on which it was read in the House or Senate chamber, its referral to committee, the action taken by the committee, its delivery to the other legislative chamber, and its progress through that chamber.[38] The history of successful bills includes their presentation to the governor and ultimate enactment. The history of unsuccessful bills ends with their defeat in committee or chamber, or, in the case of some bills, their failure to inspire a committee vote before the legislature adjourns to end the session. As discussed above in Section V.A., the House of Representatives archives the video of House proceedings and House committee meetings held during a session.

A researcher may also use commercial databases to access legislative history. In Fastcase, click the link that takes you to "Search Bills and Resolutions" on the General Assembly's website. The Lexis "Advance Legislative Service"[39] provides historical information under "Arkansas Legislative Bill History."[40] Similarly, the Westlaw "Arkansas Proposed & Enacted Legislation" databases contain legislative history information for Arkansas legislation.[41]

B. Print Sources for Arkansas Legislative History

Unlike the United States Congress, whose legislative process is discussed below, the Arkansas General Assembly does not publish a written record of its legislative proceedings, debates, or committee reports. The only written records are tallies of the votes taken on each measure, which are recorded in each chamber's official journal, along with any gubernatorial vetoes.[42] Infrequently,

---

38. See Figure 6-2.

39. The same materials are available online in the Lexis.com Arkansas Advance Legislative Service (ARALS) database.

40. This Lexis database includes the text of the governor's veto messages to the legislature.

41. Under the "Tools & Resources" side bar for "Arkansas Proposed & Enacted Legislation," you will find a link to the database "Arkansas Legislative History," which in turn links to the search windows for "Bill Analysis & Other Reports" and "Journals."

42. See Ark. Const. art. 5, § 12; Ark. Const. art. 6, § 15. For a description of the electronic voting process used in the Arkansas House of Representatives, go to www.arkansashouse.org/about-the-house.

Figure 6-2. Bill History on the Arkansas General Assembly Website

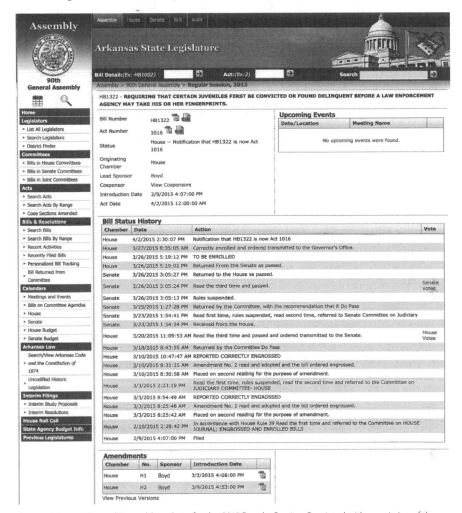

a bill may direct that the clerk of the chamber record additional information in the chamber's journal. House and Senate journals are located on the home page of the General Assembly's website for the session.

To track the origin of a current statute published in the *Arkansas Code of 1987 Annotated*, researchers can consult the historical notes or publisher's notes immediately following the statute, which cite the acts creating and amending the statute. These citations refer to the original legislation from the session laws, and they can be used to retrieve an act from the session laws for that year.

Additional legislative history is located in annotations provided by the Arkansas Code Revision Commission in the *Arkansas Code of 1987 Annotated*. In the course of codifying acts, the Commission indicates each act from which a statute is derived (including amendments) and publishes any emergency clauses.[43] Other annotations are included when new legislation receives special attention in the Code. For example, the General Assembly may designate that an act is "not to be codified" because it only relates to but does not amend a current statute. In that event, the Commission publishes the text of the uncodified legislation in annotations to the *Arkansas Code of 1987 Annotated* in close proximity to the related statute or at the beginning of the chapter or subchapter where the related statute is codified.[44] Also, if two or more legislative acts amend the same Code section, the Commission publishes the last of the acts and annotates the earlier act(s).[45]

VIII. Federal Legislative Materials

Much as they are in Arkansas, federal bills are introduced in one of the two legislative houses, the House of Representatives or the Senate, and both houses must pass them before the bills are sent to the president for signing. Bills are numbered sequentially in each chamber of Congress. When a federal bill is enacted, it becomes a *public law,* published in consecutive order by Congressional session, and assigned a *public law number* in the *United States Statutes at Large*.[46] Finally, the new public law is assigned a statute number when it is codified with

---

43. *See supra* note 27. The Commission is not required to publish emergency clauses. Ark. Code Ann. § 1-2-303(e)(2) (2008). The publication is useful, however, because an emergency clause may be used to determine legislative intent. *Farm Bureau Mut. Ins. Co. v. Wright*, 285 Ark. 228, 232, 686 S.W.2d 778, 781 (1985) (citing *Mo. Pac. R.R. Co. v. Kincannon*, 203 Ark. 76, 156 S.W.2d 70 (1941)).

44. The General Assembly's website contains a searchable database of uncodified historic legislation. A print version of the historic uncodified act may be obtained only from sources such as the Secretary of State, the Supreme Court library, or from an Arkansas law school. To access the database, locate "Arkansas Law" on the home page, then select "Uncodified Historic Legislation."

45. *See* Ark. Code Ann. § 1-2-207 (2008).

46. The *United States Statutes at Large* is the federal counterpart of *Acts of Arkansas*.

statutes on similar topics in the *United States Code*. For more detailed information concerning the federal legislative process, a researcher can access nine videos describing the legislative process on Congress's official website.[47]

A. Federal Online Sources

Congressional material is daily becoming ever more available via the Internet, and using Internet sources for bill tracking is often easier than using print resources. The official website for federal legislative action is Congress .gov,[48] which provides bill summaries and status, committee reports, activities of both chambers, biographical and contact information for legislators, the *Congressional Record*, and many more resources.[49] The Government Publishing Office website[50] also contains bills, selected hearings and reports, and the *Congressional Record*. Select the "Customers" link on the left pane of the home page, then select "Official Journals of Government."

In addition, both Lexis and Westlaw maintain databases with federal legislative history materials. The Lexis databases are located by browsing for the U.S. Federal source, then selecting the category "Statutes and Legislation."[51] The databases include bill tracking, committee reports, full text of bills, and the *Congressional Record*. You may also browse or search voting records, hearings, and bill summaries.

---

47. The address for the official website is www.congress.gov. The legislative process videos are available at https://www.congress.gov/legislative-process.

48. The Library of Congress maintains and updates Congress.gov, and it is presently transferring legislative materials from THOMAS, a website created in 1994 for free public access to these materials, to the new official site. The address for THOMAS is http://thomas.loc.gov/home/thomas.php. Once all the materials have been transferred, the THOMAS site will be closed.

49. The official website contains a wealth of information. It provides a robust search engine for searching legislation. For an overview, see Andrew Weber, *Now over 1,000,000 Items to Search on Congress.gov: Communications and More Added*, Library of Congress: In Custodia Legis (Oct. 7, 2015), https://blogs.loc.gov/law/2015/10/now-over-1000000-items-to-search-on-congress-gov-communications-and-more-added/.

50. The address is www.gpo.gov.

51. On Lexis.com, use the "Federal Legal — U.S.>Legislative Histories & Materials" library to locate specific databases for current legislation and legislative history in committee reports or the *Congressional Record*. For example, researchers can use the BLTEXT database to retrieve the full text of current bills and the BLTRCK database to track current federal legislation. To find archived legislation from previous sessions of Congress, select from several databases in the "Federal Legal — U.S.> Archived Bill Text & Tracking" library.

On Westlaw, federal legislative history may be found either by accessing the statute or the "Federal Proposed and Enacted Legislation" database. When viewing a statute, look for the session law and public law numbers in the statute's annotation. You can also locate legislative history information by clicking the "History" tab for the statute. The "Federal Proposed and Enacted Legislation" database includes the full text of bills and public laws. The "Tools & Resources" sidebar for that database provides bill tracking, bill summaries, committee schedules, and historical information.

B. Federal Print Sources

Federal legislative history research in print begins with the statute number. If you do not know the number, use an annotated code to find it. After you locate the statute, you can find the session law citation and public law number in the annotation following the statute. You may then use the session law citation and public law number to find the legislative history of the bill as it worked its way through Congress.

In researching federal legislative history, look for committee reports, material from committee hearings, and transcripts of floor debates. Committee reports are considered the most persuasive authority. Congressional committee reports are often lengthy documents published in soft-cover format. These reports contain the committee's analysis of the bill, the reasons for enacting it, and the views of any members who disagreed with those reasons. Congressional hearing materials include transcripts from the proceedings as well as documents such as prepared testimony and exhibits. Floor debates are published in the *Congressional Record*. Be wary of relying on these so-called debates, as they may not have actually been delivered in the House or Senate. Members of Congress can amend their remarks and even submit written statements that are published in transcript form in the *Congressional Record* as if they had been spoken. Table 6-3 on the following page contains the most common print sources for researching federal legislative history. Additional information for researching federal legislative history is addressed in chapter 6 of *Federal Legal Research*.[52]

Understanding how the legislative process works is key to successfully researching new legislation and legislative history. Table 6-4 provides an overview of important steps in researching legislation.

---

52. Mary Garvey Algero, Spencer L. Simons, Suzanne E. Rowe, Scott Childs & Sarah E. Ricks, *Federal Legal Research* (2d ed. 2015).

Table 6-3. Selected Print Sources for Federal Legislative History

Source	Contents
United States Code Congressional and Administrative News (USCCAN)	Selected reprints and excerpts of committee reports; references to other reports and to the *Congressional Record*
Congressional Information Service (CIS)	Full text of bills, committee reports, and hearings on microfiche; print indexes and abstracts in bound volumes
Congressional Record	Debate from the floor of the House and Senate

Table 6-4. Research Process for Legislation and Legislative History

1. Identify the title or number and year of the legislation you are researching. You may also search under the name of the legislation's sponsor.

2. If you do not have the title or number of the bill or act, identify the subject matter area of the law to generate a list of research terms, from broad to narrow.

3. If this area of law is new to you, consult secondary materials such as treatises or periodical articles to improve your understanding of the issues and to help you identify additional research terms.

4. Federal legislation may have a popular-name bill title, such as the "No Child Left Behind Act of 2001." Consult the popular name table in the U.S.C. or an online source.

5. When conducting research in online sources, use research terms to construct natural language or Boolean searches in relevant databases or their fields or segments.

6. Once you have located the bill or act and the number and year of the legislative session where it was introduced or enacted, you can consult sources compiled during the session to obtain information on the history of the bill or act, such as journals, bill summaries, committee reports, and bill-tracking information.

7. While a useful source is on the screen, obtain all necessary information for constructing its full citation, should this be a source you later decide to cite. Download sources or save them in online folders.

8. Retrieve relevant authorities, and read them carefully. Select appropriate authorities to support your analysis of the legislation, and construct citations to those sources.

9. Confirm currency and validity of all selected sources, as described in Chapter 9.

Chapter 7

Administrative and Executive Law

I. Introduction to Administrative and Executive Law

The executive branch of government is charged with carrying out the law enacted by the legislative branch, which it typically performs through the actions of its *agencies*. Although agencies are part of the executive branch of government, they are generally created by the legislature through *enabling statutes*. An enabling statute defines the scope of a particular agency's authority in a delimited subject area to promulgate rules. Thus, an agency is empowered to act only within the scope of that authority. The legislature may also grant an agency the authority to create rules to adjudicate disputes. Although the separation-of-powers doctrine ordinarily prevents one branch of government from exercising the kind of authority belonging to another branch, administrative agencies typically combine functions of the legislative, executive, and judicial branches.[1]

Administrative law is a form of primary authority, just as are cases and statutes, although it is published in sources that are not as standardized as are reporters and codes. The most common forms of administrative law are the rules and decisions of governmental agencies. Other law from the executive branch of government include *executive orders* of the governor and *opinions* of the attorney general.

Under the Arkansas Administrative Procedure Act ("APA"), an administrative "rule" is "any agency statement of general applicability and future effect that implements, interprets, or prescribes law or policy, or describes the

---

1. For an in-depth examination of the ways the separation-of-powers principle is implicated in powers exercised by Arkansas administrative agencies and the legislative and judicial branches of the state government, see L. Scott Stafford, *Separation of Powers and Arkansas Administrative Agencies: Distinguishing Judicial Power and Legislative Power*, 7 U. Ark. Little Rock L.J. 279 (1984).

organization, procedure, or practice of any agency and includes, but is not limited to, the amendment or repeal of a prior rule."[2] The terms "rule" and "regulation" are used interchangeably by Arkansas agencies, although technically speaking, Arkansas has administrative rules, and the federal government has administrative regulations.

II. Arkansas Administrative and Executive Law

A. The Executive Department

The Executive Department of Arkansas includes the offices of governor, lieutenant governor, secretary of state, state treasurer, state auditor, attorney general, and commissioner of state lands, all of whom are elected to four-year terms.[3] The two most important sources of law in the Executive Department are the governor and the attorney general.

1. The Governor

Executive power is the authority to enforce laws or appoint the agents charged with the duty of enforcement.[4] As chief executive of the state, the governor may exercise his authority through executive orders, grants of clemency, or proclamations.

The most common executive document is the *executive order*. A governor typically uses the executive order to address certain management or administrative issues.[5] Neither the Arkansas Constitution nor Arkansas statutory law specifically authorizes executive orders. Instead, the governor's power to issue executive orders derives from the Arkansas Constitution, which endows the governor with "supreme executive power."[6]

A second type of executive act sometimes exercised by the governor is a grant of clemency to a person convicted of a crime. Under the Arkansas

---

2. Ark. Code Ann. § 25-15-202(9)(A) (2014).

3. Ark. Const. amends. 56, 63.

4. *Clinton v. Clinton*, 305 Ark. 585, 590, 810 S.W.2d 923, 926 (1991).

5. A list of the governor's executive orders is found at http://governor.arkansas.gov/ executive-orders.

6. Ark. Const. art. 6, § 2. The Arkansas Attorney General opined that the power is "attendant the otherwise express or implied powers granted the Governor by the constitution or statutes over particular topics." Ark. Atty. Gen. Op. No. 93-435 (Jan. 20, 1994) (citing 81A C.J.S. *States* § 130(b)).

Constitution, the executive branch has the sole authority and discretion to grant such "reprieves, commutations of sentence, and pardons."[7]

A gubernatorial proclamation typically honors or draws attention to an event or organization worthy of public recognition. Examples of recent proclamations by the governor include recognition of Black History Month, Congenital Heart Defects Awareness Week, and Firefighter Recognition Day.[8]

2. The Attorney General

Administrative and legislative decision-makers often confront questions calling for interpretation of the law. When they need a legal opinion, they call upon the office of the attorney general for advice. Pursuant to statute and upon specific request, the attorney general will prepare legal opinions for certain members of state government: (a) the governor or the heads of the executive departments of the state upon any constitutional or other legal question that concerns their official actions; (b) prosecuting attorneys concerning legal questions about the financial interests of the state or its counties or any matters relating to the administration of criminal laws; (c) members of the General Assembly about the constitutionality of any proposed bill; and (d) state boards or commissions concerning the discharge of their duties.[9]

The attorney general's office is charged with responsibility for approving ballot titles and popular names for initiatives and referenda,[10] for giving initial approval of inter-local cooperation agreements,[11] and for responding to opinion requests concerning release of personnel records pursuant to the Freedom of Information Act.[12] The attorney general is not authorized to issue opinions to local officials or to private citizens or other private entities. Although the attorney general is a member of the executive branch, an opinion is advisory only; it is not binding.

---

7. Ark. Const. art. 6, § 18; *see also Smith v. Huckabee*, No. 06-917, 2007 WL 701045 (Ark. Mar. 8, 2007) (per curiam) (unpublished).

8. Find the most recent proclamations at http://governor.arkansas.gov /proclamations.

9. Ark. Code Ann. § 25-16-706(a) (2014).

10. Ark. Code Ann. § 7-9-107 (Supp. 2015).

11. Ark. Code Ann. §§ 25-20-101 to -108 (2014).

12. Ark. Code Ann. § 25-19-105(c)(3)(B) (Supp. 2015).

Table 7-1. Names and General Statutory Provisions of Major Departments of Arkansas State Government

Department Name	General Statutory Provisions
Department of Aeronautics	Ark. Code Ann. §§ 27-115-101 et seq.
Agriculture Department	Ark. Code Ann. §§ 25-38-201 et seq.
Department of Arkansas Heritage	Ark. Code Ann. §§ 25-3-101 et seq.
Assessment Coordination Department	Ark. Code Ann. §§ 25-28-101 et seq.
Department of Career Education	Ark. Code Ann. §§ 25-30-106 et seq.
Department of Correction	Ark. Code Ann. §§ 25-5-101 et seq.
Department of Economic Development	Ark. Code Ann. §§ 25-11-101 et seq.
Department of Education	Ark. Code Ann. §§ 25-6-101, et seq.
Department of Emergency Management	Ark. Code Ann. §§ 12-75-1011 et seq.
Department of Environmental Quality	Ark. Code Ann. §§ 25-14-101 et seq.
Department of Finance & Administration	Ark. Code Ann. §§ 25-8-101 et seq.
Department of Health	Ark. Code Ann. §§ 25-9-101 et seq.
Department of Higher Education	Ark. Code Ann. §§ 25-7-101 et seq.
Department of Human Services	Ark. Code Ann. §§ 25-10-101 et seq.
Department of Information Systems	Ark. Code Ann. §§ 25-4-101 et seq.
Department of Labor	Ark. Code Ann. §§ 25-12-101 et seq.
Department of Parks & Tourism	Ark. Code Ann. §§ 25-13-101 et seq.
Securities Department	Ark. Code Ann. §§ 23-42-101 et seq.
State Bank Department	Ark. Code Ann. §§ 23-46-201 et seq.
State Highway & Transportation Department (administered by State Highway Commission)	Ark. Code Ann. §§ 26-65-101 et seq.
State Insurance Department	Ark. Code Ann. §§ 23-61-101 et seq.
Department of Veterans Affairs	Ark. Code Ann. §§ 20-81-102 et seq.
Department of Workforce Services	Ark. Code Ann. §§ 11-10-301 et seq.

B. Arkansas State Agencies

The term *state agency* in Arkansas is typically used to refer to an agency, authority, board, bureau, commission, council, department, institute, or office.[13] Most agencies have been created pursuant to legislative enactment, although three commissions were created by amendments to the Arkansas Constitution: the Arkansas State Game and Fish Commission, the State Highway Commission, and the Judicial Discipline and Disability Commission.[14] Table 7-1 sets out the names of the main departments of Arkansas state government and citations to the primary statutory provisions affecting them. These departments are the largest administrative units. There are literally hundreds of smaller administrative agencies, boards, offices, councils, and commissions.[15]

The scope of government covered by the state's administrative agencies is vast, and it is always evolving. By law, soon after each regular session of the General Assembly concludes, each agency is obligated to review any newly enacted law to determine whether any of its existing rules should be repealed or amended, or whether it should adopt any new rules.[16] Similarly, the Bureau of Legislative Research assists the Arkansas General Assembly's Legislative Council in reviewing and approving current, proposed, and amended rules to ensure that they conform to legislative intent.[17]

---

13. The *Arkansas Code of 1987* contains several definitions of "state agency." For purposes of the Administrative Procedure Act, the term "agency" includes every "board, commission, department, officer, or other authority of the government of the State of Arkansas, whether or not within, or subject to review by, another agency, except the General Assembly, the courts, and Governor." Ark. Code Ann. § 25-15-202(2)(A) (2014). This definition includes the Division of Child Care and Early Childhood Education of the Department of Health and Human Services, and for purposes of administrative appeal, the Child Care Appeal Review Panel, but it excludes the Arkansas Public Service Commission, the Arkansas Pollution Control and Ecology Commission, the Workers' Compensation Commission, and the Department of Workforce Services, as the General Assembly has deemed that "the existing laws governing those agencies provide adequate administrative procedures for those agencies." *Id.* § 25-15-202(2)(B), (C).

14. *See* Ark. Const. amends. 35, 42, 66.

15. A complete alphabetical list of all Arkansas agencies, including departments, boards, commissions, committees, and councils, with links to their websites, if any, is available at www.arkansas.gov/government/agencies.

16. Ark. Code Ann. § 25-15-216 (2014).

17. Ark. Code Ann. § 10-3-309 (Supp. 2015). This amended code section implements changes to process-of-rules review by the General Assembly as a result of the passage of Amendment 92 in 2014. The amendment created a significant change to

Researching administrative law is challenging because the publication of agency rules and decisions is less standardized than the publication of statutes and judicial opinions and because some agencies are authorized to use their own internal procedures and policies. In addition to the general research processes described in Chapter 1, Table 7-2 adds more steps needed for researching administrative law.

Table 7-2. Additional Steps for Researching Administrative Rules

1. Find and review the agency's enabling statute and judicial or administrative cases interpreting the enabling statute.

2. Determine whether the agency is subject to the APA. If so, review the relevant procedures of the APA. If not, locate and review the agency's own statutory procedures.

3. Locate and review the agency's rules, as well as judicial or administrative cases interpreting or applying those rules.

The first step in researching an agency's administrative law is to locate the agency's *enabling statute* to determine the extent and limits of the powers the agency is authorized to exercise.[18] By gaining some familiarity with the agency's basic role and functions, the researcher will better understand the kinds of administrative materials associated with that agency.

The agencies subject to the APA include most, but not all, of the state's boards, commissions, departments, and other administrative offices.[19] The Arkansas Public Service Commission, the Arkansas Pollution Control and Ecology Commission, the Workers' Compensation Commission, and the De-

---

Arkansas's separation of powers doctrine to require legislative approval of state agency rules before they become effective. *See* Ark. Const. art. 5, § 42. Further, under an executive order issued by the current administration, the governor must approve a rule before an agency can submit it to the General Assembly, unless the governor grants an exemption. *See* Ark. Exec. Order No. 15-02 (Jan. 14, 2015), *available at* http://governor.arkansas.gov/executive-orders.

18. For a helpful overview of the adjudicative processes of Arkansas administrative agencies, including judicial review of agency decisions, see Gregory L. Crow & Warren T. Readnour, *The Arkansas Administrative Procedure Act: A Practitioner's Guide to the Adjudication and Judicial Review Process*, 39 Ark. Law. 9 (Winter 2004).

19. Ark. Code Ann. § 25-15-202(2)(A) (2014).

partment of Workforce Services are not subject to the APA, however, because separate statutes govern their operation and procedures.[20]

One purpose of the APA is to establish procedures for hearings and notice "in those functions of the executive branch which are basically adjudicatory or quasi-judicial, particularly with respect to rule making, renewal or revocation of licenses and where, under law, an agency must make orders based on the adjudication process."[21] Agency actions governed by the APA are exempt from the Rules of Civil Procedure because the APA provides a different procedure for the parties to follow.[22]

Researchers can locate the administrative rules, decisions, and orders of Arkansas state agencies, boards, and commissions through either print or online sources.

1. The *Arkansas Register*

The official print source for administrative law is the *Arkansas Register*, which contains all the adopted rules of every state agency.[23] The *Arkansas Register* is published at least once a month, and its cumulative index is published annually.[24] Although electronic copies of the current versions of these rules are maintained on the secretary of state's website,[25] they are not viewed as "official" copies. The official copies remain the paper copies housed in the *Arkansas Register* division of the secretary of state's office.

Since 2003, the secretary of state has published current rules, including proposed rules, on that office's website.[26] Full text searches of the online version of the *Arkansas Register* are only available for the period from September 1, 2001, to the present. The website does not maintain superseded rules.

---

20. *Id.* § 25-15-202(2)(C).

21. *Ark. Livestock & Poultry Comm'n v. House*, 276 Ark. 326, 329, 634 S.W.2d 388, 389 (1982).

22. *See* Ark. R. Civ. P. 81(a).

23. *See* Ark. Code Ann. § 25-15-205(a) (2014). The *Arkansas Register* is available online at www.sosweb.state.ar.us/admin_rules_ar_register.html, but only for issues published since September 1, 2001.

24. *Id.* § 25-15-205(b).

25. The Secretary of State's website is found at www.sos.arkansas.gov/admin _rules.html.

26. *See* Ark. Code Ann. § 25-15-218(a) (2014).

2. The *Code of Arkansas Rules*

An unofficial but important source of Arkansas's administrative rules is the multi-volume, looseleaf *Code of Arkansas Rules*, which is updated monthly.[27] To find rules in a particular area, check the *Index* volume of the *Code of Arkansas Rules*, as the contents of the print volumes are not arranged in alphabetical or other recognizable order. Each binder provides a "Volume Content List" at the beginning. For example, Volume 4 contains rules of the Insurance Department, the Private Investigators and Private Security Agencies Board, the Board of Massage Therapy, the State Medical Board, the Manufactured Home Commission, the Board of Nursing, and the Board of Optometry.

Rules are indexed by subject and by rule number. Another useful feature of the index is a table linking administrative rules to specific provisions of the *Arkansas Code of 1987.* For example, Ark. Code Ann. § 8-4-201 is linked to the reference number 014 08 007, indicating a civil penalties rule from the Arkansas Department of Environmental Quality. The index also contains monthly updates for emergency rules promulgated by any agency and citations to recent court decisions relating to administrative law and procedure. The *Code of Arkansas Rules* is also available online in Lexis.

C. Additional Sources for Administrative and Executive Materials

Although the *Arkansas Register* is the official print source for administrative materials, an easy place to find current information about Arkansas agencies is the state's official website.[28] Arkansas's administrative bodies are too numerous to list here, but you can find an alphabetical list of all Arkansas agencies with links to their websites on the state's official website. Although not all agencies have websites, those who do typically make their rules available online.

You may be able to locate citations to rules by checking the enabling statute for an agency in the unofficial *West's Arkansas Code Annotated*: "Code of Arkansas Rules that are authorized by or interpretive of the Arkansas Code are identified with appropriate references at the beginning of titles, subtitles,

---

27. The *Code of Arkansas Rules* was formerly published by Weil Publishing Company and is still commonly referred to as "Weil's Code." You may find the old Weil binder covers still in use, even though their content now comes from LexisNexis Matthew Bender.

28. The address is www.arkansas.gov.

chapters, or subchapters or under the sections that authorize the rules or are interpreted by them."[29]

For example, directly beneath Subtitle 3, "Mental Health," in Volume 28 of *West's Arkansas Code Annotated*, researchers will find the heading "Administrative Code References," followed by a citation to State Health Department regulation, Code Ark. R. 007 00 001 et seq. The regulation is not reprinted in the statutory code, so you will need to retrieve it from one of the other sources discussed in this Section.

The APA also requires state agencies to file a copy of each proposed, final, or emergency rule with the Arkansas State Library.[30]

In Lexis, administrative rules are searchable in the "Arkansas Administrative Code" (ARDSM, corresponding to the *Code of Arkansas Rules*). Lexis also provides more specialized databases, such as "AR Public Service Commission Decisions" (ARPUC), "AR Department of Finance Regulations" (ARTXRG), and "AR Division of Securities; Decisions, Releases and Letters" (ARSEC), to name a few.[31]

To find administrative rules in Westlaw, search the "Regulations" directory.[32] Westlaw also provides an "Administrative Decisions & Guidance" database for specific agency decisions, such as "Arkansas Environmental Records" (EDR-AR), "Arkansas Blue Sky Regulations" (ARSEC), or "Arkansas Insurance Bulletins" (ARIN), among others.

Several administrative agencies publish their decisions and orders. While the decisions of a few agencies are available on Lexis or Westlaw, it is increasingly common to find these materials online on the websites of the agencies themselves.[33] Table 7-3 lists sources for the decisions and orders of several Arkansas agencies.

---

29. Ark. Code Ann., Vol. 1, *Preface*, at v (West 2015).

30. Ark. Code Ann. § 25-15-204(e)(1) (Supp. 2015).

31. These databases are found in Lexis by selecting "Browse," then selecting the category "Administrative Materials" followed by selecting the jurisdiction, Arkansas. Lexis subscribers may also use a regulation tracking feature, "AR State Regulation Tracking" (ARRGTR), which provides dates of proposed rules, dates of adoption, effective dates, withdrawal dates, and hearing dates.

32. You may find these files in Westlaw by searching "Regulations" then the jurisdiction "Arkansas" or by searching the jurisdiction first. By searching the jurisdiction first, you will more readily see other databases such as the "Arkansas Proposed & Adopted Regulations — Current" database.

33. The Fastcase database "Administrative Opinions and Orders" provides a limited number of state sources, but Arkansas is not included.

**Table 7-3. Sources for Decisions and Orders of
Selected Arkansas Agencies**

Agency Name	Decision & Order Publication Sources
Office of the Arkansas Attorney General	http://www.arkansasag.gov/opinions/index.php (searchable database of opinions)
Arkansas Department of Environmental Quality	https://www.adeq.state.ar.us/legal/orders.aspx (searchable database of orders)
Arkansas Ethics Commission	http://www.arkansasethics.com/ (decisions in contested matters; attorney general ethics opinions 1989–90; ethics commission opinions, after 1991)
Arkansas Public Service Commission	ARPUC (Lexis database), http://www.apscservices.info/ (searchable database of orders, testimony, or "all documents")
Arkansas Securities Department	ARSEC (Lexis database), www.securities.arkansas.gov (orders and legal opinions; website is searchable)
Arkansas Workers' Compensation Commission	ARWORK (Lexis database); ARWC-ADMIN (Westlaw database), http://www.awcc.state.ar.us/opinionmain .html (opinions of administrative law judges and full commission opinions sine July 1, 2003; listed by year)

The governor's executive orders, clemency orders, and proclamations are filed with the secretary of state, but are not otherwise published. Copies of some executive orders may be found on the governor's office website[34] and at the Arkansas State Library.[35]

Formal opinions of the attorney general are published in the *Arkansas Register*. In addition, print copies of opinions going as far back as September 1, 2001, may be downloaded in .pdf format from the secretary of state's website.[36]

---

34. The address is www.governor.arkansas.gov.

35. The website for the Arkansas State Library is www.library.arkansas.gov. The library holds some executive orders from 1969 to the present in the Arkansas Documents Collection.

36. The Secretary of State's website is found at www.sos.arkansas.gov.

Another good source for attorney general opinions is the attorney general's website.[37] Attorney general opinions are also available on the commercial databases. Fastcase provides a link to the Arkansas Attorney General's web page for an opinions search. On Lexis, use the "AR Attorney General Opinions" (ARAG) file. Westlaw's database for Arkansas Attorney General Opinions is "AR-AG."

III. Federal Administrative and Executive Law

The federal government's agencies function in much the same way that state agencies do. Agencies such as the Civil Rights Division of the Department of Justice, the Internal Revenue Service, and the U.S. Fish and Wildlife Service are invaluable parts of the executive branch.

The federal Administrative Procedure Act is codified at 5 U.S.C. §§ 551 et seq. An online version of the Administrative Procedure Act is maintained by the National Archives.[38] Like Arkansas's Administrative Procedure Act, its goal is to promote uniformity, public participation, and public confidence in the fairness of the procedures used by agencies of the federal government.

A. The *Code of Federal Regulations*

Federal administrative rules are called "regulations." Federal regulations are codified in the *Code of Federal Regulations* ("C.F.R."), which is published by the Government Publishing Office. C.F.R. regulations are divided into 50 titles, organized by agency and subject. The titles of C.F.R. do not necessarily correspond topically to the titles of the *United States Code* ("U.S.C."), although some topics do fall under the same title number. For instance, Title 7 in both C.F.R. and U.S.C. pertains to agriculture, but U.S.C. Title 11 addresses bankruptcy, while C.F.R. Title 11 deals with federal elections. Each title is subdivided into chapters that usually bear the name of the agency whose regulations they contain.

C.F.R.'s soft-bound volumes are updated annually, as indicated by a change of color on the covers. In addition, specific titles of C.F.R. are updated quarterly:

---

37. The "Opinions Search" page of the Arkansas Attorney General's website is found at www.ag.arkansas.gov/opinions.

38. The National Archives website is found at www.archives.gov/federal-register /laws/administrative-procedure/.

in the first quarter, Titles 1–2 and 4–16;[39] in the second quarter, Titles 17–27; in the third quarter, Titles 28–41; and in the fourth quarter, titles 42–50.

To research a topic in C.F.R., use the general index to look up research terms or the relevant agency's name, and then read the regulations referenced. It may be more efficient to begin your research, however, in an unofficial annotated statutory code that contains references to related regulations for each statute. After finding a statute on point, review the annotations following the statutory language for cross references to relevant regulations; you may notice that *United States Code Service* tends to provide more references to regulations than does *United States Code Annotated*. Look up the citations given and review the regulations.

On Lexis, the C.F.R. is found under federal materials. For each section of the C.F.R., Lexis provides a tab for the table of contents for the section, the history of the section, and annotations. Lexis also provides access to the *Federal Register* and the "USCS — Federal Rules Annotated."

When viewing a C.F.R. section on Westlaw, you will see tabs labeled "History" (containing prior versions of the regulation); "Notes of Decisions" (with links to all cases dealing with the C.F.R. section); "Citing References" (containing links to every case, court document, law review article, or treatise in Westlaw databases that cites the C.F.R. section); and "Context & Analysis" (providing links to the *United States Code Annotated*, and summaries, references, and cross-references within the *Federal Register*).

Federal regulations are available to the public on the Internet, at the Government Publishing Office's *GPO Access* website.[40] This site not only gives researchers free electronic access to the current version of C.F.R., but also lets researchers look for regulations dating back to 1996. The site allows searching by key word, citation, or title.

Another useful website for researchers of regulations is *Regulations.gov*, a regulatory clearinghouse.[41] This website, launched in January 2003 as the first milestone of the Federal E-Government eRulemaking Initiative, provides public access to view rules from more than 160 different federal agencies, to read full texts of the rules' accompanying documents, and to submit comments to the federal department or agency proposing the rule.

---

39. Unlike other C.F.R. titles, Title 3, "The President," containing executive orders, is not updated annually.

40. The C.F.R. is found on the Government Publishing Office web page at www.gpo.gov/fdsys.

41. The address is www.regulations.gov.

B. The *Federal Register*

The *Federal Register*, published daily, is the United States government's official first source for rules, proposed rules, and notices of federal agencies and organizations, as well as executive orders and other presidential documents. Before they are published in C.F.R., new federal regulations and proposed changes to existing regulations appear in the *Federal Register*.

Print copies of the *Federal Register* are maintained throughout the United States at Federal Depository Libraries. The online version of the *Federal Register*, containing material from 1994 to the present, is available at both the Government Publishing Office website[42] and the website of the *National Archives*.[43] The online *Federal Register* is searchable by key words, including Boolean connectors, or by *Federal Register* page number, C.F.R. citation, date, or specific sections such as "Final Rules and Regulations," "Notices," or "Presidential Documents." The site provides free listserv subscription service to daily emails with the *Federal Register*'s Table of Contents.

Online commercial services also search the *Federal Register*, the C.F.R., and other federal administrative materials. Fastcase provides an external link to the *Federal Register* and has searchable databases for specific federal agency decisions. The Lexis database "Administrative and Agency Materials" provides access to the *Federal Register* and federal agency materials, including decisions, forms, bulletins, and news releases. On Westlaw, the C.F.R., *Federal Register*, and materials under "Federal Administrative Decisions & Guidance" are available.

C. Federal Executive Materials

Like the governor, the president issues executive orders and proclamations. Both are published in the *Federal Register*, and they are reprinted in the *United States Code Congressional and Administrative News* ("USCCAN") and in the annual compilation of Title 3 of the *Code of Federal Regulations*. Online resources for presidential documents include databases on Lexis and Westlaw, each called "Executive Office of the President."[44]

---

42. The *Federal Register* is found on the Government Publishing Office website at www.gpo.gov/fdsys.

43. The address is http://www.archives.gov/research/start/online-tools.html.

44. Fastcase does not contain a database for presidential documents or opinions of the U.S. Attorneys General.

Opinions of the U.S. attorney general are published in *Official Opinions of the Attorneys General of the United States*, and they can be found online on the U.S. Department of Justice website.[45] Lexis provides a searchable database for the Department of Justice under its "Federal Administrative Materials." You may also search Westlaw's "Federal Administrative Decisions & Guidance," then selecting "Department of Justice," then "U.S. Attorney General Opinions."

Additional information for researching federal administrative and executive law is addressed in *Federal Legal Research*.[46]

---

45. https://www.justice.gov/olc/opinions.
46. Mary Garvey Algero, Spencer L. Simons, Suzanne E. Rowe, Scott Childs & Sarah E. Ricks, *Federal Legal Research* (2d ed. 2015).

Chapter 8

Court Rules

I. Introduction to Court Rules and Rules of Professional Conduct

While questions of substantive law are the most common objects of legal research, sometimes issues arise that involve the application or interpretation of rules governing the handling of cases in the courts.[1] Rules of practice and procedure (commonly known as *court rules*) are often promulgated by states' highest courts under their power to supervise the administration of justice within their jurisdiction, although in many jurisdictions, such rules are the product of legislation or legislatively delegated authority. Closely related to court rules are the rules governing professional conduct, i.e., the way attorneys conduct themselves in the practice of law.

II. Arkansas Court Rules

Amendment 80 of the Arkansas Constitution gives the Arkansas Supreme Court superintending power over the state's judicial system.[2] The court exercises this power by the creation and enforcement of rules governing practice and procedure. Before the adoption of these rules, common law and statutes dictated the way the courts would operate. Amendment 80, however, "settled

---

1. Administrative agencies have their own rules of procedure, utilizing the Arkansas Administrative Procedure Act. *See* Chapter 7, Part B.

2. Under Amendment 80, § 3, of the Arkansas Constitution, "[t]he Supreme Court shall prescribe the rules of pleading, practice and procedure for all courts; provided these rules shall not abridge, enlarge or modify any substantive right and shall preserve the right of trial by jury as declared in this Constitution."

the question whether the Supreme Court's rulemaking power is exclusive or shared with the General Assembly."[3]

Because the *Arkansas Code of 1987* contains many procedural statutes,[4] Arkansas courts seek to interpret them in a way that is harmonious with the intent of the court rules. Statutes are subject to review on a case-by-case basis; when a challenge comes before the Arkansas Supreme Court, it decides whether the statute deals with a procedural or a substantive issue, ruling that a statute in conflict with procedural rules is unconstitutional in violation of Amendment 80.[5]

The history, development, and features of certain sets of Arkansas court rules warrant special mention: the rules of appellate procedure, civil procedure, criminal procedure, evidence, and professional conduct. Table 8-1 on the facing page lists titles of current Arkansas court rules.[6]

A. Appellate Procedure

Depending on the nature of the case being appealed, an attorney will need to consult either the Arkansas Rules of Appellate Procedure–Civil or the Arkansas Rules of Appellate Procedure–Criminal for basic information concerning the timing and methods to employ in pursuing an appeal.[7] With

---

3. David Newbern, John J. Watkins & D.P. Marshall, Jr., *Arkansas Civil Practice and Procedure* § 1:3 (5th ed. 2015):

> First, so long as a legislative provision dictates procedure, it need not directly conflict with one or more of the Court's rulemaking procedural rules to be unconstitutional. This proposition follows from the exclusivity of the Court's rulemaking authority under Section 3 of Amendment 80. Second, a statute is invalid if it "bypasses [court-adopted] 'rules of pleading, practice and procedure' by setting up [its own] procedure."
>
> *Id.* (footnotes omitted) (quoting *Johnson v. Rockwell Automation, Inc.*, 2009 Ark. 241, at 9, 308 S.W.3d 135, 141).

4. The majority of these procedural statutes are located in Title 16, Practice, Procedure, and Courts.

5. *See, e.g., Johnson v. Rockwell Automation, Inc.*, 2009 Ark. 241, at 6, 308 S.W.3d 135, 140 (holding that statutory procedure set out in Ark. Code Ann. § 16–55–202 was unconstitutional violation of separation of powers provisions of Arkansas Constitution Article 4, § 2, and Amendment 80, § 3).

6. Rules, regulations, and administrative orders affecting entities related to legal professionals are available at https://courts.arkansas.gov.

7. Several statutory provisions affecting appeals were previously included in Title 16, Chapter 67 of the *Arkansas Code of 1987*, but they were either repealed or super-

Table 8-1. Arkansas Court Rules

Arkansas Code of Judicial Conduct

Arkansas District Court Rules

Arkansas Rules for Minimum Continuing Legal Education

Arkansas Rules of Appellate Procedure–Civil

Arkansas Rules of Appellate Procedure–Criminal

Arkansas Rules of Civil Procedure

Arkansas Rules of Criminal Procedure

Arkansas Rules of Evidence

Arkansas Rules of Professional Conduct

Rules of the Supreme Court and Court of
Appeals of the State of Arkansas

Rules Governing Admission to the Bar

regard to requirements for motions, petitions, briefs, and oral argument, regardless whether the case is civil or criminal in nature, consult the Rules of
the Supreme Court and Court of Appeals of the State of Arkansas, which apply to all proceedings before the state's appellate courts.

B. Civil Procedure

Until the Arkansas General Assembly passed Act 38 of 1973, Arkansas civil
procedure was governed solely by statute.[8] Act 38 of 1973, however, recognized the Arkansas Supreme Court's inherent constitutional power to regulate procedure in the courts, and consequently, by per curiam order, the court
adopted the Arkansas Rules of Civil Procedure, expressly superseding a number of statutory procedural rules. Fortunately, many statutory provisions that
were inconsistent with rules of civil procedure have been repealed.[9] Even so, a
number of statutes governing civil procedure remain; be careful to check
both current court rules and Chapters 55 through 68 of the *Arkansas Code of
1987* for provisions affecting procedural issues.[10] The Arkansas Rules of Civil
Procedure "apply to all civil proceedings cognizable in the circuit courts of

---

seded by court rule.

    8. Newbern et al., *supra* note 3, at § 1:2.

    9. *See, e.g.,* 2003 Ark. Acts 1185 (repealing Ark. Code Ann. §§ 16-57-101 to -109).

    10. For example, one important statutory rule of procedure that does not con-
flict with court rules is the long-arm statute, Ark. Code Ann. § 16-58-120 (2005).

Table 8-2. Articles of the Arkansas Rules of Civil Procedure

Article I. Scope of Rules — One Form of Action

Article II. Commencement of Action; Service of Process, Pleadings, Motions, and Orders

Article III. Pleadings and Motions

Article IV. Parties

Article V. Depositions and Discovery

Article VI. Trials

Article VII. Judgment

Article VIII. Counsel; Provisional and Final Remedies; Suits *in Forma Pauperis*

Article IX. Circuit Courts and Clerks

Article X. General Provisions

this state except in those instances where a statute which creates a right, remedy or proceeding specifically provides a different procedure[,] in which event the procedure so specified shall apply."[11] In adopting the Rules of Civil Procedure, the Arkansas Supreme Court "intended . . . to except from the rules [of civil procedure] *special proceedings* created by statute which established different procedures from those applicable to civil actions."[12]

The Arkansas Rules of Civil Procedure are similar to the Federal Rules of Civil Procedure in most respects and often use language identical to that found in the federal rules. The 86 Arkansas rules are divided into ten articles arranging the rules by subject; these articles are identified in Table 8-2.

For specific information about similarities and differences between Arkansas and federal rules or for explanation of amendments to the rules, see the Reporter's Notes following each rule.

C. Criminal Procedure

Act 470 of 1971 authorized creation of the Arkansas Criminal Code Revision Commission and directed the Arkansas Supreme Court to prescribe rules

---

11. Newbern et al., *supra* note 3, at § 1:4 (quoting *Weidrick v. Arnold*, 310 Ark. 138, 144, 835 S.W.2d 843, 846 (1992)); *see, e.g., Swenson v. Kane*, 2014 Ark. 444, at 4, 447 S.W.3d 118, 121 (holding that guardianship determinations are special proceedings "excepted" from the Arkansas Rules of Civil Procedure).

12. *Weidrick v. Arnold*, 310 Ark. 138, 144, 835 S.W.2d 843, 846 (1992).

of pleading, practice, and procedure in criminal matters. These rules, known as the Arkansas Rules of Criminal Procedure, went into effect on January 1, 1976. Their purpose is "to provide for a just, speedy determination of every criminal proceeding."[13] In addition to these rules, many statutes governing criminal procedure are codified in the *Arkansas Code of 1987*, Title 16, Chapters 80 through 98.[14]

Like the rules of civil procedure, the criminal rules are divided into articles, but they follow a different numbering format. Moreover, while the criminal rules are not supplemented by Reporter's Notes, many are explained in extensive Commentary sections.[15] The Commentaries cross-reference co-existing statutes, but these references are to the old *Arkansas Statutes Annotated* that were in effect at the time the rules were drafted. Use the parallel reference charts in Tables, Volume A, of the *Arkansas Code of 1987* to translate these citations to their current versions. Table 8-3 sets out the 11 articles of the Arkansas Rules of Criminal Procedure.

Table 8-3. Articles of the Arkansas Rules of Criminal Procedure

Article I. General Provisions

Article II. Procedures Commencing with Initial Contact by Law Enforcement Officer

Article III. Arrest, Citation, Summons and Pretrial Release

Article IV. Search and Seizure

Article V. Pretrial Procedures: Discovery

Article VI. Pretrial Procedures: Joinder and Severance

Article VII. Pleas of Guilty and Nolo Contendere

Article VIII. Speedy Trial

Article IX. Trial by Jury

Article X. Appeal and Other Post-Conviction Proceedings [although article's title refers to appeals, its rules concerning criminal appeals are superseded by the Arkansas Rules of Appellate Procedure – Criminal]

Article XI. News Media Coverage of Criminal Cases

---

13. Ark. R. Crim. P. 1.3.

14. For example, although Article III of the Arkansas Rules of Criminal Procedure governs arrests, statutory procedures to be followed in making arrests are set out in Ark. Code Ann. § 16-81-107 (2005).

15. The rules are based on the Model Code of Pre-Arraignment Procedure (Am. Law Inst. 1972).

D. Evidence

Conflicts between judicial and legislative rules of evidence have been particularly problematic in Arkansas. Previously, there were two different sets of
rules of evidence in the state, one judicial and one statutory; they were substantially the same, although not identical. Amendment 80 superseded and
repealed the statutory version.[16] However,

> some statutes falling outside of the repealed rules implicate eviden-
> tiary matters and remain on the books. These statutes continue to be
> questioned in the courts because Amendment 80 gives the Supreme
> Court exclusive authority to "prescribe the rules of pleading, prac-
> tice and procedure for all courts," so long as the rules do not "abridge,
> enlarge or modify any substantive right."[17]

Therefore, always consult the Arkansas Rules of Evidence, but keep in mind
that a statute might also be relevant.

E. Professional Conduct

Since 2005, Arkansas's Model Rules of Professional Conduct have mirrored
the ABA's Model Rules of Professional Conduct. As stated in its per curiam
order of March 3, 2005, the Arkansas Supreme Court declined to adopt only
one of the ABA's rules, Rule 3.8(e) (limiting the ability of prosecutors to sub-
poena lawyers in grand jury or other criminal proceedings).

Explanations of the current rules are appended as Comments, and in
many instances, a rule is also annotated with a "Code Comparison Prior to
2005 Revision," which explores differences in the current rule and its predecessor.[18]

---

16. *See* 2013 Ark. Acts 1148 (repealing dozens of procedural statutes).

17. Newbern et al., *supra* note 3, at § 1:9 (quoting Ark. Const. amend. 80, § 3).

18. Until 1985, ethical rules governing lawyers in Arkansas were set out in the
Code of Professional Responsibility. In the mid-eighties, the Arkansas Supreme Court
adopted a somewhat amended version of the Model Rules of Professional Conduct
developed by the American Bar Association. *In re Amendment to Rules of the Court
Regulating Professional Conduct of Attorneys at Law*, 288 Ark. 643, 643, 702 S.W.2d
785, 785 (1986). These rules were themselves superseded by the rules currently in effect, but you may find references to them in prior case law.

III. Federal Court Rules

Like Arkansas courts, federal courts have the power to create rules relating to the way business is conducted in the federal judicial system.[19] National rules include the Federal Rules of Appellate Procedure, the Federal Rules of Civil Procedure, the Federal Rules of Criminal Procedure, and the Federal Rules of Evidence. These rules apply uniformly to all federal courts. Some procedural requirements are found in federal statutes, primarily within Title 28 of the *United States Code.*

Besides these federal rules and statutes, some rules apply only to certain courts, such as the United States Supreme Court or the federal bankruptcy courts. Finally, all lower federal courts promulgate their own procedural rules, called *local rules.* Local rules are permitted to supplement the national rules but must not be inconsistent with them or any acts of Congress.[20]

IV. Finding Court Rules

A. Finding Court Rules in Online Sources

State court rules and federal court rules are available on Fastcase, Lexis and Westlaw. All Arkansas state court rules are available on the *Arkansas Judiciary* website, at https://courts.arkansas.gov/.

Current local rules of the federal courts are available on the respective websites of those courts:

- United States Supreme Court: www.supremecourtus.gov.
- Eighth Circuit Court of Appeals: www.ca8.uscourts.gov.
- U.S. District Court for the Eastern District of Arkansas: www.are .uscourts.gov.
- U.S. District Court for the Western District of Arkansas: www.arwd .uscourts.gov.
- U.S. Bankruptcy Court of both the Eastern and Western Districts of Arkansas: www.arb.uscourts.gov.[21]

---

19. *See* 28 U.S.C. §§ 2071(a), 2072 (2012).

20. *See* 28 U.S.C. § 2071.

21. Although online sources of court rules are typically updated on a regular basis, for guidance on updating court rules in electronic media, see Chapter 9.

B. Finding Court Rules in Print Sources

1. State Sources

The official source for state court rules of procedure is the soft-cover "Court Rules" volume of the *Arkansas Code of 1987*. This volume is updated and replaced annually, and it is supplemented by the *Arkansas Code Service*. In addition to providing the text of and annotations to all Arkansas state court rules, this volume also contains text and annotations for local rules of the federal courts in Arkansas, including the United States District Courts for the Eastern and Western Districts of Arkansas, the United States Bankruptcy Courts for the Eastern and Western Districts of Arkansas, and local rules of the United States Court of Appeals for the Eighth Circuit.

There are several unofficial sources for state court rules. *West's Arkansas Code Annotated* has a two-volume set of annotated court rules. Volume 1 contains the Rules of Civil Procedure and the Rules of Criminal Procedure; Volume 2 contains everything else, plus local rules for the Eighth Circuit and the Arkansas federal district and bankruptcy courts.

2. Federal Sources

National rules for federal courts are published in the U.S.C., and in the unofficial U.S.C.A. and U.S.C.S.

3. Using Print Sources

Each set of rules is indexed; the key to finding a court rule through an index is to use the correct index for the specific type of rule you're searching for. This may sound simple, but with similarly numbered rules and many sets of rules in one volume, it's easy to find yourself using the wrong index. Alternatively, scan the complete list of rules at the beginning of a particular set to find the rule you're looking for.[22]

---

22. For guidance on updating court rules in print sources, see Chapter 9.

Chapter 9

Updating Your Research

I. Introduction

You've invested a lot of time finding relevant sources for an issue you're researching, and you have found quite a few. Now you can relax, yes? No.

It isn't enough to find sources relevant to the issue. "Relevance" encompasses a lot of concepts, things like the following: primary law from the applicable jurisdiction, a statute defining key terms, a case with facts that are tantalizingly similar to yours, a law review article calling for the Supreme Court to alter its interpretation of a constitutional provision. Certainly finding these things means that you've successfully utilized the tools of legal research addressed in the earlier chapters of this book.

But if you haven't updated what you've found, you may be relying — and unjustifiably relying — on sources that are no longer current, no longer valid, no longer accepted, no longer convincing. Unless your research investigates whether the sources you've found are both current and valid, you aren't through yet. Updating your finds makes you a more effective researcher.

- It means you're aware of the ways primary authorities can affect one another's validity. (Remember how the structure of government relies on that system of checks and balances?)
- It means you recognize the value in knowing how an authority written (or enacted, or promulgated, or decided) at one time has been regarded by subsequent writers and decision-makers.
- It means that in predicting or advocating the outcome of a legal issue, you'll avoid making any huge errors because your analysis or argument will be grounded in current law.
- It means you're seeing connections between authorities. By discovering those connections, you can tell whether one authority has relied on or disregarded others.

- It means that you're more efficient in finding all the law relevant to the resolution of an issue, saving time and taking comfort in knowing you haven't overlooked anything that's necessary or helpful.

This chapter discusses a multitude of ways by which you can ensure that the fruits of your labor represent current and valid sources of law. It addresses both print and online tools and the means to ensure you have the most current information on the law. It demonstrates ways you can tell whether your finds represent the most current and valid representation of the law on a given topic. Finally, although this book has generally treated online research tools before addressing their print counterparts, this chapter begins with advice for updating print sources with print tools, because those methods supply the theoretical underpinning for updating via electronic means. It then addresses methods of supplementation and validation for either print or online sources, through the use of online tools.

II. Updating Print Sources by Checking for Supplements

As this book's previous chapters on specific sources demonstrate, when revisions are necessary to print sources such as books, treatises, statutory codes, and similar publications, publishers do not have many options. Due to the cost of producing a hard-bound volume, particularly when the volume is one of a series, these volumes tend not to be reprinted on a frequent basis. Instead, publishers will create a soft-bound supplement to augment the bound volume until such time as the volume (or the entire series) is reprinted.

When you use a print resource published in a hard-bound volume, check the back of the volume for a supplemental insert, also referred to as a *pocket part*. A pocket part is the publisher's way of updating the content of the printed volume with subsequent information that may affect the text itself, its history, or its impact.

Because some sources — in particular, statutory codes — are subject to frequent changes, pocket parts are a convenient form of updating their contents. A pocket part will display its date of publication, typically on the front page, but sometimes on its copyright page. If you are using a pocket part, locate that date to determine the supplement's currency, considering that the most recent pocket part may not yet have been inserted.

When a pocket part gets too large to permit the hard-bound volume to easily close, publishers will place the updated material into a separate soft-bound supplement. Supplements are typically shelved adjacent to the hard-bound volumes they accompany. Like a pocket part supplement, a soft-bound supplement will display its date of publication in a prominent location. Publications which undergo frequent changes may use both soft-bound supplements and pocket parts. Check for both. Depending on the source and the custom of its publisher, a pocket part or supplement may contain only the text of additions, revisions, and indicators of deletions. Others will reproduce the entire text of the revised section.

Looseleaf publications take advantage of their binder- or notebook-style design to insert new pages or substitute revised pages for outdated material. Many looseleaf services feature a preliminary section highlighting recent developments and other changes. As with pocket parts and supplements, look for a date indicating the currency of the service's coverage.

III. Updating Online Sources by Checking Their Currency and Validity

Prudent researchers are not satisfied with the mere appearance of an authority in an official website or an online database; they want to know whether the version represented on the screen is current, and they want to know whether the representation remains valid. To determine the extent of a database's reliability, look for a notation indicating the date through which the version represented on the screen is current. Reliable online providers continually update their sites. If you encounter outdated information, be wary of relying on the accuracy or currency of the information it provides.

In most instances, the official online or a commercial database version of a primary authority such as a constitution, a statute, or an administrative rule or regulation will have incorporated all recent changes to that authority — whether that authority has new provisions, has been amended, or has been repealed. You must determine whether the version you have found represents the current state of the applicable provision, as the provision not only governs contemporary situations but also operates prospectively. For statutory authorities in particular, depending on the customs of the online publisher, the currency notation may indicate a specific date, a specific act or public law, or the end of a specific legislative session.[1]

---

1. For guidance on how to use citations to indicate the currency of a statutory or legislative source retrieved from an online database, see Appendix A.

In contrast, a judicial opinion, once the case is finally decided by a court of law, is no longer subject to updates in the form of amendment or editing. Certainly, the written opinion of a trial court or an intermediate court of appeals may be reviewed by a higher court, but when that happens, the higher court will write its own opinion addressing the correctness of the lower court's ruling. The continuing validity of a case is determined by checking its *direct history* (also known as its *subsequent history*) to determine whether it was *affirmed* (approved), *reversed* (disapproved), or *reversed and remanded* (disapproved and sent back to the lower court for further action). In these instances, the subsequent history of the case affects the ultimate outcome of the case originating in the trial court.

A case may be *overruled*, however, in a subsequent, unrelated case when the same court or a higher court reconsiders the basis for its original holding and disagrees with the rule or reasoning as stated in the original case. An overruling cannot change the outcome of the original case, but it does change the law for new cases addressing the same issue in future proceedings.[2] Methods for determining a case's subsequent history via online tools are addressed in this chapter's Section IV, below.

As for secondary authorities, their currency and validity depend on the nature of the work. Periodical articles, for instance, are static; once published, they do not change. By noting their date of publication, the researcher can determine the likelihood of their being current.

With regard to online versions of secondary authorities such as treatises, encyclopedias, practice aids, and the like, an online database may indicate their dates of publication or most recent revisions as a means of reflecting their currency, particularly where the authority is an electronic version of a source whose print counterpart is updated through supplements. In the case of a secondary authority whose contents remain static, the database may provide links to more recent publications of that secondary authority or to related secondary sources.

No matter whether you have used a print or an online version of an authority, you are not through updating merely because you have looked for a print version's pocket part or checked a database's "current through" date. You must also use a *citator*.

---

2. A full citation to a case must include its subsequent history. See Appendix A for explanation and illustrations.

IV. Updating Primary Sources with Citators

We didn't always have citators. *Shepard's Citations* ("Shepard's") was the first American citator system, created in 1873 to help lawyers find case law citing earlier cases as precedent.[3] Originally a multi-volume and heavily supplemented print resource, Shepard's has evolved into an electronic resource available to Lexis subscribers. Today's researchers have other choices as well. Westlaw's *KeyCite* is an online citator that produces results comparable to Shepard's in terms of its wide scope and analytical depth. Limited citator services are available from *BCite* (Bloomberg Law) and *Authority Check* (Fastcase), and new applications for conducting and updating online legal research continue to be developed.[4]

A citator provides three important kinds of information about an authority. First, it indicates an authority's *subsequent history*, i.e., whether the authority has been amended, repealed, affirmed, reversed, overruled, modified, or otherwise treated in a way that affects its scope or validity. For example, the electorate may approve an amendment that repeals an existing provision of the constitution. A legislature may amend or repeal a statute. An agency may adopt a regulation that supersedes existing rules. The holding of a case decided by the Arkansas Court of Appeals may later be overruled by the Arkansas Supreme Court. In any of these situations, you must determine whether the specific source you found is still good law and whether it still can be relied upon.

A citator also indicates an authority's *treatment* and the number of its *citing references*. Researchers want to know whether the authority has been discussed to any degree by later sources. For example, when a secondary source or a court from a different jurisdiction discusses a statute or a case, it's useful

---

3. Shepard's longevity (and for decades, its lack of competitors) is responsible for the phrase "Sheparding" as a synonym for using a citator to check for an authority's subsequent history, treatment, and citing references. If you are asked to "Shepardize" a citation, you are being asked to use a citator, not necessarily to use the Shepard's product.

4. For example, the Ravel legal research system (begun in 2012) can retrieve every case from the United States Supreme Court, plus all *published* cases from the federal circuit courts of appeal since 1925, from federal district courts since 1933, and from state appellate courts since 1950. Ravel also provides access to all federal and state *unpublished* cases since May 15, 2015. *Ravel*, https://www.ravellaw.com/ (last visited Feb. 11, 2016). While Ravel does not feature a citator per se, it lists a case's citing references, and it graphically maps those references with timelines and variously sized circles that indicate the case's influence on later cases in terms of the number of their citations to it, similar to the system used in Fastcase for Authority Check.

to see their treatment of that statute or case. Do the later authorities discuss the earlier authority to any degree, and if so, to what degree? Do they criticize it? Do they adopt its reasoning? Do they simply cite it as one more example of an established principle?[5]

Whether you have used print or online research techniques to locate relevant authority, use an online citator to confirm its currency and its validity. Online citators have replaced the cumbersome process of validating sources in print. Today's researchers use online citators because they are fast, convenient, and for the two leading services (Shepard's and KeyCite), comprehensive. In addition, because they are not constrained by the limits of size, online citators need not employ the complicated abbreviation systems used by print citators to indicate the status of the material being checked. And rather than having to consult volumes and supplements of a citator in print, each covering a different time period, when you use an online citator you can access all the citing references in no more than a few clicks.

Citator services such as Shepard's, KeyCite, Authority Check, and BCite use colorful *status icons* (e.g., symbols in the form of flags or geometric shapes) to signal that a primary authority's validity has been subsequently affected, whether negatively or positively, by a later development; at the very least, all services utilize some method to indicate how a case has been treated by subsequent sources and how often it has been cited, and they furnish hyperlinks to those subsequent sources for easy access. Today's citator services display these icons whenever you retrieve an authority on the screen; you don't have to leave the page to access the citator function. It is not enough, however, merely to observe the presence of a positive or negative icon. Effective researchers take the next step, retrieving and reading the later source in order to determine the basis for its notation in the citator.

The particular features of Shepard's, KeyCite, Authority Check, and BCite citators are discussed below. Note that the descriptions of citators in this chapter represent their appearance and functions as of the time this book was published. Because these services are continually being upgraded, they may employ new or modified features that cannot be described here. Fortunately, the services are designed to be user friendly, and they offer tutorials or other instructional materials to help you navigate their current features.

---

5. While learning that a later authority has merely cited your source tells you nothing about its subsequent history, the citing authority furnishes you a tool to find more recent authorities weighing on the topics or issues addressed by the original.

A. Lexis: Shepard's

When you retrieve a case on Lexis, look for a Shepard's status icon adjacent to the case name. The absence of an icon isn't necessarily a positive thing; it simply means that no subsequent authority has said anything about the case (a somewhat rare occurrence). If an icon is present, your screen will also display a brief synopsis of results retrieved by the citator. Although you may see other icons represented in the results, the adjacent icon carries the most significance for determining the case's history or treatment. As of this writing, Shepard's signals for case law are represented by the following icons:

- a red octagon (resembling a stop sign), warning you that the case has been treated negatively by later cases;
- an orange square enclosing the letter "Q," advising you that the precedential value of the case has been questioned by later cases;
- a yellow triangle, cautioning you of the existence of possible negative treatment by later cases;
- a green diamond enclosing a plus ("+") sign, indicating that your case has been followed as precedent by later cases;
- a dark blue octagon enclosing the letter "A," indicating neutral treatment (neither positive nor negative) by later cases; and
- a dark blue circle enclosing the letter "I," serving as notice that the case has been cited by some other source(s).

Should one of these symbols be displayed in the synopsis accompanying the case, it will be followed by a figure in parentheses indicating the number of later sources who have accorded the case the treatment in question. When you click a symbol, you are presented with a page containing citations and brief summaries of the authorities who have given the case the treatment indicated by the symbol. Citing sources include sources of primary law such as later case law and annotated statutes, as well as secondary sources such as law reviews, treatises, restatements, and other commentary.

Shepard's citator entries for statutes use the same symbols and notations as those used for cases — with one addition. When a statute has been found unconstitutional or received negative treatment by a court, you will see a different symbol: a red-outlined circle enclosing a red exclamation mark ("!"). Shepard's citator results for statutes also indicate their legislative history and where any exist, archived copies of previous versions of the statutes. Just as with cases, you can narrow the results, and whatever the results you obtain, all will include brief summaries and links to citing references.

Additional editorial features provide another boon to researchers. You can filter results with the "narrow by" option, limiting them to particular topics (the "headnotes" feature), to specific jurisdictions or courts, and even to specific types of authority. Shepard's "Timeline" feature uses a bar graph to depict the increasing (or decreasing) number of citing references within a range of dates (e.g., from the date of the decision or date of enactment to the present). Annotations for citing references include a horizontal bar made of four cells, indicating the citing reference's "Depth of Discussion." The greater the number of filled-in cells, the greater the discussion of the Shepardized authority.

B. Westlaw: KeyCite

When you retrieve a case on Westlaw, look for a KeyCite symbol in the page header. If the case has negative history or treatment, you will see a colored flag:

- a red flag indicates that the case has significant negative history, alerting the researcher that one or more points of law addressed by the case should no longer be followed (typically because the case has been reversed or overruled on that point);
- a yellow flag cautions that the case has received some form of negative treatment, such as criticism or disapproval by another court which lacks the power to overrule the case; and
- for cases in the federal courts, a striped blue flag indicates a pending appeal.

Whether or not a flag is present, you can narrow the citator results by choosing one of the tabs shown above the text of the case — "Notes of Decisions," "History," "Citing References," "Context & Analysis" — each label being followed by a number in parentheses indicating how many items are addressed under that category. Click the tab to see a list of the sources in its category. The Citing References tab provides links to any and all resources on Westlaw that have directly cited the case you are checking, whether they are other cases, other statutes, administrative regulations or decisions, secondary authorities, or court documents. The Context & Analysis tab contains links to sources that deal with or bear some relation to the case's issues and topics, including annotations, encyclopedias, and commentaries, among others.

Subsequent cases are the most common citing references, and a single case may have several Notes of Decisions, corresponding to the topic/key number headnotes associated with it. Citing references may also include materials such as attorney general opinions, secondary sources, and court documents (e.g., briefs). Each citing reference is accompanied by a "depth of treatment" bar displaying one to four colored blocks to indicate the extent to which the case is discussed in the citing reference; a quotation mark icon indicates a source that has quoted the cited case.

When you retrieve a statute in Westlaw, you may see a flag adjacent to the statute's citation, accompanied by a brief notation of its significance. Red and yellow flags carry significance similar to those used for case law. A red flag alerts the researcher that the statute has been repealed or found unconstitutional. A yellow flag indicates that the provision has been modified or affected in a way meriting the researcher's attention.

No matter whether the statute is flagged, above the statutory text on screen, just as with cases, you'll see the tabs for "Notes of Decisions," "History," "Citing References," and "Context & Analysis." And just as they do for case law, the Notes of Decisions for a statute (sometimes represented in a table by the acronym "NOD") represent headnotes in cases interpreting or applying the statute, accompanied by citations to the cases and the topic/key number for each headnote.

The History tab operates differently. Clicking this tab opens an overview presenting an array of choices: a graphical depiction of the statute's legislative history and any proposed legislation that may affect it in the future; the version of the statute as it existed on a particular date; all drafts of the bills that preceded the statute's enactment; links to cases, session laws, public laws, and proposed legislation connected to the statute; analyses of the statute prepared by West editors; and additional legislative history resources relating to the processes of debate and consideration of the bill as it worked its way through the legislative process.

C. Fastcase: Authority Check

Authority Check is Fastcase's abbreviated citator equivalent. It searches for positive or negative references to a case cited in a subsequent case. As Fastcase explains, "Authority Check is an automated system that identifies later-citing cases, but it is not a citator, and does not include editorial information telling you whether your case is still good law."[6] For a statute, click Authority Check to access a list of cases that have cited it. As of this writing, Fastcase does not provide researchers with indications of positive treatment, nor does it provide commentary, analysis, or links to non-case-law authorities. It does, however, provide links to cases that have cited a statute.

---

6. Fastcase, *Authority Check*, https://apps.fastcase.com/Research/Help/Authority CheckHelp.htm (last visited Feb. 17, 2016).

D. Bloomberg Law: BCite

Similar to the icons used by Shepard's and KeyCite, BCite's colored geometric shapes adjacent to a case citation symbolize its direct history or treatment by later authorities:

- a red square containing a minus ("−") sign tells researchers that the authority has negative direct history or treatment;
- a yellow square enclosing a triangle signals direct history or treatment that warrants caution in relying on the authority;
- a blue square containing a plus ("+") sign represents positive treatment of the authority;
- a blue square containing a diagonal slash ("/") indicates that the authority has been treated as distinguishable from the citing reference;
- an orange square enclosing a dot means that the authority has been superseded, typically by legislative enactment; and
- a gray square containing a plus sign indicates that the authority has no citing references.

Each citing reference retrieved by BCite is rated by a "strength of discussion" indicator (strong, moderate, or weak) or a "citation frequency indicator" (showing the number of times it has been cited). Strong or moderate ratings or a high number of citations should prompt the researcher to consult those citing references to determine how in fact they have treated the authority.

E. Comparing Services

As the preceding discussion has explained, each service has its advantages and disadvantages. While cost is always a factor in selecting resources, the necessity of using some reliable resource to ensure you are using current and valid sources of law is imperative. If you are a student with free access to multiple kinds of citators, take advantage of that access to familiarize yourself with their attributes, and compare the results you get.

This chapter concludes with tables comparing citator results for an Arkansas case and an Arkansas statute.[7] Using Shepard's, KeyCite, Authority Check, and BCite, Table 9-1 illustrates the differences in citator results for *Madison v. Osburn*, 2012 Ark. App. 212, 396 S.W.3d 264, a case concerning whether the purported grandparents of a child could seek visitation rights; its reliance on a fitness standard for guardianship proceedings over a statu-

---

7. The entries in Tables 9-1 and 9-2 reflect citator results displayed on February 13, 2016.

tory preference for natural parents was later overruled by the Arkansas Court of Appeals.[8]

Table 9-1. Comparing Citator Results for
***Madison v. Osburn*, 2012 Ark. App. 212, 396 S.W.3d 264**

Citator service	Shepard's (Lexis)	KeyCite (Westlaw)	Authority Check (Fastcase)	BCite (Bloomberg Law)
Status icon	Red octagon	Red flag	None	Red square containing minus sign
Explanation of icon's significance	"Warning"	"Severe Negative Treatment"	None	"Negative"
Summary of history or treatment	"Overruled in part by Furr v. James"	"Overruled by Furr v. James, Ark.App., March 13, 2013"	Displays portion of opinion from *Furr v. James* stating, "Though neither party here relied on *Madison*, we take this opportunity to overrule *Madison* . . . ."	"No negative subsequent direct history" "Overruled in Part in Furr v. James, 2013 Ark. App. 181, 427 S.W.3d 94"
Number of citing authorities (with breakdown, if available)	Two 1 case (*Furr*) 1 law review	Nine 1 case (*Furr*) 7 secondary sources (including 1 law review and 6 practice aids or legal encyclopedias) 1 trial court document	One 1 case (*Furr*)	One 1 case (*Furr*)

---

8. *Furr v. James*, 2013 Ark. App. 181, at *6, 427 S.W.3d 94, 98.

Table 9-2. Comparing Citator Results for Ark. Code Ann. § 6-18-702

Citator Service	Shepard's (Lexis)	KeyCite (Westlaw)	Authority Check (Fastcase)	BCite (Bloomberg Law)
Currency	"Current through the 2015 Regular Session and First Extraordinary Session."	"Current through 2015 Reg. Sess. and 2015 1st Ex. Sess. of the 90th Arkansas General Assembly, including changes made by the Ark. Code Rev. Comm. received through 11/1/2015."	"Arkansas Code (2015 edition)"	"Current through Act 12 of the First Extraordinary Session 2015"
Indication of enactment, repeal, or amendment	"Acts 1967, No. 244, §§ 1-3; 1973, No. 633, § 1; 1983, No. 150, § 1; A.S.A. 1947, §§ 80-1548 — 80-1550; Acts 1997, No. 871, § 1; 1999, No. 1222, §§ 1 , 2; 2003, No. 999, § 1; 2005, No. 1994, § 185."	"Enacted Legislation Acts of 2005, Act 1994, § 185, eff. Aug. 12, 2005"	"Acts 1967, No. 244, §§ 1-3; 1973, No. 633, § 1; 1983, No. 150, § 1; A.S.A. 1947, §§ 80-1548 — 80-1550; Acts 1997, No. 871, § 1; 1999, No. 1222, §§ 1, 2; 2003, No. 999, § 1; 2005, No. 1994, § 185."	"Document Last Updated 2005, No. 1994, § 185."
Status icon	Red circle enclosing exclamation mark	Yellow flag	None	None
Explanation of icon's significance	"Warning: Negative case treatment is indicated for statute"	"Negative Treatment"	None	None

Summary of history or treatment	"Warning 2 Unconstitutional by 2 Unconstitutional in part by 1" "Positive 1 Constitutional by 1" "Neutral 2 Interpreted or construed by 2"	"Unconstitutional or Preempted | Prior Version Held Unconstitutional by Boone v. Boozman | E.D.Ark. | Aug. 12, 2002"	None	None
Total citing authorities (breakdown, if available)	36 3 federal courts (Eighth Circuit) 1 state court (Arkansas) 32 other citing sources (including 26 law reviews, 6 statutory annotations)	91 19 Notes of Decisions (drawn from 5 cases) 1 statute 4 regulations 3 administrative decisions & guidance 34 secondary sources (including 30 law reviews, 1 legal encyclopedia, 3 "other") 6 appellate court documents 30 trial court documents	4 4 cases, all federal (1 Eighth Circuit, 2 E.D. Ark., 1 W.D. Ark.)	None

Table 9-2 compares citator results for a current Arkansas statute addressing immunization requirements for children, Ark. Code Ann. § 6-18-702. A prior version of § 6-18-702 was held unconstitutional by the United States District Court for the Eastern District of Arkansas,[9] information that is of critical importance to researchers who need to know whether they can rely on cases referring to the statute's prior version. Because Authority Check indicates nothing more than the date through which its publication of a statute is current, it cannot be used to check a statute's subsequent history or treatment. BCite similarly gives no indication of a statute's later treatment, but in addition to the currency information, it advises the researcher of the most recent modification to the statute.

---

9. *Boone v. Boozman*, 217 F. Supp. 2d 938, 950 (E.D. Ark. 2002).

Appendix A

Essentials of Legal Citation

I. Introduction

A legal citation conveys more information than just the name and location of the referenced source. Case citations, for example, contain important clues about the hierarchy, currency, and value of the precedent. Moreover, a case citation may direct readers to an official or an unofficial version of a court's opinion, or to both. Statutory citations similarly indicate whether the writer relied upon an official or an unofficial code; they also reveal whether the writer is relying on the most current version of a statute. Citations to secondary sources such as law review articles distinguish between student-written and more authoritative commentary.

The most widely used national guides to citation are the *ALWD Guide to Legal Citation* and *The Bluebook: A Uniform System of Citation*. The citations produced via these texts are virtually the same. The main differences between the texts stem from each book's primary focus and its intended users.

ALWD focuses on the citation formats used by practicing lawyers in every-day legal documents such as office memoranda or briefs, whether those citations appear in the body of the text or in footnotes. However, because academic writing places citations into footnotes, employing a different type-face for certain citation components, *ALWD* citation rules are supplemented with specially marked subsections that demonstrate the formatting changes required for academic footnotes.

Bluebook, in contrast, focuses on academic writing, and its basic citation formats are those used in footnotes to scholarly works, such as law review articles, academic textbooks, and treatises. To convert a scholarly *Bluebook* citation into the format used by practicing lawyers, a writer consults the "Bluepages" section in the front of the book to determine any necessary formatting changes.

Pay attention to the presence of local court rules affecting citation. While some states expressly mandate the citation system to use, *ALWD* and *Bluebook* citations are equally acceptable in Arkansas practice. Local rules are addressed below in certain subsections. The only local rule significantly affecting Arkansas citation practice is one requiring a case citation to include reference to both official and unofficial case reporters (a practice known as *parallel citation*) in briefs submitted to the Arkansas Supreme Court or the Arkansas Court of Appeals. Other local rules in Arkansas allow for optional abbreviations. Many Arkansas lawyers don't realize it, but the common abbreviation "A.C.A." used to refer to the *Arkansas Code of 1987 Annotated* is in fact authorized by statute. Similarly, you may abbreviate the Arkansas Rules of Civil Procedure as "ARCP," and the Arkansas Rules of Evidence as "A.R.E." It's fine to use these optional abbreviations within the state. If your document has a wider audience, however, stick with national standards of citation, as this book does.

Accurate citations make it easy for your readers to locate the authorities upon which you have relied. Whether your writing is intended to objectively analyze an issue or to persuade a court, its citations should refer to the precise sources relied upon, and they should be constructed according to standardized conventions of the legal profession.

II. Citing Specific Sources

This section sets out examples of citations to the most common types of legal authorities, and for each type, it will direct you to specific *ALWD* and *Bluebook*/Bluepages rule numbers, tables, and appendices. Tables in the subsections illustrate citations in practitioner format, such as you would use in a brief, contrasted with the same citations in academic footnote format. Note that in both practitioner and academic formatting, some citation components use *italics*. In academic formatting, a few citation components use LARGE AND SMALL CAPITALS. No matter what kind of source you cite, give your readers a *pinpoint reference* pointing to the specific location (page, section, or paragraph) of the cited information.

A. Constitutions

To cite a constitution currently in force, abbreviate its name and the article or amendment. Unless you are citing an entire article or amendment, cite specific section number(s).

Table A-1. Citing Constitutions Currently in Force

Practitioner Format	Academic Format
Ark. Const. art. 2, § 15.	Ark. Const. art. 2, § 15.
U.S. Const. amend. XXIII.	U.S. Const. amend. XXIII.

To cite a constitution no longer in force or a constitutional provision which has been superseded, amended, or repealed, the citation must indicate that it does not refer to the *current* document. Indicate either the date of repeal or amendment or the specific provision amended or repealed by later amendment.

Table A-2. Citing Constitutional Provisions No Longer in Force

Practitioner Format	Academic Format
Ark. Const. of 1836, art. 2.	Ark. Const. of 1836, art. 2.
Ark. Const. amend. 3 (repealed 1982).	Ark. Const. amend. 3 (repealed 1982).
Ark. Const. art. 5, § 1, *amended by* Ark. Const. amend. 7.	Ark. Const. art. 5, § 1, *amended by* Ark. Const. amend. 7.
U.S. Const. amend. XVIII, *repealed by* U.S. Const. amend. XXI.	U.S. Const. amend. XVIII, *repealed by* U.S. Const. amend. XXI.

B. Secondary Sources in Print

This section discusses citations for secondary sources having the highest persuasive value in legal writing: books, treatises, restatements, and periodical articles.

1. Books, Treatises, and Practice Manuals

Key components of a citation to a book, treatise, or practice manual are references to the author(s); the title; the specific pages, paragraphs, or sections referred to; and the date of publication.

When a work has three or more authors, you may replace names following the first named author with the phrase "et al." (meaning "and others"). When a title ends in a number, add a comma and the preposition "at" before the pinpoint reference. If the work is published by an entity other than the original publisher or published in a later edition than the original, add the newer publisher's name and/or the later edition's number to the date parenthetical. A citation to material in a single volume of a multi-volume work indicates the volume number in front of the author's name.

Table A-3. Citing Books, Treatises, and Practice Manuals in Print

Practitioner Format	ACADEMIC FORMAT
John Wesley Hall, Jr., *Search and Seizure* 102 (5th ed. 2013).	JOHN WESLEY HALL, JR., SEARCH AND SEIZURE 102 (5th ed. 2013).
Bernadette Cahill, *Arkansas Women and the Right to Vote: The Little Rock Campaigns, 1868-1920*, at 32 (2015).	BERNADETTE CAHILL, ARKANSAS WOMEN AND THE RIGHT TO VOTE: THE LITTLE ROCK CAMPAIGNS, 1868-1920, at 32 (2015).
Robert B. Buckalew et al., *Maximizing Damages in an Arkansas Personal Injury Case: From Start to Finish* 34 (2014).	ROBERT B. BUCKALEW ET AL., MAXIMIZING DAMAGES IN AN ARKANSAS PERSONAL INJURY CASE: FROM START TO FINISH 34 (2014).
Louis Fisher, *Constitutional Conflicts Between Congress and the President* 104 (Univ. Press of Kan. 3d rev. ed. 1991).	LOUIS FISHER, CONSTITUTIONAL CONFLICTS BETWEEN CONGRESS AND THE PRESIDENT 104 (Univ. Press of Kan. 3d rev. ed. 1991).
2 Austin Wakeman Scott, William Franklin Fratcher & Mark L. Ascher, *Scott and Ascher on Trusts* § 11.3 (5th ed. 2006).	2 AUSTIN WAKEMAN SCOTT, WILLIAM FRANKLIN FRATCHER & MARK L. ASCHER, SCOTT AND ASCHER ON TRUSTS § 11.3 (5th ed. 2006).

2. Restatements

A restatement's citation includes its title, a pinpoint reference, and in parentheses, the year of publication. The *Bluebook* adds the abbreviated name of the publisher.

Table A-4. Citing Restatements

Practitioner Format	ACADEMIC FORMAT
Restatement (Second) of Torts § 324A (1965).	RESTATEMENT (SECOND) OF TORTS § 324A (AM. LAW INST. 1965).

3. Periodical Articles

To cite an article in a periodical, first determine its system of page numbering (i.e., its *pagination*). This determination is essential because of differences in the components and their order.

A periodical uses *consecutive pagination* when it begins with page 1 in a volume's first issue and continues that numbering through the volume's entire series of issues. Law reviews typically employ consecutive pagination. For example, a volume's third issue can *begin* on page 543. A typical citation to an article in a consecutively paginated journal shows the name of the author(s), the article's title, the volume number of the journal, the journal's abbreviation, the page on which the article begins, the page(s) on which the specific information is located, and in parentheses, the year of publication. Student-written articles are indicated by inserting a descriptive noun for the work (e.g., "Note," "Comment") immediately after the author's name.

A periodical uses *non-consecutive pagination* when it starts page numbering on page 1 in each new issue. A typical citation to an article in a non-consecutively paginated journal shows the author name(s), the article's italicized title, the periodical's volume number, its abbreviation, the specific date of the issue (abbreviating month names), and following the preposition "at," the specific page(s) cited.

Table A-5. Citing Periodical Articles

Practitioner Format	ACADEMIC FORMAT
Lindsey P. Gustafson, *Making the Peg Fit the Hole: A Superior Solution to the Inherent Problems of Incorporated Definitions*, 37 U. Ark. Little Rock L. Rev. 363, 367-68 (2015).	Lindsey P. Gustafson, *Making the Peg Fit the Hole: A Superior Solution to the Inherent Problems of Incorporated Definitions*, 37 U. ARK. LITTLE ROCK L. REV. 363, 367-68 (2015).
Patricia Medige, *Immigrant Labor Issues*, 32 Denv. J. Int'l L. & Pol'y 735 (2004).	Patricia Medige, *Immigrant Labor Issues*, 32 DENV. J. INT'L L. & POL'Y 735 (2004).
Stephan R. Leimberg & Leo C. Hodges, *The Income Tax and Estate Planning Advantages of Private Annuities*, Est. Plan., Feb. 2006, at 3.	Stephan R. Leimberg & Leo C. Hodges, *The Income Tax and Estate Planning Advantages of Private Annuities*, EST. PLAN., Feb. 2006, at 3.

C. Case Law

A citation to case law conveys an abundance of information, including both the case name and the physical location of the case, i.e., its reporter address, and also important information about its weight, including which court decided it, how recent it is, and whether its impact has been subsequently altered due to its being affirmed, reversed, or overruled.

Be cautious about copying citations as they appear in other published sources, as the citation formats used there may not comply with current citation rules. In particular, do not copy case citations as they appear in digests or online commercial publishers' databases, as those publishers use their own in-house formats, including abbreviations that do not match national standards. Moreover, such in-house citations typically omit essential references to any subsequent history the case may have undergone.

A *full citation* to a case sets out the italicized or underlined names of the adversarial parties, the volume of the regional reporter in which the case is published, an abbreviation for that reporter, the page number on which the case begins, the specific page(s) referenced, and in parentheses, an abbreviation for the court issuing the opinion, the date the opinion was released, and if applicable, a reference to the case's significant subsequent history.

Arkansas court rules require the use of parallel citations in briefs to the Arkansas Supreme Court or the Arkansas Court of Appeals. To construct a parallel citation, give the volume, reporter abbreviation, initial page, and pinpoint page from the official reporter, and then do the same for the unofficial South Western Reporter, followed by the date of the opinion in parentheses. If the case is published in an online database but not the South Western Reporter, the court rules require citation to the online version in the parallel citation, including the exact date of its publication. Because the official reporter shows the reader which court decided the case, omit the court's abbreviation from the date parenthetical.

Beginning in July 2009, the Arkansas Supreme Court and the Arkansas Court of Appeals stopped publishing their official opinions in print; instead, the official opinions are available online at the *Arkansas Judiciary* website, https://courts.arkansas.gov/, under the "Opinions and Disciplinary Decisions" link. Cite an online official opinion using the case name, the year of the opinion's issuance, the court, the case's sequential number, and a pinpoint reference.

To cite the non-majority part of an opinion, in addition to the citation elements listed above, add a parenthetical that indicates the surname of the author of the minority opinion, followed by the abbreviation "J." (which stands for "Judge" or "Justice"), and indicate what kind of opinion it is—concurring or dissenting.

If the court that originally issued the case or a higher court has subsequently released a ruling that affects the weight or validity of the case, the citation appends an explanatory clause setting out that *subsequent history*. Subsequent history indicates the action taken by the later court and the volume, reporter, initial page, and parenthetical reference to the later court and the date of its action.

Table A-6. Citing Cases

Practitioner Format	Academic Format
State v. Bostick, 856 S.W.2d 12, 13 (Ark. 1993). [regional reporter citation]	State v. Bostick, 856 S.W.2d 12, 13 (Ark. 1993).
State v. Bostick, 313 Ark. 596, 598, 856 S.W.2d 12, 13 (1993). [Arkansas parallel citation]	Citations in academic footnotes do not conform to local citation rules for briefs.
Huffman v. Fisher, 976 S.W.2d 401, 404 (Ark. Ct. App. 1998), *rev'd*, 987 S.W.2d 269 (Ark. 1999). [regional reporter citation]	Huffman v. Fisher, 976 S.W.2d 401, 404 (Ark. Ct. App. 1998), *rev'd*, 987 S.W.2d 269 (Ark. 1999).
Huffman v. Fisher, 63 Ark. App. 174, 180, 976 S.W.2d 401, 404 (Ark. Ct. App. 1998), *rev'd*, 987 S.W.2d 269 (Ark. 1999). [Arkansas parallel citation]	Citations in academic footnotes do not conform to local citation rules for briefs.
Lacy v. State, 44 S.W.3d 296, 298 (Ark. 2001), *overruled by Grillot v. State*, 107 S.W.3d 136 (Ark. 2003). [regional reporter citation]	Lacy v. State, 44 S.W.3d 296, 298 (Ark. 2001), *overruled by* Grillot v. State, 107 S.W.3d 136 (Ark. 2003).
Furnas v. Kimbrell, 2014 Ark. 501, at 1-2, 2014 WL 6852040, at **1. [Arkansas parallel citation; case not published in regional reporter]	Furnas v. Kimbrell, 2014 Ark. 501, at 1-2, 2014 WL 6852040, at **1.
Wilson v. Norris, 879 F. Supp. 936, 937 (E.D. Ark. 1994).	Wilson v. Norris, 879 F. Supp. 936, 937 (E.D. Ark. 1994).
United States v. Keenan, 753 F.2d 681, 683 (8th Cir. 1985) (per curiam).	United States v. Keenan, 753 F.2d 681, 683 (8th Cir. 1985) (per curiam).

D. Statutes, Session Laws, and Local Ordinances

Citations to statutory authorities—including statutes, session laws, and local ordinances—are less standardized than citations to other types of primary authority, due to the particular requirements of a particular juris-diction, whether the statute has an official or popular name, whether the code is annotated or unannotated, whether the code contains numbered titles or subject-matter designations, and whether the cited material is of-ficial or unofficial, in print or online. This section focuses on citations to Arkansas and federal statutory sources in print and online, whether they are codified statutes or uncodified session laws, as well as citations to local ordinances.

1. Statutes Currently in Force

Codified Arkansas statutes are published in official and unofficial print versions and in unofficial electronic versions. Because a legislature has the power to modify an existing statute, be sure you are citing its most current version, and if possible, cite its official version. Use the abbreviation for the *Arkansas Code of 1987* (Ark. Code Ann.), followed by the section symbol (§), the section number, and in a parenthetical, the date. Even though the official code is published by Lexis, it is not necessary to identify the publisher in the official code's date parenthetical. The unofficial code in print is *West's Arkansas Code Annotated*; its date parenthetical component indicates the publish-er's name.

Although the official code is named the *Arkansas Code of 1987*, all of its original volumes have been updated and republished. Therefore, use the date on the spine of the specific volume that contains the referenced statute, or if the statute has been enacted or modified since that volume was published, the date of the *supplement* (a pocket part or separately bound volume) that con-tains it. Similarly, the date component of citations to West's unofficial code reflects the date on the title page or the copyright date of the specific volume or supplement containing the referenced statute. If you cite the electronic version of the code, the date parenthetical indicates the database provider and the legislative session through which the statute is current in that specific database.

Citations to the *United States Code* are similarly published in official and unofficial versions, and the preference is to cite the official version ("U.S.C.") if possible. Unofficial versions are published by Lexis—the *United States Code Service* ("U.S.C.S.")—and by West—the *United States Code Annotated* ("U.S.C.A."). Because the *United States Code* is divided into titles, a citation to a federal statute begins with the title number, followed by the code abbreviation, a section symbol and number, and the date. Add the publisher name to the date parenthetical if you cite an unofficial version.

Attorneys in Arkansas commonly use the abbreviation A.C.A. for the *Arkansas Code of 1987*, an abbreviation authorized by Ark. Code Ann. § 1-2-113(c) (2008) ("Sections of the Code may be cited by the abbreviation 'A.C.A.' followed by the number of the section."). All other components of the citation are the same as those following national standards. Feel free to use the A.C.A. abbreviation in documents intended for readers within the state of Arkansas. Clients or courts in other jurisdictions, however, might not recognize the abbreviation, and it is therefore advisable to follow national standards when writing for out-of-state readers.

Table A-7. Citing Official and Unofficial Codes

Practitioner Format	Academic Format
Ark. Code Ann. § 5-26-308(a) (2013).	Ark. Code Ann. § 5-26-308 (2013).
A.C.A. § 5-26-308(a) (2013). [local format]	Citations in academic footnotes do not conform to local citation formats.
Ark. Code Ann. § 5-37-208 (Supp. 2015).	Ark. Code Ann. § 5-37-208 (Supp. 2015).
A.C.A. § 5-37-208 (Supp. 2015).	Citations in academic footnotes do not conform to local citation formats.
Ark. Code Ann. § 5-26-308(a) (West 2008).	Ark. Code Ann. § 5-26-308 (West 2008).
Ark. Code Ann. § 5-65-103(a)(2) (West Supp. 2015).	Ark. Code Ann. § 5-65-103(a)(2) (West Supp. 2015).
Ark. Code Ann. § 5-65-103(a)(2) (West, Westlaw through 2015 Reg. Sess. & 2015 1st Extraordinary Sess. of 90th Gen. Assemb.).	Ark. Code Ann. § 5-65-103(a)(2) (West, Westlaw through 2015 Reg. Sess. & 2015 1st Extraordinary Sess. of 90th Gen. Assemb.).
30 U.S.C. § 28-1 (2012).	30 U.S.C. § 28-1 (2012).
30 U.S.C.S. § 28-1 (Lexis 1995).	30 U.S.C.S. § 28-1 (Lexis 1995).
30 U.S.C.A. § 28-1 (West 2007).	20 U.S.C.A. § 28-1 (West 2007).

2. Statutes No Longer in Force

Should you need to cite a statute that is no longer in force, the citation must clearly demonstrate to the reader that you are not citing the current statute. Parenthetically indicate the year of the statute's repeal. If reference to the repealing act would be particularly relevant, it may be appended as shown in the second example in Appendix A, Table A-8.

Table A-8. Citing a Statute No Longer in Force

Practitioner Format	Academic Format
Ark. Code Ann. § 5-27-228 (repealed 2001).	Ark. Code Ann. § 5-27-228 (repealed 2001).
Ark. Code Ann. § 5-27-228, *repealed by* 2001 Ark. Acts 414, § 2.	Ark. Code Ann. § 5-27-228, *repealed by* 2001 Ark. Acts 414, § 2.

3. Session Laws

For recent legislative enactments that have not yet been codified, cite *session laws* (sometimes referred to as *slip laws*). To cite an Arkansas session law in the official publication *Arkansas Acts*, set out the name of the act (if any), the year of enactment, the abbreviation "Ark. Acts," and the page on which the text of the act begins. Unofficial publications of the state's session laws are available in the *Arkansas Code of 1987 Annotated Legislative Service* ("Ark. Adv. Legis. Serv.") or *West's Arkansas Legislative Service* ("Ark. Legis. Serv."); for either, indicate the publisher name in a parenthetical.

Citations to federal session laws indicate the official or popular name of the act, the public law number, the volume and initial page number where the act is published in *United States Statutes at Large* ("Stat."), the pinpoint page, and the date of enactment.

Table A-9. Citing Session Laws

Practitioner Format	Academic Format
An Act to Amend Various Sections of the Law Regarding Massage Therapists, 2015 Ark. Adv. Legis. Serv. 1083 (LexisNexis).	An Act to Amend Various Sections of the Law Regarding Massage Therapists, 2015 Ark. Adv. Legis. Serv. 1083 (LexisNexis).
Wounded Warriors Federal Leave Act of 2015, Pub. L. No. 114-75, 129 Stat. 640, 641 (2015).	Wounded Warriors Federal Leave Act of 2015, Pub. L. No. 114-75, 129 Stat. 640, 641 (2015).

4. Local Ordinances

A local ordinance is the municipal equivalent of a statute; some are codified, but others are not. The citation to a codified ordinance begins with the abbreviated name of the town or county promulgating the ordinance, followed by an abbreviation for the state. Next comes an abbreviation of the name of the code, followed by a pinpoint reference, and the publication date in parentheses. An uncodified ordinance will also begin with the name of the town or county and its state, followed by the term "Ordinance" and its number (preceded by the abbreviation "No.") or its name, a pinpoint reference (if the ordinance has subdivisions), and a parenthetical indicating the month, day, and year of enactment.

Local ordinances are increasingly available on the Internet; to cite an ordinance published online, substitute a parenthetical indicating its publisher and an indication of its currency, followed by the URL for the website.

Table A-10. Citing a Local Ordinance

Practitioner Format	ACADEMIC FORMAT
Little Rock, Ark., Code of Ordinances § 17.5-24 (Municode through Ordinance No. 21,028, adopted Apr. 21, 2015), https://www.municode.com.	Little Rock, Ark., Code of Ordinances § 17.5-24, (Municode through Ordinance No. 21,028, adopted Apr. 21, 2015), https://www.municode.com.
Saline Cnty., Ark., Ordinance No. 2014-09 (Apr. 15, 2014).	Saline Cnty., Ark., Ordinance No. 2014-09 (Apr. 15, 2014).

E. Legislation

Legislative chambers, whether state or federal, consider and vote upon various types of legislation: bills, resolutions, concurrent resolutions, or joint resolutions. If enacted, a bill, resolution, or joint resolution should be cited as a statute, as described above in Section D.1. Otherwise, pending or unenacted bills and resolutions, or any concurrent resolutions, have their own citation formats.

A citation to pending or unenacted Arkansas legislation begins with an abbreviation for the type of legislation (indicating its origin in the House of Representatives or the Senate, and if applicable, its status as a concurrent or joint resolution), followed by the bill or resolution number, the legislature's number, a designation of the legislative session, and in parentheses, the state's abbreviation and the year.

Citations to pending or unenacted federal legislation similarly begin with an abbreviation for the House or Senate, an abbreviation for a joint or concurrent resolution (if applicable), the number of the bill or resolution, the number of the Congress in which the bill was introduced, the section (if any), and in parentheses, the year.

Table A-11. Citing Bills and Other Forms of Legislation

Practitioner Format	ACADEMIC FORMAT
H.R. 1009, 90th Gen. Assemb., 1st Extraordinary Sess. (Ark. 2015).	H.R. 1009, 90th Gen. Assemb., 1st Extraordinary Sess. (Ark. 2015).
S. 1150, 89th Gen. Assemb., Reg. Sess. (Ark. 2013).	S. 1150, 89th Gen. Assemb., Reg. Sess. (Ark. 2013).
Fairness in Class Action Litigation and Furthering Asbestos Claim Transparency Act of 2015, H.R. 1927, 114th Cong. § 3 (2015).	Fairness in Class Action Litigation and Furthering Asbestos Claim Transparency Act of 2015, H.R. 1927, 114th Cong. § 3 (2015).
S. Res. 4, 113th Cong., 1st Sess. § 2 (2013).	S. Res. 4, 113th Cong., 1st Sess. § 2 (2013).

F. Administrative and Executive Law

Determining how to cite the variety of administrative and executive materials and the sources in which they are published is a challenging task, as there is no single template that works for all. This section instead presents multiple examples of materials such as administrative rules, regulations, notices, and agency adjudications, as well as materials such as advisory opinions and executive orders. Refer to your chosen citation manual's specific rules for more guidance in citing these materials.

1. Administrative Rules and Regulations

Citations to agency rules and regulations are typically made to a governmental administrative code or register. In Arkansas, citations to codified rules indicate their location in the *Code of Arkansas Rules* (published by LexisNexis). Otherwise, rules are cited to the *Arkansas Register* (published by the state). The latter is also available in an unofficial publication, the *Arkansas Government Register*, published by LexisNexis.

Citations to the compiled administrative rules in Arkansas use a three-part hyphenated number representing the agency–sub-agency (if any)–chapter number, followed by the code's abbreviation ("Code Ark. R."), a pinpoint reference, and a date parenthetical. Citations to materials in official or unofficial registers begin with the volume number, followed by the register's abbreviation ("Ark. Reg." or "Ark. Gov't Reg."), a pinpoint page reference, and a parenthetical indicating the month and year of publication. Add the publisher's name to this parenthetical when you cite an unofficial register.

Citations to federal agency rules are made to the official *Code of Federal Regulations* (if codified) or to the *Federal Register*. Citations to codified regulations begin with the specific title number, the code's abbreviation ("C.F.R."), a section symbol, the section number, and a date parenthetical indicating the year of publication. Citations to materials in the *Federal Register* begin with the volume number of that issue of the register, the register's abbreviation ("Fed. Reg."), a pinpoint page reference, and a date parenthetical indicating the month, day, and year of publication.

Table A-12. Citing Administrative Rules and Regulations

Practitioner Format	Academic Format
178-00-001 Ark. Code R. B-16 (Matthew Bender & Co. 2007).	178-00-001 Ark. Code R. B-16 (Matthew Bender & Co. 2007).
30 Ark. Reg. 5 (Nov.–Dec. 2006).	30 Ark. Reg. 5 (Nov.–Dec. 2006).
49 C.F.R. § 605.11 (2014).	49 C.F.R. § 605.11 (2014).
72 Fed. Reg. 4961, 4963 (Feb. 2, 2007).	72 Fed. Reg. 4961, 4963 (Feb. 2, 2007).

2. Executive Documents and Advisory Opinions

Executive documents include items such as executive orders, proclamations, memoranda, and reorganization plans. Therefore, it is essential to first identify the form of the document, as its identification will affect the citation. Begin with the document's title, if any, followed by an abbreviation for the identification and the number of the document. Executive documents are typically published in administrative codes or registers (in Arkansas, the *Code of Arkansas Rules* or the *Arkansas Register*; in the federal government, the *Code of Federal Regulations* or the *Federal Register*). Indicate the volume number of the code or register, followed by the abbreviation for the code or register, a pinpoint reference, and a parenthetical reference to the date of publication. Register citations refer to the exact date shown on the issue's front cover. Add the publisher's name to this parenthetical when you cite an unofficial source.

A citation to an advisory opinion, such as that issued by the government's attorney general, begins with its title, if any, abbreviated as indicated by the writer's chosen citation manual. Rather than being identified by its title, an opinion may be identified by number; in that case, designate the document as an opinion of the attorney general and indicate its number. The next components of the citation are the volume number and abbreviation for the publication that contains the opinion, the initial page and a pinpoint reference, ending with a parenthetical identifying the year of publication. Advisory opinions may appear in official publications dedicated to publishing only those opinions (e.g., *Opinions of the Office of Legal Counsel of the Department of Justice*) or in general administrative registers (e.g., the *Arkansas Register*).

Table A-13. Citing Executive Orders and Advisory Opinions

Practitioner Format	Academic Format
Exec. Order No. 05-08, 62 Ark. Gov't Reg. 2 (LexisNexis July 2005).	Exec. Order No. 05-08, 62 Ark. Gov't Reg. 2 (LexisNexis July 2005).
Exec. Order No. 13389, 3 C.F.R. 203 (2006).	Exec. Order No. 13389, 3 C.F.R. 203 (2006).
Ark. Att'y Gen. Op. 2005-175, 29 Ark. Reg. 4 (LexisNexis July 2005).	Ark. Att'y Gen. Op. 2005-175, 29 Ark. Reg. 4 (LexisNexis July 2005).
Immunity of the Assistant to the President and Director of the Office of Political Strategy and Outreach From Congressional Subpoena, 38 Op. O.L.C. 3-4 (July 15, 2014).	Immunity of the Assistant to the President and Director of the Office of Political Strategy and Outreach From Congressional Subpoena, 38 Op. O.L.C. 3-4 (July 15, 2014).

G. Court Rules

To cite a rule of practice, procedure, or professional conduct, begin with an abbreviation of the controlling jurisdiction, followed by an abbreviation for the type of rule and the rule number. Add a pinpoint reference to a subsection if necessary. No date is necessary in citations to rules currently in force.

Two sets of Arkansas court rules have local rules that permit different abbreviations and formats from those found in *ALWD* or *Bluebook*. Arkansas Rule of Civil Procedure 85 authorizes the abbreviation "ARCP." Similarly, Arkansas Rule of Evidence 1102 authorizes the abbreviated (although redundant) format "A.R.E. Rule ___."

Table A-14. Citing Court Rules

Practitioner Format	ACADEMIC FORMAT
Ark. R. Civ. P. 56.	ARK. R. CIV. P. 56.
ARCP 56. [local rule format]	Citations in academic footnotes do not conform to local citation rules.
Ark. R. Evid. 503.	ARK. R. EVID. 503.
A.R.E. Rule 503. [local rule format]	Citations in academic footnotes do not conform to local citation rules.
Ark. R. Prof'l Conduct 1.6.	ARK. R. PROF'L CONDUCT 1.6.
Fed. R. App. P. 32.1.	FED. R. APP. P. 32.1.
Fed. R. Civ. P. 52(a)(3).	FED. R. CIV. P. 52(a)(3).

III. Short Forms

The first time you cite any source in a piece of legal writing, provide a *full citation*, one that contains all of the components required for a citation to that particular source. Subsequent citations to the same authority, however, typically use a *short-form citation* that takes less room while still guiding readers to a specific location within the source.

The handiest of all short forms is the abbreviation *id.*, meaning "the same thing just cited." *Id.* tells a reader to look at the immediately previous citation in the very same location, because the writer is citing that source and that specific location again. When the source is the same but the pinpoint reference has changed, the writer simply adds the new pinpoint reference immediately after *id.* If the pinpoint reference refers to a page number, add the preposition "at" before the pinpoint page number; if the pinpoint reference refers to a paragraph or section number, do not use "at."

You cannot use *id.*, however, if a citation to another source follows the original source's citation, because you are no longer citing "the same thing just cited." In that instance, you will need to use a *longer* short form, directing your readers to the original source but also providing enough information for them to recognize what you're citing for the second (or third or tenth time).

In parallel case citations, *id.* refers only to the first-cited reporter (i.e., the official reporter); the unofficial reporter's citation in the parallel citation must use the longer short form because it has its own page numbering.

The short reference *supra* (meaning "above") should never be used in citations to primary sources in practitioner writing because it tells readers only that the writer cited the source *somewhere earlier*, but it doesn't provide any other clue to the location of the full citation. In citations to secondary sources, however, *supra* is an acceptable short form provided it contains enough other information for readers to locate the cited material (author's surname or title of work, plus pinpoint reference). In academic writing, writers can use *supra* to refer to any type of source, because academic writing will employ a numbered footnote containing the source's first full citation, and *supra* plus the note number will lead readers to the footnoted citation without difficulty.

Table A-15 illustrates the use of *id.* and acceptable longer short forms for several of the sources previously illustrated in this appendix. The table features short forms employed in practitioner format and, using footnote references, academic format.

Table A-15. Using Short Forms for Later Citations

Full Citations–Practitioner Format	Short Forms–Practitioner Format
Ark. Const. art. 2, § 15.	*Id.* *Id.* art. 2, § 14.
John Wesley Hall, Jr., *Search and Seizure* 102 (2012).	*Id.* *Id.* at 100. Hall, *supra*, at 101.
Lindsey P. Gustafson, *Making the Peg Fit the Hole: A Superior Solution to the Inherent Problems of Incorporated Definitions*, 37 U. Ark. Little Rock L. Rev. 363, 367-68 (2015).	*Id.* *Id.* at 365. Gustafson, *supra*, at 366.
Stephan R. Leimberg & Leo C. Hodges, *The Income Tax and Estate Planning Advantages of Private Annuities*, Est. Plan., Feb. 2006, at 3.	*Id.* Leimberg & Hodges, *supra*, at 3.
State v. Bostick, 856 S.W.2d 12, 13 (Ark. 1993). [regional reporter citation]	*Id.* *Id.* at 597. *Bostick*, 856 S.W.2d at 597.
State v. Bostick, 313 Ark. 596, 598, 856 S.W.2d 12, 13 (1993). [parallel citation]	*Id.* at 599, 856 S.W.2d at 13. *Bostick*, 313 Ark. at 599, 856 S.W.2d at 14.

Ark. Code Ann. § 14-14-903 (2013).	*Id.* *Id.* § 14-4-903. Ark. Code Ann. § 14-4-903.
Wounded Warriors Federal Leave Act of 2015, Pub. L. No. 114-75, 129 Stat. 640, 641 (2015).	*Id.* 129 Stat. at 641. Wounded Warriors Federal Leave Act, 129 Stat. at 641.

FULL CITATIONS–ACADEMIC FORMAT	SHORT FORMS–ACADEMIC FORMAT
[15] JOHN WESLEY HALL, JR., SEARCH AND SEIZURE 102 (5th ed. 2013).	[16] *Id.* [21] HALL, *supra* note 15, at 104.
[31] Lindsey P. Gustafson, *Making the Peg Fit the Hole: A Superior Solution to the Inherent Problems of Incorporated Definitions*, 37 U. ARK. LITTLE ROCK L. REV. 363, 367-68 (2015).	[32] *Id.* [37] *Id.* at 365. [42] Gustafson, *supra* note 31, at 366.
[25] State v. Bostick, 856 S.W.2d 12, 13 (Ark. 1993). [regional reporter citation]	[26] *Id.* [33] *Bostick*, 856 S.W.2d at 597.
[56] ARK. CODE ANN. § 14-14-903(b)(1) (2013).	[57] *Id.* [58] *Id.* § 14-14-903 (b)(3). [61] ARK. CODE ANN. § 14-14-903.

Appendix B

Resources for Arkansas Legal Research

I. Free Online Resources

A. Arkansas Governmental Entities

- Administrative Agencies, http://www.arkansas.gov/government/agencies
- Attorney General, http://www.arkansasag.gov/
- Circuit Courts, https://courts.arkansas.gov/courts/circuit-courts (trial courts of general jurisdiction)
- Court of Appeals, https://courts.arkansas.gov/courts/court-of-appeals
- District Courts, https://courts.arkansas.gov/courts/district-courts (trial courts of limited jurisdiction)
- General Assembly, http://www.arkleg.state.ar.us/
- Governor, http://governor.arkansas.gov/
- House of Representatives, http://www.arkansashouse.org/
- Judiciary, https://courts.arkansas.gov/
- Secretary of State, http://www.sos.arkansas.gov/
- Senate, http://www.arkansas.gov/senate/
- Supreme Court, https://courts.arkansas.gov/courts/supreme-court

B. Arkansas Primary Law

Administrative Rules & Regulations

- Arkansas Legislature, *Administrative Rules and Regulations*, http://www.arkleg.state.ar.us/bureau/legal/Publications/Administrative%20Rules%20and%20Regulations.htm
- Arkansas Secretary of State, *Administrative Rules*, http://www.sos.arkansas.gov/rules_and_regs/index.php/rules/search/new

- Arkansas Agriculture Department, http://aad.arkansas.gov/Pages
/default.aspx

Cases

- Official opinions of the Arkansas Court of Appeals, http://opinions
.aoc.arkansas.gov/WebLink8/Browse.aspx?startid=37576 (spring term
2009–present)
- Official opinions of the Arkansas Supreme Court, http://opinions
.aoc.arkansas.gov/WebLink8/Browse.aspx?startid=39345 (spring
term 2009–present)
- Unofficial opinions of the Arkansas Court of Appeals, http://
opinions.aoc.arkansas.gov/WebLink8/Browse.aspx?startid=101895
(spring term 1981–spring term 2009)
- Unofficial opinions of the Arkansas Supreme Court, http://opinions
.aoc.arkansas.gov/WebLink8/Browse.aspx?startid=101893 (1837–
spring term 2009)

Constitution

- Arkansas Constitution of 1874, http://www.arkleg.state.ar.us
/assembly/Summary/ArkansasConstitution1874.pdf
- *Arkansas Constitutions Collection*, Arkansas History Commission,
Little Rock, Arkansas, at http://ahc.digital-ar.org

Court Rules

- *Arkansas Rules of Appellate Procedure–Civil*, https://courts.arkansas
.gov/rules-and-administrative-orders/rules-of-appellate
-procedure%E2%80%94civil
- *Arkansas Rules of Appellate Procedure–Criminal*, https://courts
.arkansas.gov/rules-and-administrative-orders/rules-of-appellate
-procedure%E2%80%94criminal
- *Arkansas Rules of Civil Procedure*, https://courts.arkansas.gov
/rules-and-administrative-orders/rules-of-civil-procedure
- *Arkansas Rules of Criminal Procedure*, https://courts.arkansas.gov
/rules-and-administrative-orders/rules-of-criminal-procedure
- *Arkansas Rules of Evidence*, https://courts.arkansas.gov/rules-and
-administrative-orders/arkansas-rules-of-evidence
- *Arkansas Rules of Professional Conduct*, https://courts.arkansas.gov
/rules-and-administrative-orders/%5Bcurrent%5D-arkansas-rules

-of-professional-conduct (current; supersedes Arkansas Model Rules of Professional Conduct)
- *Rules of the Supreme Court and Court of Appeals of Arkansas*, https://courts.arkansas.gov/rules-and-administrative-orders/rules-of-the-supreme-court-and-court-of-appeals-of-the-state-of-arkansas

Executive Orders of the Governor

- http://governor.arkansas.gov/executive-orders/ (current administration)

Jury Instructions

- *Arkansas Model Jury Instructions – Civil*, https://govt.westlaw.com/armji/ (free access furnished as joint project of Arkansas Committee on Model Jury Instructions—Civil and Thomson Reuters) (includes Table of Contents, text of instructions, Notes on Use, and Comments; searchable by natural-language query)
- *Arkansas Model Jury Instructions—Criminal*, http://www.lexisnexis.com/hottopics/arcrimji/ (free access furnished as joint project of Arkansas Committee on Model Jury Instructions—Criminal and LexisNexis) (includes Table of Contents, text of instructions, Notes on Use, and Comments; search by terms and connectors or natural-language query)

Statutes & Session Laws

- *Arkansas Code*, http://www.lexisnexis.com/hottopics/arcode/Default.asp

C. Attorneys

- Administrative Office of the Courts, Office of Professional Programs, *Arkansas Bar Examination*, https://courts.arkansas.gov/administration/professional-programs/bar-exam
- Arkansas Bar Association, www.arkbar.com

D. Federal Materials

Administrative Rules & Regulations

- *Code of Federal Regulations*, http://www.gpo.gov/fdsys/browse/collectionCfr.action?collectionCode=CFR
- *Federal Register*, http://www.gpo.gov/fdsys/browse/collection.action?collectionCode=FR (1994–present)

Cases

- Supreme Court of the United States, http://www.supremecourt.gov/
- United States Courts Opinions, http://www.gpo.gov/fdsys/browse
  /collection.action?collectionCode=USCOURTS
- United States Court of Appeals for the Eighth Circuit, *Opinions*,
  http://www.ca8.uscourts.gov/all-opinions
- Law Librarian's Society of Washington, D.C., *Quick Links and
  Sources to U.S. Court Opinions*, http://www.llsdc.org/quick-links-to
  -us-court-opinions

Constitution

- *The Constitution of the United States of America*, https://www.gpo
  .gov/fdsys/pkg/CDOC-110hdoc50/pdf/CDOC-110hdoc50.pdf (United
  States Government Publishing Office, authenticated text)

Court Rules

- Rules of the Supreme Court of the United States, http://www
  .supremecourt.gov/ctrules/rulesofthecourt.pdf
- United States Courts, *Current Rules of Practice & Procedure*, http://
  www.uscourts.gov/rules-policies/current-rules-practice-procedure
  (includes appellate rules forms, bankruptcy forms, and national
  court forms)
- United States Court of Appeals for the Eighth Circuit, *Local Rules*,
  http://media.ca8.uscourts.gov/newrules/coa/localrules.pdf
- United States Court of Appeals for the Eighth Circuit, *Rules &
  Procedures*, http://www.ca8.uscourts.gov/rules-procedures

Executive Orders of the President

- *Presidential Documents/Executive Orders*, https://www.federal
  register.gov/executive-orders

Regulations

- United States Government Publishing Office, *Electronic Code of
  Federal Regulations*, http://www.ecfr.gov/ (unofficial; Boolean search
  capability)

Statutes & Session Laws

- *Public and Private Laws*, http://www.gpo.gov/fdsys/browse
  /collection.action?collectionCode=PLAW (slip laws)
- *United States Code*, http://www.gpo.gov/fdsys/browse/collection
  UScode.action?collectionCode=USCODE

Other

- Federal Judicial Center, *Guide to Research in Federal Judicial History* (2010), http://www.fjc.gov/public/pdf.nsf/lookup/guidereshist .pdf/$file/guidereshist.pdf
- Federal Judicial Center, *History of the Federal Courts*, http://www.fjc .gov/history/home.nsf/page/index.html

E. Miscellaneous

- Agricultural law resources, http://law.uark.libguides.com/c .php?g=367803
- American Immigration Council, *New Americans in Arkansas*, http:// immigrationpolicy.org/just-facts/new-americans-arkansas
- Arkansas Attorney General, *Children and Families*, http://www .arkansasag.gov/programs/children-and-families/
- Arkansas Attorney General, *Keeping Criminals in Jail*, http://www .arkansasag.gov/programs/criminal-justice/keeping-criminals -in-jail/
- Arkansas Attorney General, Consumer Protection Division, *Got Your Back, Arkansas*, http://gotyourbackarkansas.org/
- Arkansas Bar Association, *Arkansas Government and Law*, http:// www.arkbar.com/for-public/legal-links/ar-gov-law
- Arkansas Crime Information Center, http://acic.org/Pages/default .aspx
- *Arkansas Freedom of Information Handbook* (16th ed. 2014), *available at* https://static.ark.org/eeuploads/ag/foi-handbook-16ed-final.pdf
- *Arkansas Law Review*, http://media.law.uark.edu/arklawreview/
- Arkansas Legal Index (ARLI), http://themis.law.ualr.edu:81/
- Arkansas Supreme Court Library, *Databases & Electronic Resources*, https://courts.arkansas.gov/sites/default/files/tree/Databases%20 %26%20ElectronicResources_20150803.htm
- *Arkansas Territorial Briefs and Records* (Lynn C. Foster, ed.), University of Arkansas at Little Rock, Special Collections, http://ualr.edu /law/library/special-collections/ (digitized and transcribed territorial records from 1809 to 1836)
- Central Arkansas Library System, *Encyclopedia of Arkansas History and Culture*, http://www.encyclopediaofarkansas.net/
- Findlaw, Legal Dictionary, http://dictionary.lp.findlaw.com
- *Legal Information Institute*, https://www.law.cornell.edu/

- *Oxford English Dictionary*, http://www.oed.com/
- *UALR Law Review*, http://ualr.edu/lawreview/
- University of Arkansas at Little Rock William H. Bowen School of Law, http://ualr.edu/law/
- University of Arkansas School of Law, http://law.uark.edu/
- UALR Bowen School of Law, Law Library, *Databases & Other e-Resources*, http://ualr.edu/law/library/databases-and-other-e-resources/
- University of Arkansas School of Law, Law Library, http://law.uark.edu/library/research/

II. Commercial Services

- Arkansas Business, *Government and Politics*, http://www.arkansasbusiness.com/industry/government-politics
- *Arkansas Court Bulletin*, https://www.courtbulletin.com/
- *HeinOnline*, http://home.heinonline.org/subscriptions/subscription-options/ (periodicals, including full coverage of *Arkansas Lawyer*)
- PACER, *Public Access to Court Electronic Records*, https://www.pacer.gov/ (U.S. district, bankruptcy, and appellate court cases)

III. Other (Including Print Resources, CD-Roms, PDFs)

- Administrative Office of the Courts, *Arkansas Circuit Courts Judges' Benchbook Civil & Criminal Divisions* (2014).
- Administrative Office of the Courts, *Arkansas Circuit Courts Judges' Benchbook Domestic Relations Division* (2014).
- Administrative Office of the Courts, *Arkansas Circuit Courts Judges' Benchbook Juvenile Division* (2014).
- Administrative Office of the Courts, *Arkansas Circuit Courts Judges' Benchbook Probate Division* (2014).
- *Arkansas Bankruptcy Handbook* (Ark. Bar Ass'n 2009).
- *Arkansas Debtor-Creditor Relations Handbook* (Kevin P. Keech & Jeffrey Ellis eds., 4th ed. 2012).
- *Arkansas Domestic Relations Handbook* (Ark. Bar Ass'n 2007).
- *Arkansas Elder Law Desk Manual* (Ark. Bar Ass'n 2013).
- *Arkansas Model Jury Instructions, Civil* (Thomson Reuters 2016 ed.) (Arkansas Practice Series).

- *Arkansas Model Jury Instructions, Criminal* (2d ed., LexisNexis 1994–) (looseleaf).
- *Arkansas Probate System Handbook* (Ark. Bar Ass'n 2005).
- *Arkansas Workers Compensation Desk Book* (Ark. Bar Ass'n 2013).
- *Business Associations Handbook* (Ark. Bar Ass'n 2014).
- Junius Bracy Cross, Richard Downing & Stephen Niswanger, *Construction Lien Law in Arkansas* (2009).
- *Domestic Violence: An Arkansas Practical Guide for Attorneys, Judges and Court Clerks* (Ark. Bar Ass'n 2016).
- *Eighth Circuit Manual of Model Jury Instructions–Civil* (Thomson West 2005).
- *A Guide to Arkansas Inheritance,* http://law.uark.edu/faculty/buehler/2012Spring/Arkansas-Guide-to-Inheritance.pdf
- *A Guide to Arkansas Statutes of Limitations* (Ark. Bar Ass'n 2011).
- *Handling Appeals in Arkansas* (Ark. Bar. Ass'n 2015 ed.).
- Howard R. Brill & Christian H. Brill, *Law of Damages* (Harrison Co. 6th ed. 2014–2015) (Arkansas Practice Series).
- Murray Claycomb, *Arkansas Corporations* (Harrison Co. 1992) (with forms).
- Frances S. Fendler, *Private Placements and Limited Offerings of Securities: A Guide for the Arkansas Practitioner* (Ark. Bar Ass'n 2010).
- Kathryn C. Fitzhugh, *Arkansas Practice Materials II: A Selective Annotated Bibliography,* 21 U. Ark. Little Rock L. Rev. 363 (1998-99).
- Lynn Foster, G.S. Brant Perkins & S. Renee Brida, *Probate and Estate Administration* (Lawyers Coop. Publ'g 2010-2015) (Arkansas Practice Series, with forms).
- Kay C. Goss, *The Arkansas State Constitution: A Reference Guide* (2011).
- John Wesley Hall, *Trial Handbook for Arkansas Lawyers* (Thomson Reuters 2006 ed.) (Arkansas Practice Series, 2 volumes).
- Michael E. Miller, Brent Watson & Rick Worth, *Sales and Use Tax in Arkansas* (2014).
- David Newbern, John J. Watkins, D. Price Marshall & Brandon Harrison, *Arkansas Civil Practice and Procedure* (Harrison Co. 5th ed. 2010–2015) (Arkansas Practice Series, multi-volume).
- *Poverty Law Practice Manual: A Desk Reference for Legal Services Program Staff, and Private Attorneys Working with the Legal Services Programs in Arkansas* (2005) (looseleaf).

- *Race and Ethnicity in Arkansas: New Perspectives* (John A. Kirk ed., 2014).
- *Revocable Trust Handbook for Arkansas Practitioners* (Ark. Bar Ass'n 2007 & Cum. Supp. 2014).
- Rachel Runnels, *Family Law and Practice* (Thomson West 2015) (Arkansas Practice Series).
- *Standards for Examination of Real Estate Titles in Arkansas* (Ark. Bar Ass'n 2013).
- John J. Watkins & Richard J. Peltz, *The Arkansas Freedom of Information Act* (Ark. L. Press 5th ed. 2010).

About the Authors

Coleen M. Barger is the Ben J. Altheimer Distinguished Professor of Law at the University of Arkansas at Little Rock William H. Bowen School of Law. She has taught courses in basic and advanced legal research, legal writing, and appellate advocacy since 1992.

Cheryl L. Reinhart is an administrative law attorney with the Arkansas Department of Education and serves as Director of the Office of Educator Licensure. She is also adjunct faculty at Pulaski Technical College for Business Law and the Paralegal Technology Program. She served as a legislative attorney for seven years with the Arkansas General Assembly.

Cathy L. Underwood is a paralegal instructor at Pulaski Technical College in North Little Rock, Arkansas, where she teaches legal research and writing. She has served as a consultant to the Arkansas Bar Association for over 30 years, and provides Fastcase training for its members.

Index